Truth on Fire

From:- Mary

With love.

x.

Truth on Fire

1998 Keswick Ministry

Edited by David Porter

OM
publishing

First published 1998 by OM Publishing

02 01 00 99 98 97 98 7 6 5 4 3 2 1

OM Publishing is an imprint of Paternoster Publishing,
P.O. Box 300, Carlisle, Cumbria, CA3 0QS, UK.
http://www.paternoster-publishing.com

British Library Cataloguing in Publication Data

A catalogue record for this book is available from
the British Library

ISBN 1-85078-322-5

Cover Design by Mainstream, Lancaster
Typeset by David Porter Text & Editorial, Greatham, Hampshire
Printed in the UK
by Caledonian International Book Manufacturing Ltd, Glasgow

Contents

The Bible Readings

'Renew My Life Through Your Word'
  by Rev. Dr Chris Wright

Readings in 2 Timothy
  by Rev. Alistair Begg

The Addresses

Introduction by the Chairman
of the 1998 Convention

A memorable image from the summer of '98 was a group of eight-year-old lads, wearing the right trainers and Nike T-shirts, marching through the Keswick streets one evening armed with large NIV Bibles. Not something you see every day, at least not where I live. But it was a strong image which says something about the growing impact of the Convention. They were joining well over a thousand other young people to learn how God's Word can impact their lives as they come to know its author.

Whether it was the youth programme or the main tent, there was something dynamic about being exposed to Truth on Fire. It shouldn't surprise us. When God's word first came to Ezekiel it left him unable to do anything but sit 'overwhelmed' for a whole week. He had understood that there was a unity between the word of God and God Himself, who is personally at work through the word He speaks.

The following pages introduce this explosive theme, and represent much of what challenged our guests, young and old. It is not about a holy book which can be tamed and domesticated, but a living God who draws us into His presence, a living God who speaks His word with absolute authority and convicting power, transforming our lives by His Spirit.

It is always easy for Christians to read the Bible and stop at the text. That might improve our knowledge, but it is a missed opportunity. The purpose of these addresses, opening a range of sections of the Bible, is to bring us into the presence of the living God, to know Him more fully and serve Him more energetically. There is no other way to get to know the heart of God than through the word He has spoken. As Luther once expressed it, we come to the Bible as we would come to a cradle: to discover the baby. We are here to meet Christ, the Living Word.

That's why I was so heartened to see the streets full of young people, compact Bibles in the pockets of their jeans or large Bibles under their arms. In a generation that has lost its bearings, confused about what really matters in life and desperate to discover the foundation for moral decision-making, here were thousands of people not just opening God's word, but meeting Him in life-transforming ways. I hope you capture something of that dynamic as you read these pages.

I would want to express our thanks to all of the speakers who gave themselves wholeheartedly to explaining scripture powerfully and relevantly.

Finally, a special word of thanks to David and Tricia Porter who provided the careful editing of this selection of the summer's teaching. This represents their final year of work, after editing the book for twenty-one years, and so the Convention Council wishes specially to underline its gratitude to them.

Jonathan Lamb
Chairman, Keswick Convention

Editor's Introduction

Twenty-one years ago I went with Dave Brown, then Manager of O M Publishing, to an office in Waterloo to be interviewed for the job of Editor of the annual Keswick Volume. The Chairman was Canon Neech, and I was interviewed by the Secretary, Maurice Rowlandson.

I'd grown up with Keswick, which was a revered name in my home; books by Keswick speakers were prominent among the thousands of volumes that lined my father's shelves. Keswick is also prominent in the background of my wife Tricia, who has worked with me on this task. We began with an ancient typewriter on a kitchen table, laboriously cutting and pasting by hand; the present volume was produced entirely on computers, in our home, from audio tapes to finished typesetting.

We missed one year, 1983, when we took a summer out and Anthea Cousins edited the volume. That apart, I estimate that we have put into print around 1,500,000 words of Keswick ministry, and that Tricia (making allowance for the small army of volunteers who did much of the typing in the early years) must have typed at least a quarter of a billion words. From which you will gather that as editor I have listened to almost a quarter of a century's worth of the Keswick Convention with the primary aim of deciding what can be cut out, and there aren't many who can say that ...

We have been privileged to be doing this work during years of major change at Keswick, change which has been accepted with such good humour and initiated with such grace that the Convention will always be a model for me of how to bring about change biblically. It has also been for both of us an annual feast of biblical ministry. We began in the year that John Stott and Dick Lucas took the Bible Readings, and there have been numerous highlights since.

The editorial method has never changed. So here are the rules one last time: I have endeavoured to keep the flavour of the occasion without attempting to produce the book the speakers would have produced had they been preparing a published text rather than a spoken address. Every Bible reference has been retained, though often severely pruned. You really do need to have an open Bible by you as you read, but then that was so at the Convention too! I have tracked down what speakers' quotations I could in the time available: the rest will make an enjoyable Boxing Day quiz for the whole family (I've found the easy ones). This year we have used both the pre-1984 and post-1984 editions of the NIV, for reasons that are explained in the text, so your copy might not always exactly match a particular quotation. The Keswick preference for capitalising pronouns referring to the Persons of the Trinity is observed as usual, as is the NIV's preference the other way when we quote directly from Scripture. The occasional odd combination that results can be useful in identifying speakers' paraphrases ('cf' before a reference also signifies a paraphrase).

Many people have helped this book into print year by year. I'm going to mention just two: Dave Brown (and STL), for getting me the job in the first place and for much counsel afterwards; and Peter Cousins, wisest and most knowledgeable of friends, and encyclopaedic and disrespectful source of reference on all matters from Bauer-Arndt-Gingrich to Newt Gingrich.

On which scholarly note I'll say 'Goodbye', but not before giving the warmest editorial thanks to Tricia for her many years of typing and to our daughters Eleanor and Lauren for their years of patience during summer holidays dominated by Keswick.

We leave 'the Keswick book' in the safe hands of Hilary Price, a sensitive editor whose Keswick credentials could hardly be more impeccable. If she receives as much help and kindness from the Keswick Council, speakers and staff that we have had over the years, she will certainly enjoy the task as much as we have done.

David (and Tricia) Porter
Keswick Volume Editorial Team

THE BIBLE READINGS

'Renew My Life Through Your Word'
Psalm 119

by Rev. Dr Chris Wright

1. Personal Sin and the Word of God's Grace
Psalm 119:9-16

Around about the middle of the eighteenth century, about the time of John and Charles Wesley, there was a Puritan minister called William Grimshaw in the parish of Howarth, which is not far from Keswick but is more famous for the Brontë sisters. Grimshaw was disturbed by the number of people who stayed in the village pubs instead of coming to church on Sunday. So while the choir was singing or chanting a psalm, he would go outside the church with a large stick and beat people in from the pubs. And if there were a particularly large number of people missing he would set the choir to sing Psalm 119, which gave him a little more time to get them in.

Everybody knows that Psalm 119 is the longest psalm in the Bible, and most people know that almost every verse refers to the word of God, the law of God, or some similar phrase. For that reason some people don't pay it the attention that they should. They feel, 'It keeps repeating the same thing; and where is it leading?' But that's rather like looking at a tapestry and saying, 'I keep seeing the colour red again and again, so this doesn't mean very much.' The thread will keep coming through, but I hope the picture becomes a little clearer as you look at the whole thing.

Psalm 119 is actually a very cleverly constructed piece of work.

You may know that some of the psalms are 'acrostics', spelling out the Hebrew alphabet just as we would be doing if we started the first line of a poem with 'A', the next with 'B', and so on. The psalmist in Psalm 119 chose to create a grand acrostic to finish all acrostics; he set eight lines to each letter of the alphabet, so each of the sections of the psalm which you can see laid out there in the NIV begins with a new letter of the Hebrew alphabet.

On top of that, he chose to use eight different words or expressions to describe the word of God. The first seven of them come in the opening verses, so it's quite easy to see what they are. In verse 1 he talks about 'the law of the LORD', the whole law. In verse 2 he talks about 'the statutes', or the testimonies, or witnesses, that God has given. In verse 4 he talks about the 'precepts' that God has set, the detailed instructions. In verse 5 he talks about 'decrees' that have been inscribed and are binding upon us. Then in verse 6 he talks about 'commands', the orders that God gives. In verse 7 the NIV has 'laws' – a better translation would be His 'judgements'. In verse 9 he talks about the 'word' of God, plain and simple. And the next one comes a little later in verse 38, where he talks about God's 'promise', the promises of God. The eight expressions are woven together quite beautifully, coming again and again and again to impart a rhythm and a beat to the music of this psalm.

It's often called a psalm in honour of God's law. But I think that's a mistake, because it's not actually about the law at all. The law is always in the third person. In this psalm, God is being prayed to. In fact, apart from the first three verses the whole of the other 173 verses are directly addressed to God – 'You, O LORD' ... 'Your word' ... 'Your promises' ... 'Your law' – and concern our response to these things, so it's a deeply personal psalm as well.

The question then with which I want to begin is this: How will spending five whole mornings at Keswick, this week in 1998, be helpful to you and to me? I suggest that this psalm, with which I have lived over these last months, will probably mirror a common experience for many of you. Most of you have come with a strong love for God. You are here because you want to be, because you know God and you want to know more about Him. And you have a strong love for God's word, otherwise you probably would not come to Keswick. It is the same with the psalmist: he loves God and he loves God's word.

We find here, too, a person with a deep desire to live his life in a way that will please God, that will give joy to the Lord and blessing to himself. And I imagine that's probably true for most of us here also.

But as you read this psalm you also discover that here is a person living with a real experience of stress, difficulty, exhaustion, failure and very great need. In fact, in the very last verse of the psalm he's still saying, 'Lord, I'm going astray like a lost sheep here and I need You to seek me and find me and help me out.' There's no triumphalism in the psalm whatsoever. It comes out of a person who has a deep longing that God will renew him and give him fresh strength, new energy, renewal of life, and zeal for God and for God's work.

If those things find any kind of echo in your life today, I think you'll find that this psalmist will make a very good travelling companion for this week.

We're going to be looking at five themes in the course of the week. Let me tell you what they are now so that you can begin to think about it and come prepared. This morning, we will think about personal sin and the word of God's grace. Tomorrow, personal struggle and the word of lament. On Wednesday, personal guidance and the word of light. On Thursday, personal commitment and the word of love. And finally on Friday, personal renewal and the word of life. So I think we have plenty to discover in the psalm as we go through it together.

Each morning as we study this psalm I shall give you a recommended section to read before we begin, though our exposition will range through the whole psalm and beyond it. So please read now verses 9 to 16, the section of the psalm in which all the verses begin with the Hebrew letter 'B', *beth*.

Psalm 119 is not a confession psalm as such, unlike Psalms 32 or 51, for example, where the psalmist is speaking of deep and profound conviction of sin. Those are psalms that emerge out of a very specific sin. Psalm 51 is associated with David's adultery, and the deep, terrible contrition and conviction of wrongdoing that leads to a person being flat on their face before God saying, 'God, I've sinned and I need specific forgiveness for what I have done.' Such times, of course, are deeply painful. Yet by God's grace they can also be sobering and restoring.

But the psalmist of Psalm 119 is not desperately sorry because he has sinned. Rather, here is someone who is desperately anxious *not* to sin. Perhaps the one arises out of the other. Here is a person who has known exactly what it feels like to stand under God's conviction, to be prostrate before the wrath of God in fear and trembling and in shame. Perhaps out of that experience he has known God's forgiveness and God's grace in healing, and here he is determined with all his heart not to go that way again. So it's not so much a confession of sin as a consciousness of sin that emerges through this psalm.

I want us to look at three expressions that I think will help us to summarise this.

First of all,

The awareness of sin

What is this person's experience and assessment of sin? What does it do to you, that makes him so anxious to avoid it?

First of all, he says,

Sin can lead to shame and disgrace

Those are words that come several times. Let me give you a few examples, as I shall often be doing in these Bible Readings. Look at verse 6: 'Then I would not be put to shame when I consider all your commands.' Verse 31: 'I hold fast to your statutes, O LORD; do not let me be put to shame.' And verse 39: 'Take away the disgrace I dread, for your laws are good.'

Sin produces shame and disgrace, as it did in the Garden of Eden. In the original description of how sin came into human life, we find that Adam and Eve immediately wanted to cover themselves in the God's presence, because sin produces shame – that urgent desire to be hidden. The last thing you want to do is show your face, when you are conscious of sin in your life. You want it to be covered; there is a terrible fear of being found out, of being put to shame. Some of the psalms express that very profoundly indeed. Since childhood one of my favourite psalms has been Psalm 25, which speaks about trusting in the Lord and the Lord's blessing on our lives. But some of the verses that are more meaningful to us as we grow older are like those in Psalm

119. 'Do not let me be put to shame, nor let my enemies triumph over me' (25:2). 'Guard my life and rescue me; let me not be put to shame, for I take refuge in you' (25:20). It's that same fear of being found out and disgraced.

And it's an absolutely right and proper reaction. Sin *should* produce shame in us. When it doesn't, we have a very advanced case of hardness of heart. Sin is that which ought to be covered, which should produce blushes of shame. One of the most awful things that the prophets – especially Jeremiah – said about the sin of their people was, 'Are they ashamed of their sin? Not a bit of it, they don't even know how to blush, because they've lost the sense of shame.' When we know something of shame and disgrace within us because of what we have done or have failed to do, then, I would suggest, the cross of Christ also takes an even deeper meaning; when we begin to recognise that not only did Jesus bear my sin, but He also bore my shame. All that Jesus went through – the public humiliation, being treated as if He were a criminal which He wasn't, being treated as though He were under the wrath of God which He was, but not because of His own sin but for ours; the shame, the spitting, the disgrace, the mockery, the contempt that He bore – it was our shame, my shame, that put Him there. That's what sin does. And the psalmist says, 'That's why I want to avoid it.'

Secondly, he acknowledges,

Sin will lead you astray

One of the most frequent metaphors in this psalm is the metaphor of the pathway – the path itself or a way of walking. The psalmist wants above all to avoid taking a wrong path, and he knows that's what sin will do to him. Verse 67: 'Before I was afflicted I went astray' – he took the wrong path – 'but now I obey your word.' Or verse 101: 'I have kept my feet from every evil path so that I might obey your word.' Verse 104: 'I hate every wrong path.' And verse 128: 'I consider all your precepts right, I hate every wrong path.'

You see, when you sin and do deliberately what you know to be displeasing to God, you are taking the first of many steps that will, before you know where you are going, lead you to walk carelessly and shamelessly down a road that you knew, and know, displeases God. It is a wrong path, it's dangerous and it ultimately leads to judgement. And when you are on a wrong path, there's only one thing to do: to turn round and get back to where you first went wrong. The further you go, the harder it gets, and the best thing is not to take the first step at all. Sin leads you down a wrong path.

Thirdly, the psalmist is aware that,

Sin eventually will rule you and dominate you

In verse 133, staying with the picture of the footpath, he says, 'Direct my footsteps according to your word; let no sin rule over me.' Which of course is what God said it would do. At the very beginning, He warned Cain: 'Sin ... desires to have you' (Gen. 4:7). Sin will want you to serve the sinful purpose rather than serve God. Bob Dylan wrote a song in which he pointed out that you have to serve somebody. He is right: we serve somebody in life, and if God is not our master then sin will be. And you will end up enslaved by it and the chains will have to be broken before you can be free.

That is a theological truth – it's told us by the Bible – and also a truth that is confirmed by personal experience. Sin will dominate you if you let it.

That is just about all that this Psalm says about sin. But of course it's not all the Bible has to say about sin, and I'm quite sure it's not all that this psalmist could have said about sin if he'd wanted to. From our own reflections we could add many more examples of what sin does to us. The world always promises us more than it can ever deliver. It promises us fun and excitement and it delivers pain and tragedy. It promises us freedom and delivers slavery and bondage. It promises us life and fulfilment and all the things we think are great, and it ends up in emptiness and death. It tells us there is something else you can have, something you can add to your life, something from which you can gain. And in the end it brings loss and takes away even the good things you thought you had. It tells you that you can get away with it. The fact is, you can't.

So the psalmist tells us, 'Let's be aware of sin. Let's acknowledge it, let's know our enemy for what it is and face up to it. Let's be real, and be aware of the reality of sin. That's my starting point in this psalm.'

The avoidance of sin

And so we need to avoid sin. The psalmist clearly fears it; you could say that he fears God more than sin, which is how it should be. Verse 120: 'My flesh trembles in fear of you; I stand in awe of your laws.' This is a man (or woman) who knows God, who loves God, who knows something of the grace and forgiveness and the mercy of God! But still he says, 'Lord, when I think of your law I think of my sin; I shudder and I tremble.' And if we've lost something of that reality, then let's get back to where we should be. Here is a person who says, 'Lord my flesh shudders, my hair stands on end' – that's the language being used here – 'I actually tremble when I think of the reality of my sin and the wrath of God.' And so he is absolutely determined to avoid sin.

How is he going to do it? Well, perhaps because he remembers Genesis 6:5 (where it tells us that every inclination of the thoughts of man's heart was 'only evil all the time'; in other words every aspect of our human life and person is infected in some way by sin), and because he is determined to avoid sin and to fight it with every aspect of his being, he's going to use his mind, his will and his emotions in the fight against sin. This is a man who is serious about what he's in conflict with.

The exercise of the mind

In verse 9 he asks, 'How can a young man keep his way pure?' How do you actually avoid sin? He supplies the answer: 'By living according to your word.' Perhaps the NIV does not give us the best translation here. The Authorised Version reads, 'By taking heed thereto according to thy word'; by watching it, paying attention, constantly bringing your life under the spotlight of the word of God and asking yourself, 'What does the Scripture say, what does the law say, what does the Bible say about this course of action that I'm thinking of?' He's using his mind.

Verse 11: 'I have hidden your word in my heart that I might not sin against you.' He is talking about careful memorising of the Scriptures. He is going to have the word of God stored away, building up a rich resource from which he can fight against sin. Verse 13: 'With my lips I recount all the laws that come from your mouth.' Here he's talking about the physical, literal, speaking; learning the word of God. There's a lot still to be said for careful reading and speaking and knowing the Scriptures – out loud, in our prayer times, in our times of temptation. And verse 15: 'I meditate on your precepts and consider your ways.' That describes inner reflection, deep pondering, thinking, wrestling with the word of God.

There are many, many more verses which say exactly the same thing all through this psalm. Here was a man (or a woman) who very clearly wanted to exercise his or her mind upon the word of God, and to do so not in order to obtain a degree in theology, but as a prophylactic against sin. 'I have hidden your word in my heart', not so that I win the Bible competition (which was some of my motivation when I was in a Crusader class in my teens), and not so so that I can pass exams and become a theological expert. 'I have hidden Your word in my heart – so that I won't sin against You.'

How does the Bible do that? How does studying the Bible with our minds and becoming familiar with it effectively prevent us from sin? First of all, by *keeping us in touch with the mind of God*. If God has poured His mind and His word into Scripture and we fill up our hearts with the Scripture, then we're going to have a much more sensitive understanding of what sin actually is. We will be aware of what is and is not sin; what God likes and what God does not like. And our minds and our thoughts will be beating with the heart and mind of God Himself.

Secondly, *by giving us a rich store of examples of both success and failure in relation to sin*. Some of us, I am sure, were brought up on the Scripture Union method of reading our Bibles, where you read the passage and then were asked all sorts of questions about it. Among the questions was, 'Is there an example to follow, or an error to avoid?' Good questions - examples of those who resisted sin and examples of those who tragically fell into sin and in some cases were rescued by God's grace. So there's plenty of stories there to fill our hearts and minds.

Thirdly, *by building up our moral muscles to resist temptation*. How did Jesus resist the temptations of the evil one, in the wilderness? Wasn't it through His knowledge of the Scripture? 'It is written,' He said, every time He was tempted. On each occasion He quoted from the book of Deuteronomy upon which He was probably meditating. It is a book that claims the people of God for obedience. He quotes that at the devil. The Scriptures give us ammunition. To use Paul's word, it is the 'sword of the Spirit' that enables us to fight back against temptation (Eph. 6:17).

And fourthly, *by helping to counteract that tendency within us to rationalise and to excuse our sin*. What clever people we are! And there's a sense in which the more intelligent you are the more vulnerable you are to rationalising your sin. We want always to do what is wrong but to have good reasons for it. It too goes back to the Garden of Eden. And the Bible unmasks us. It takes away our pretence and our sham. We say, 'Well I can get away with it, it'll be all right.' The word of God says, 'Be sure your sin will find you out.' We think to ourselves, 'Well God doesn't mind too much, I'm a child of God, He's forgiven me anyway.' The word of God says, 'Don't be deceived, God is not mocked.'

There is something about the Bible that, as the writer to the Hebrews said, is sharper than a double-edged sword (Heb. 4:12). It cuts into those corners of our lives where we do exactly that; where we will find any and every reason why it doesn't apply to us and we are above it and it won't matter anyway. Again and again the word comes back to us and says, 'Don't be daft, that's not how it is.' God sees, God knows, and God is not fooled. So the more our minds are filled with the Scriptures, the more there will be that which will enable us to avoid sin, or, where we fall into sin, to find our way back to the right path and to the grace of God and the healing of His forgiveness.

The exercise of the will

Psalm 119 is full of deliberate, purposeful, determined choosing of what is good, choosing not to sin and choosing to avoid evil. The language of determination breathes through the tapestry of this psalm again and again. Look for example at verse 30, a positive choice: 'I have chosen the way of truth; I have set my heart on your laws.' In verse 101 there is a negative choice: 'I have kept my feet from every evil path so that I might obey your word.' The choice in verse 106 is deadly serious, because he takes an oath: 'I have taken an oath and confirmed it, that I will follow your righteous laws.' In Old Testament terms that's a serious matter. It wasn't just 'Oh yes, Lord, I'll do it, I promise.' This is a man who puts his life upon the line: 'Lord, you hear what I'm saying; and may I, one way or another, obey You.' And he is determined to make it a life-long choice: verse 112, 'My heart is set on keeping your decrees to the very end.'

So it's a matter of the will, of commitment. I think it's very important these days for us to be reminded that sin is a matter of choice and of the will. Of course it is also a matter of temptation. Of course we are moved by the wicked one, there is a satanic demonic element dragging us down. But temptation is not compulsion, and we need to remember that the very first sin that is recorded in the Bible, in Genesis 3, was an act of deliberate choice that is echoed in us all every time we sin. Yes, the devil came into the Garden of Eden and tempted Eve: 'Has God *really* said this? You don't really want to believe it, do you? He didn't really mean it.' But then, as it were, he slides off and he plays no further role in the story until God comes to declare His punishment. Eve stood before that tree, and we read that she saw and she thought and she decided and she took and she ate and she gave; and he ate and they both ate. These are acts of choice. We choose to sin. Let's not minimise that. We could do otherwise; you don't have to sin.

Let me be very careful to explain that. I'm not saying that it's possible to be perfect, that any of us could live without sin and be morally perfect in that sense. We do sin. As John rightly tells us, 'If we claim we have not sinned, we make him out to be a liar' (1 John 1:10). But let's remember, that never removes our responsibility for our choices and our actions. Yes, we do sin. But we sin because we choose to. The very essence of sin is that we choose it – if we had no choice in the matter, it wouldn't really be sin. It is sin because we have moral choice, and standing in the presence of God in God's world, knowing God's will and knowing God's righteousness, we choose to do what we know is wrong and not do what we know is right. That is a matter of our choice and our wills, brothers and sisters. Let us never go back to the Garden of Eden, and take up Adam's attitude when he said to the Lord, 'Oh, it's all this woman's fault – You put her here with me!' Or the woman's attitude, 'Oh, it's all this snake's fault, that You put in the creation.' Shifting the blame elsewhere is almost the archetypal sin of our culture. The last thing anybody will do is accept blame or responsibility.

That is why we have so little repentance and so little forgiveness.

When you reduce a person's responsibility, you remove the very first opportunity they have to step back towards repentance and forgiveness and grace. Remember, it is our wills that lead us to sin. And that is why this psalmist is so determined to strengthen his will against sin. He wants to think, to decide, to take steps, to determine what he will or will not do.

He would, I'm sure, have been the first to confess – as I will and you will too – that no matter how determined we are, we still fail. Of course we do. But that doesn't mean that we stop trying, that we turn round to God and say, 'Oh God, it doesn't matter. I can't help it, I'm just going to go on sinning anyway.' That is a very dangerous condition to be in.

Do you remember, in Daniel 1, how Daniel and his three friends resolved not to eat the food from the king's table? They made it a matter of will and determination, which then enabled them to stand up to the king and to his politicians. That choice that they made in chapter 1 was what sustained them in chapter 3 in the context of a burning fiery furnace, and in chapter 6 in the context of the lions' den. Possibly a whole lifetime later, Daniel has gone through life resolving, determining that he is not going to bow down to idols. He is going to serve God.

'I have kept my feet from the place of temptation, I have refused to stand in the way of sinners,' says the psalmist. Be ruthless on yourself! Remember, Jesus said, 'If your eye causes you to sin pluck it out. If your hand causes you to sin cut it off' (cf Mark 9). Be ruthless, be determined in your will. The choices that we make are so utterly vital. Moses said to the people of Israel, 'I set before you blessing and cursing, obedience and disobedience, life and death; now you choose,' he says. 'And for God's sake, choose life.' (cf Deut. 30:19).

The exercise of the emotions

The psalmist is not just a cold intellectual, whose head is full of the Bible and who has all the right verses and all the right doctrines. Nor is he a cold disciplinarian with a stern, unyielding, iron will. He is a person who feels very deeply. (Tomorrow we are going to look at some of his depths of feeling and emotion.) And among the deepest and most frequently expressed of his emotions are his reactions against sin, wickedness and evil in the world that he sees

around him and indeed in himself. Listen to some of the verses
that express these emotions, rather than merely the mind and the
will.

Verse 53: 'Indignation grips me because of the wicked, who
have forsaken your law.' Verse 104: 'I hate every wrong path.' Verse
128, the same thing: 'I hate every wrong path.' Verse 158 he says,
'I look on the faithless with loathing, for they do not obey your
word.' Verse 163, 'I hate and abhor falsehood but I love your law.'

We may not like those emotions. 'Hatred, loathing, indignation
– isn't that what's causing all the problems today in the world?'
Well, yes – when we hate the wrong thing. But here is a person so
saturated with the word of God that what he's actually doing is
reflecting or echoing the emotions of God Himself. Because God
is a God who hates sin, who is indignant because of the way the
world is going against Him. Indeed I find in Psalm 119 some of
the language of the prophets. You know how the prophets reflect
all the dealings of God, as they come out in their words against the
wickedness and sin of Israel? God's anger, God's grief, God's tears,
God's sense of betrayal by the people He loved – God's sheer
disbelief: 'How can you be like that?'; His disgust at the dirt and
the filth of sin, and His utter and total rejection of it. That's how
God feels, and that's how the prophets felt. And I think that is part
of what is welling up within the psalmist.

It challenges us, therefore, to ask the question: 'Isn't that how we
ought to feel about sin?' When we can sin without being bothered,
then, I suggest, we've lost touch with the heart of God. When we
can witness sin and see it in the lives of others, or watch it on the
television or in the world around us without a sense of pain or grief
– then we have lost touch with the heart of God.

Perhaps the most poignant verse is verse 136: 'Streams of tears
flow from my eyes, for your law is not obeyed.' Not because he was
hurting, though that was true; not just because people were against
him, though that was also true (as we'll see tomorrow). He is
grieved and hurt because of the sin of society around him. If we
were as filled with the word of God as this person is, then surely
our emotions need to be touched also by the heart of God against
sin.

So that is what the psalmist wants to tell us about avoiding sin.
How can a young man keep his way pure? How can an old man

keep his way pure – or a young man, or woman for that matter? The psalmist responds, 'By using your mind and filling it with the word of God; by using your will and watching your choices; and also by the exercise of your emotional feelings, to make sure they are in tune with God Himself.

The answer to sin

Psalm 119 speaks not only of the awareness and the avoidance of sin, but of the answer to sin. You see, the psalmist is not saying, 'Look, here are the rules. Just keep them and you'll have no problem with sin.' There are some books and some preachers around today that teach that all you need is forty quick steps to leading a victorious life and there you are. I don't think that our psalmist is saying that. He's not just saying, 'Just read your Bible every day, make your mind up, think positive, keep in touch with your inner feelings and all will be well.' He is not that naive. The idea that rules or techniques alone can solve the problem of sin is in fact the essence of legalism. Legalism is something of which Psalm 119 is often accused of, but in fact it's a million miles from legalism. In fact, it's altogether a very false idea that the Old Testament is all about legalism.

Do you remember that I said at the outset, Psalm 119 is not primarily about the law at all but about God? Verse 11, at the very beginning: 'I have hidden your word in my heart that I might not sin against you.' The psalmist does not say, 'I have memorised all the rules so that I won't break any of them,' as if that were all that matters. He says, 'No, Lord it's Your word in my heart and I don't want to sin against You.' This is relational language. So the only answer to the problem of sin that this psalmist is going to come up with is actually God Himself.

But then we might be tempted to say, 'Well, in that case can there be any real answer for him? Because isn't the God of the Old Testment the God of wrath, the God of judgement, the God of whom you should be afraid – as, indeed, we saw in verse 120? I mean, this poor fellow's going to have to wait till the New Testament; he's not going to find any answer to his sin until he's able to read the gospels and hear the word of grace and salvation that will come through the cross of Calvary and the blood of Christ.' What a lie, what a travesty! What a mistaken view of

Scripture is this idea that somehow in the Old Testment there's nothing but law and wrath, and there's no grace until you get to the New Testament. If I can do anything this week, I hope I can correct that impression.

But let the psalmist speak for himself. If this is a psalm about the law of God, then listen to what he has to say. Verse 29: 'Keep me from deceitful ways; be gracious to me through your law.' Verse 41: 'May your unfailing love come to me, O LORD, your salvation according to your promise.' Verse 58: 'I have sought your face with all my heart; be gracious to me according to your promise.' Verses 76 and 77, 'May your unfailing love be my comfort, according to your promise to your servant. Let your compassion come to me that I may live, for your law is my delight.' Verse 132: 'Turn to me and have mercy on me, as you always do to those who love your name.' And finally, verse 156: 'Your compassion is great, O LORD; renew my life according to your laws.'

Did you hear those words? Grace, love, kindness, salvation, comfort, compassion, mercy – and this is the Old Testament! Oh, let's get hold of this, because this is what made this psalmist come to life. He wants to praise and love God for His law, but he says, 'Lord, I find in Your word that You are this God – grace, love, compassion and mercy; and that's the answer to my sin. I can do all that I can do with my mind, my heart, my will, my emotions, to keep my feet away from sin; but I know that at the end of the day I've got to come back to You Lord, because You are the God of compassion and love and mercy.' This is the character of God that this psalmist knew and loved.

And we have to ask the question: How did he know? Here's a man who lived before Calvary, before the cross, before all the things that we celebrate at Keswick. How did he know that God was this kind of God? 'You ask me that?' he says. 'I'm telling you all the way through this psalm! "Be gracious to me according to your law."' We say, 'But that doesn't make sense. How can you have grace and law in the same sentence?' Well, that just exposes how silly is some of our systematic theology. We write books of systematic theology with all the law in one chapter and all the grace in another chapter as if they are somehow totally different. And yet here, in the Old Testament, this person is so filled with his gratitude for what he finds in God's law that he says, 'Lord, I know

You can be gracious to me because I've read it in Your law.'

Where did he read that? Where does the law talk about the grace, love and mercy of God? Of course we need to remember that when he was talking about 'the law' he meant the whole of the Torah – Genesis, Exodus, Leviticus, Numbers and Deuteronomy. It's there that we read about God's mercy when He saved Noah and his family from judgement. It's there, in the law of the Lord, that we read this story of the Exodus, that great act of God's redemption and salvation; such that when a son says to his father, 'Hey dad, what's this law about? Why should I keep it?' (cf Deut. 6:20), the father is to answer with the story of the gospel: 'We were slaves of Pharaoh in Egypt, but the LORD brought us out of Egypt; that's why we keep the law.' He tells his son, 'You ask me why we keep the law? I'll tell you the old, old story of Yahweh and His love, and I'll tell you the story of grace and salvation and redemption; that's where law comes from.' In the law we read the very definition of God.

In Exodus 34:6, God, speaking to Moses says, 'The LORD, the LORD, the compassionate and gracious God, slow to anger, abounding in love and faithfulness'. That verse bounces its way all the way through the Old Testament. You'll find it in the book of Numbers, in the Psalms, in Nehemiah, in Daniel, in the Prophets; 'the gracious, the compassionate God'.

So if you ask the psalmist, 'How do you know that God is gracious?', he will say, 'Let me take you to the law, let me tell you these stories. Let me fill you with the knowledge of this God, of love and grace and mercy and forgiveness.'

Of course you and I today know of the righteous mercy of God ultimately from the cross. Please don't misunderstand me, I don't want to minimise that. But it's the Old Testament believers, including psalmists like this, who would have said, had they stood at the cross – and indeed, as some of their successors did say – 'Yes, it's as we expected. That's our God: the God of love, patience, grace and mercy whom we knew in our Scriptures, in our history.'

And they would also say to us, if they were here to tell us today, 'Look, it is we who gave you all the words you need to express this – words like grace, love, forgiveness and mercy, which flow through the scriptures of the Old Testament and flood on into the New.' You won't find any better way of expressing the forgiveness of God's answer to sin than Psalm 103:9: 'He [the LORD] will not always accuse, nor will he harbour his anger for ever; he does not treat us as our sins deserve or repay us according to our iniquities.' Thank God for that. That's the gospel, and it's the gospel in the Psalms.

Or look at the very similar Isaiah 57:16-17 – 'I will not accuse for ever, nor will I always be angry, for then the spirit of man would grow faint before me – the breath of man that I have created. I was enraged by his sinful greed; I punished him, and hid my face in anger, yet he kept on in his wilful ways.' That's the wilful choice of sin. And yet, God says, 'I have seen his ways, but I will heal him; I will guide him and restore comfort to him' (57:18). That's the word of grace, the pure grace of the Lord Himself.

The answer to sin is not to be found in the rules, but in the Lord.

I'm told that it's quite traditional at Keswick that we begin with a reminder of our sin and of the need of God's cleansing, and that is a good way to start. And as go through this week with this psalmist, let us begin in the same way as he did, by acknowledging the reality of sin. I don't know what that will mean for you. I know what it means in my own heart, my own life, standing before you as a sinner saved by grace, like any of the rest of us. You know before God what it means to you.

It will be good if we start this week either literally or spiritually on our knees before God, saying, 'God, I know the sins I've committed. I know where I'm coming from, I know my problem. And Lord, I'm here because I want to avoid it. I want to use my mind and my heart and my emotions to avoid sin. But Lord, I know that at the end of the day I have to come to You because You alone have the words of eternal life, You alone have the words of grace.' And then as this psalmist did, to cast ourselves upon His mercy and His forgiveness, and plead again the old, old story of Jesus and His love – just as for the psalmist it was the old, old story that he knew, from the stories that he'd heard from his father, of the God who was the Saviour and the healer and the restorer of Israel, and his God too.

May the Lord enable us to do that this week.

2. Personal Struggle and the Word of Lament
Psalm 119:81-88

Today we move on to our second theme, and the word flowing through here is the word of lament. I want us to take as a focus for our reflection this morning the section from verse 81 to verse 88 – the part of Psalm 119 in which all the lines begin with the Hebrew letter *kaph*, 'K'. Please read these verses as we begin our study.

One of the ironies of the book of Psalms is that although its Hebrew title is actually 'The Praises', the largest single group of psalms are actually laments. The characteristic form of these laments is that in effect they are saying, 'God, I am hurting; and God, everyone else is laughing. And God, You are not helping very much either; and how long is it going to go on?' That is the essential form of the laments of the book of Psalms.

Dreadful experiences

And Psalm 119 has got a lot of it. Clearly the psalmist is a believer who is having a very tough time. He is struggling with a lot of stuff in his life. I use the word 'stuff', because at college we have a visiting lecturer called Bill Taylor (he is chairman of the World Evangelical Fellowship's Mission Commission), and he told us about a WEF study of why a considerable number of mission partners return to their home countries earlier than planned. It's a phenomenon called 'missionary attrition'. He says that sometimes, all you can say is 'Stuff happens.'

Stuff happens. Things go wrong in life. And for this person, a lot of stuff was happening. In fact it begins near the beginning of the psalm in verse 19. 'Lord,' he says, 'I feel like a stranger on the earth, I don't belong here, I'm like an alien.' In the very last verse, when you would have thought he might have reached some sort of resolution to his problems, he says, 'I have strayed like a lost sheep' (verse 176) – 'I'm still astray, I still need God to come and find me and help me.' So, from being like a stranger to being like a lost sheep, this is clearly a person with a far from happy state of mind.

Perhaps that rings some bells for some of us; we have come to Keswick not just to sing God's praises but also with that song of lament in our hearts that has a minor key: 'Lord, how long have I got to go on like this? How long are these problems going to be with me? When are You going to act?'

I want in this Bible Reading to begin by looking at some of the dreadful experiences this psalmist went through, and we will look at a number of things that he has to say. As I've said, it is summed up in the opening section, verse 19: 'Lord, I am a stranger here. So often I feel that I just don't belong. It feels like I'm not at home. I'm out of place, I'm uncomfortable.' Many Christians feel like that in their workplace, or as they live in a non-Christian family. 'Lord, I'm so different.'

The psalmist may well have been a young person, if verse 9 is at all autobiographical. He may be talking there about himself, feeling inexperienced, and vulnerable, possibly having been thrust while young into the public arena. It seems that may have been the case, because occasionally he talks about his involvement with kings, princes and leaders. So perhaps he's in a rather vulnerable state of anxiety and self-doubt, wondering if he will really make it and yet somehow confident that God will help him through.

Verse 99 again suggests that he's a younger person: 'I have more insight than all my teachers.' So he's still at school, as it were, perhaps a student. And in verse 100, 'I have more understanding than the elders.' So it is very probable that this is a person who speaks, yes, from experience, but from an early experience of life, though of course that doesn't make it irrelevant to those of us who are older.

Contempt and scorn

There are at least two elements in his suffering. The first is the pain of contempt and scorn. In verse 22 he says, 'Remove from me scorn and contempt.' In verse 42 he says, 'Then I will [be able to] answer the one who taunts me.' And in verse 141 he says, 'Though I am lowly and despised'. Scorned, taunted and despised. That's the language that this person uses of himself.

Now it is a terribly hard thing in life to be treated as a butt of other people's mockery or humour. Some of us may have experienced that in great measure, others of us are fortunate enough only perhaps ever to have experienced it very occasionally and have gone through life, generally speaking, with people's respect and encouragement. But there are those who suffer greatly because of other people's mockery. It is hard enough in life not to be treated with respect. It's doubly hard to be laughed at, to be treated with contempt and arrogance. That is deeply painful. And yet how common it is, and how early it starts. How our hearts go out when we witness children being bullied or laughed at in school. How utterly cruel children can be to one another, even before they can really understand what it is they are doing to each other! They are laughing, mocking, abusing one another; and we see it in schools and in playgrounds, in families and between families. It starts early. Sometimes, tragically, it can go on through childhood, even from the hands of those who should be honouring and respecting them; that is, from their parents. And people sometimes enter adult life with all the pain of having being mocked and laughed at, by parents saying, 'You weren't any good at this, you couldn't do that,' and so on. And then there are those who suffer abuse at work, perhaps racist humour which can be so cruel, or abuse of all kinds because we are Christians.

Well, here in this psalm we have a person who's been through that. And as we can tell, he was still going through it.

Slander and conspiracy

The other side of his suffering was more violent. Some people can live with scorn and contempt, though it's very damaging. But he also experiences the pain of slander and conspiracy, and what we have here is an even longer catalogue of abuse. Let me take you through some of the verses that express this.

Verse 23: 'Though rulers sit together and slander me...' – people are telling lies about him in high places. Verse 69: 'Though the arrogant have smeared me with lies...' – that's the language of the mud-heap or the manure-heap. He's getting plastered with dirt and muck and lies. That's the language he uses. Verse 78: 'May the arrogant be put to shame for wronging me without cause' – an unjustified attack. Verses 84 to 87: beginning, 'When will you punish my persecutors? The arrogant dig pitfalls for me ... Help me, for men persecute me without cause. They almost wiped me from the earth.' Verse 95: 'The wicked are waiting to destroy me.' Verse 110: 'The wicked have set a snare for me' – traps, snares, holes dug in the ground to trip him up. Verse 121: 'Do not leave me to my oppressors.' Verse 122: 'Let not the arrogant oppress me.' Verse 134: 'Redeem me from the oppression of men.' Verse 157: 'Many are the foes that persecute me.' And finally verse 161, 'Rulers persecute me without cause.'

Now, either this psalmist was paranoid – in other words, he just thought everybody was against him – or, if there remotely any truth in what he is saying, then he was having a very tough time at the highest level. It seems to suggest that he was in political leadership, young for his age but put into a position of authority. Many of us know that any position of leadership will expose you to the jealousies of others, to misinterpretation or to attacks and slander campaigns. And the Christian world, sadly, is no different. In fact sometimes it's even worse.

Remember Daniel's political enemies in Daniel 6? We read that because Daniel was a man of such integrity and hard work his enemies said, 'We'll never find anything against this man! We'll never be able to label him with any corruption, nothing will stick to him. We can't find any weaknesses. So we'll pull him down by his strength.' And they attacked him on grounds so blatantly racist and discriminatory in religion that they were quite unconstitutional.

That was Daniel's experience. I wonder whether it reflects any of yours? Perhaps you are a Christian minister; I'm sure you have gone through that experience of struggling with opposition, criticism, of never being able to do anything right and never seeming to be able to please. You know that experience of being in a position of wanting to lead people who do not want to be led and of having a vision which you believe is from the Lord. You want to move people forward into that vision, and they can't see it and they won't share it. You feel sometimes like the leading mountain climber with all the others tethered to the rope; and it's not so much that you are moving at the speed of the slowest climber (which is of course what you should do) – but there is somebody at the bottom end of the rope who has tied it to a tree and doesn't want to go up that particular mountain at all. So every obstacle and every rock is not a fresh challenge that you can overcome together with joy, but a reason why you shouldn't be climbing that mountain anyway.

Some of you are missionaries and suffer and struggle in positions of literally physical danger, and in some cases religious and political opposition. You have to endure that, and in a sense that would be all right; but what you also experience sometimes is misunderstanding and misinterpretation of your motives by those with whom you want to share and live and serve. That too can be a desperately painful thing. As the psalmist sometimes also pointed out, he could have borne it if his suffering was coming from his enemies, but when it was coming from those who he thought were his friends it was even worse. To be in Christian service and in Christian mission is no recipe for an easy life.

My wife tells me that the first time she ever saw me really angry was when we were in India together serving God in a theological college. After several years there we came up against a situation in which I became aware that things were being said about me and about my family. We were being accused, we were being misinterpreted, our motives were being called into question and our actions were being twisted. I became desperately angry, and for some time I became quite depressed as well. It was a Christian institution, I told myself; here were people I was wanting to work with and to serve; why else did I think I was there?

It is hard sometimes to experience the slander, the conspiracy of other people who you count as your brothers and sisters. But it can happen even in a Christian environment.

But of course many of us have had the experience of being the only Christian in a secular context, just as indeed Daniel and other believers were in the Old Testament. You've suffered at work something of the mockery or discrimination against you as a

Christian, because on principled grounds you are not prepared to do certain things. You won't go along with corruption or bribery or the getting around the rules that is so common. Or you want to take a stand on something, like, for example, working on Sunday; and you discover that your contract will not be renewed, or that you aren't appointed to the post. Threat is there. Or you work in a place where to be a Christian is a constant cause of abuse and of mockery and of pin-pricks and discrimination against you.

It may be that you are a Christian in a non-Christian family, and in the West that can be hard enough because of misunderstanding. Certainly at All Nations we often agonise with students who come to us believing that God has called them into mission and who are moving forward with God in mission, but who face the keenest opposition and misunderstanding from parents, family and people who accuse them of all sorts of things because they want to follow the Lord. Of course Jesus warned us against that. But if it's tough for us in the Western world, think of those who are Christians in countries where to be a Christian can lead you into total rejection by your family by being cut off and excluded, treated as if you had died, and in some cases actually being put to death because of your faith in Christ.

Maybe you are a young person at school or at college. It can be difficult to be a Christian at university. I was fortunate in that I didn't have a lot of opposition, but I was a member of the boat club. As the regatta approached, the issue arose of rowing and training on Sunday. I believed I should not, and I didn't, which meant they had to find a substitute and I was not at all popular for taking that stand. People today suffer much worse kinds of abuse and misunderstanding and are laughed at, because they have chosen to follow Christ. If you choose to follow biblical standards of behaviour and sexual morality you will become the butt of jokes and ridicule. 'How can you be like that? Why are you so old-fashioned?' There is all the pain of scorn, contempt, slander and conspiracy that comes from human opponents. And that is what this author is talking about.

Perhaps some of us don't experience those things from human enemies but can translate some of the language of this psalm into those words of mockery and taunting, depression and sneering, that come from the pit. They come from the spiritual reality of the satanic assault upon us. Many of us know what it is to read through psalms like this one, and as we read, 'Lord, deliver me from my enemies, they have risen up against me,' to think not so much of human enemies but of those demonic, satanic forces which impinge upon us, drive us down and create within us emotions and feelings that we know do not come from the Lord and from the Holy Spirit. And yet they well up within our hearts, until we recognise where they are coming from.

Things like fear can be terrible enemies and terribly debilitating. The fear that may perhaps come through physical illness: the devil says, 'You're never going to get any better, you're never going to recover, and what's life going to be like?' Or the fear that comes from sin: 'You're going to be found out some day and you're going to be disgraced; and then what?' There's the fear that comes from guilt, from self-accusation – sometimes we are our own worst enemies.

The enemies are not external but internal. Satan plays on that fact and accuses us. 'What kind of Christian are you? What sort of a believer are you?' He will exploit any avenue he can, and intensify every shaft of guilt which we ought to turn into repentance; and he will turn it the other way. Even when we have confessed and been forgiven, he will still come back and drive us with those shafts of enmity. No wonder Paul says we should take the whole armour of God upon us, to defend ourselves against such attacks! All these things will come.

And here is this psalmist telling us: 'I know all of this. These are the things I've been through, all this mockery, contempt, accusation – human and physical, spiritual, satanic, wherever it comes from – I've been there, I've known that, I've walked where you walk, I've sat where you sit, I've wept, I've struggled as you do.'

The great thing is that this psalmist is not the only one in the Bible. We could have been doing these Bible Readings in the book of Job and found the same thing. We could have been studying the book of Jeremiah and found it there. Both Jeremiah and Job said to the Lord, 'Lord, I wish I'd never been born if I was going to suffer like this.' Jeremiah said to the Lord, 'Lord, you've cheated me.' Not a terribly evangelical thing to say! But it's the words of a prophet: 'Lord when I turn to you, you are like a deceitful brook. Is that what you are going to be to me?' He wished he'd never been born. He went through these experiences of scorn and contempt.

And of course Jesus Himself has been there. He has been there with these psalms on His lips, and He went through mockery, contempt, rejection, oppression, accusation, lies, false trial and death; and He did it for you and for me,

> Bearing shame and scoffing rude,
> In my place condemned He stood.

That's the gospel, you see. And it's because Jesus went there that Jesus also knows what it's like to be there, as this psalmist did.

So that's the experiences he's been through. I'm quite sure that some, perhaps most, of us here are saying, 'God, it's good that this is in the Scriptures. It's good that somebody knows what I'm feeling, and actually puts it into words, and that those words are in the Bible, the word of God.'

Deep reactions

One thing about this psalmist is that you always know what he is thinking. He doesn't hide anything, he lets us see his reactions very explicitly indeed. And again, he does it in two ways. We see his reaction to the external wickedness that he sees around him, but he also gives us a window on the internal emotional cost of this experience.

The external reaction

This person is no passive observer. He's not an armchair critic of society, a television commentator just sitting back mocking and throwing the hand grenades of attack and cynicism at the wickedness and foibles of others. Still less is he a gutter-press journalist with a knowing wink and a false righteousness, pointing out wickedness and flaws in others. This is a person who cares deeply about God and His law. He is deeply distressed about the blatant evil and corruption and violence and wickedness that he sees in the society around him.

Let's do another thread-tracing exercise through Psalm 119. We can begin with verse 53: 'Indignation grips me because of the wicked.' Here he is feeling that rising tide; it is red-faced indignation, there is fury in his heart because of what he sees. Verse

113: 'I hate double-minded men' – that is, people who say one thing and do another, whom you can never trust. In verse 115 he addresses them directly: 'Away from me, you evildoers.' He is repulsed by them and he rejects them. But it's not just anger, fury and rejection. There is also deep grief. Verse 136: 'Streams of tears flow from my eyes, for your law is not obeyed.' How much do we weep over what we see in the news? Verse 139 talks of zeal for the law: 'My zeal wears me out, for my enemies ignore your words' – not just because they are attacking him but because they are ignoring the word of God. And finally, in verse 158, he says, 'I look on the faithless with loathing, for they do not obey your word.'

They are strong words: indignation, hatred, repulse, grief, zeal and loathing. Nor are they pleasant words. And yet, as I was saying yesterday, they reflect God's own reaction to evil. Yesterday we saw it in relation to our own sin. Here the psalmist speaks as he does because he knows God's feelings and God's reactions to wickedness and to sin in society. He knows the way God is going to act towards those who are unrepentantly, persistently and arrogantly wicked. He's not just talking about what we might call 'everyday ordinary sinners', for of course we are all sinners on whom the love and the compassion and the grief of the Lord is poured out. He's talking rather about people who knowingly, willingly, deliberately, persistently and unrepentantly do wrong. He tells us that with such people the Lord will deal first of all: verse 21, 'You rebuke the arrogant, who are cursed.' Verse 118: 'You reject all who stray from your decrees, for their deceitfulness is in vain.' And verse 119: 'All the wicked of the earth you discard like dross.'

So here is a psalmist who looks at the wickedness of the world and who sees and feels it with the response of the Lord Himself. For me that prompts questions. What is my reaction to the sin and the evil and the wickedness in the world? Does my moral sensitivity in any way match up to the words of this psalm, let alone the rest of the Scriptures, in the prophets, Jesus and so on?

'What makes you angry?' is probably a good question if we want to check ourselves on this kind of righteousness table. Is it your own selfish interests when your pride is hurt? Or do we become angry at what we see happening in our country, because it offends our political preferences and loyalties so that we shout at the television screen, at people the colour of whose politics we dislike?

Is it our social prejudices that make us angry – are we coloured by certain views of society? It's so easy to be selective and one-sided in our moral righteousness. I think as evangelical Christians we are very good at having a mixture of moral heat spots and moral blind spots. What we need to ask is: What makes God angry, and how do we know what makes Him angry?

The answer is that we know because of the clarity and the emphases of the Scriptures themselves. Look at what God says in His word about what He is most concerned about. Sometimes, that can be a very healthy corrective to the things that we might be most concerned about.

For example, the word 'abomination' is used in Scripture. We hear it also used and lightly quoted in contemporary discussion. But it is a very strong word. It literally means 'that which stinks in God's nostrils, that which He hates with all His being'. Now yes, we know from the Scriptures that sexual immorality and sexual perversion are described as abominations to the Lord. Yes, we also know that the Scriptures describe as 'abominations' such horrors as child sacrifice. But did you know that Proverbs 11:1 also says that dishonest scales are an abomination to the Lord? Cheating in business and dishonesty in the workplace are also an abomination to the Lord. Where does that cut?

And yes, we know too that Deuteronomy 27:15 tells us that 'Cursed is the man who carves an image or casts an idol' – who worships other gods. And yes, in the same chapter we read that cursed is the one who commits a whole range of sexually perverted acts. Yes, that's all there. But also verse 19 says, 'Cursed is the man who withholds justice from the alien, the fatherless or the widow.' Are we as aware of the anger and the wrath of God on those issues of social justice and compassion, as we are in those other areas?

Yes, we know that Paul tells us in Romans 1:29-32 that the wrath of God is revealed against such things – sexual immorality and murder; but he also says that envy, greed and gossip are among the things that bring the anger and the wrath of God.

Let's be wholly biblical in the things that make us angry. Let's look at the wickedness of the world through the eyes of the Lord Himself. It is possible for evangelical moral anger to be rightly expressed at some of the things that are such burning issues in our day. Yet we are also to ask ourselves: How disturbed are we, how angry do we get, how willing are we to march in campaigns on behalf of refugees, asylum-seekers, the homeless, the elderly, the poor? – they are those about whom the Scriptures are absolutely clear. God's anger is revealed against those who mistreat such people, and deprive them of justice and compassion.

Remember the words of Jesus in the parable of Lazarus and the rich man. Remember what it was that the rich man went to hell for. He neglected what he should have done for the poor man at his gate. And remember how he said to Abraham, in that parable of Jesus, 'Why don't you please send somebody back from the dead to warn my brothers, so that they don't come to this place of torment?' And that awful reply came: 'Even if somebody comes back from the dead, they won't believe. Because if they didn't listen to the law and the prophets, they won't listen even if somebody comes back from the dead.'

The Law and the Prophets of the Old Testament Scriptures tell us what we should be angry about. They tell us what we should be concerned about in our world, and they tell us about purity, morality, righteousness, integrity, compassion and justice. So let's have our hearts touched by that which touches the heart of God in our moral campaigns, in a deep reaction, like this psalmist's, to the external wickedness of our society.

The internal cost

But what was it all doing to him? That's a very modern question that would be asked from many a counselling chair. What is all this doing to you? How does it make you feel? It's not a question perhaps that we often ask, but this psalmist is perfectly happy to tell us. In fact I would be willing to suggest that had he been living in the twentieth century, he would have been in a counsellor's office every week.

Just look at how he expresses himself. Verse 25: 'I am laid low in the dust.' Isn't that one of the best descriptions of depression you could ever get? He says, 'It's like living on the floor eating dust, that's my experience. I'm laid low on the ground, absolutely flat.' Verse 28: 'My soul is weary with sorrow' – 'I can't go on any longer.' Verse 50: 'My comfort in my suffering is this.' But he is going through pain and suffering. And then in verses 81 to 83 he says, 'My soul faints with longing' – he's passing out, this man. 'My eyes fail, looking for your promise.' In verse 83 there's the wonderful image, 'Though I am like a wineskin in the smoke ...' A wineskin would have been a leather bag used for carrying wine. Leave leather above a fire for any length of time and it will become dried out, and hard and cracked, instead of being flexible as it has to be to hold the wine. He says, 'I'm like a dried up sack.'

In verse 92 he says, 'I would have perished in my affliction.' In verse 107 he talks about suffering again, and in verse 139 about being worn out again: 'My zeal wears me out.'

Depression, exhaustion, weariness, suffering, fainting, being dried up, perishing: the language is incredible. And once again, I wouldn't be surprised to find that many of us can identify with this language and often come before the Lord saying exactly the same thing: 'Lord, I've had enough, I'm worn out.' And even before we look for the answer to this, is there not at least the precious comfort of knowing that the Bible includes that kind of expression in the word of God? – that which is not the words of God Himself, but the words of a man or woman who says, 'Lord, this is what I want to say to You.' Much of the Psalms, Jeremiah, Job and other parts of Scripture is the outpouring of a human heart and human words saying, 'Lord, I can't go on.' God is willing to take that word from our lips, and to turn it around and actually include it as part of the worshipping word of Scripture so that it is included in the word of God to us. There is at least an encouragement in that.

And I want to point out too that this is a word of desperate emotional cost, longing and suffering on the lips of somebody who was faithful to the Lord, who was trusting and obeying God, who was desperately anxious to be faithful, to be loyal, to love God, and to serve God. This is not the language of somebody experiencing suffering, depression and fear because he's being disobedient or is walking away from God in disbelief. This is the language of a person who is suffering in the midst of faithfulness and obedience.

That in turn leads me to say that if that is so, then what a lie, what a travesty of the truth, is the so-called prosperity gospel! It wants to distort and twist all the scriptures about the blessing of God and obedience and turn them upside down. 'If you are obedient and if you trust God, you are never going have pain and suffering, you are never going to be sick, you are never going to be poor, you ought to always be healthy, wealthy and successful' ...

even if not very wise. Prosperity? Rubbish.

I sometimes wonder what New Testament some people read. In what Bible do they come across that kind of thing? Here, and elsewhere through the Scriptures, we find people struggling to be faithful, who were trusting and being obedient, and yet they went through suffering, scandal, slander, pain, poverty, everything else. It just isn't true to say that if only you have faith and turn to God, everything's going to be all right. We do need to turn to God. But let's not be naive. Let's not feel that somehow all the problems will then be solved, and we'll be off to heaven there and then.

Our singing can sometimes be so trite. 'Every day with Jesus is sweeter than the day before.' I wish that were true. In a sense it can be, but is it true for you? Can you say literally that every day your Christian life has been better than the day before? Some might say so and I wouldn't want to question it, but I know that probably for every one who might say that, there are another ten who would say, 'That's not true for me. I know what this psalmist is talking about and I've been through that emotional cost. I've been depressed, I've been eating the dust of life and I don't want to deny it.'

So here is a man who's had some dreadful experiences and some very deep reactions to them, about which he is perfectly honest and open. He doesn't conceal it. He doesn't put on a smile and say, 'Isn't it great to be a believer?'

He says, 'Lord, it's tough; and just at the moment You are not helping very much.'

Double response

How did the psalmist cope with such experiences and with such crushing reactions to it? Again, his is a double response.

He cried out

First of all, he cries to God, as any of us would if we'd been where he was, and as many of us still do, frequently and regularly. Verses 81 to 88, the section called *kaph*, is almost one prolonged 'How long, O Lord? How long? When will You comfort me, how long must I wait? It's nearly wiped me out.' It's a desperate, seemingly endless, waiting for God; it's the cry of endurance. It fits with what the psalmist said in Psalm 40, 'I waited patiently for the LORD my God.' And some of us know that we don't wait patiently. 'When,

Lord, when, when, when will You do something about this problem?' We sing that lovely song, 'Faithful One so unchanging, You're my rock of hope.' And yet it contains the line, 'I call out to You again and again.' I'm sure that you've been there. I have. When it seems the Lord either isn't there, or He's gone away, or He's far off. And you say, 'Lord, when, *when*, WHEN will You do something?'

That's what this psalmist feels, and that's what he says. It is plain in the *Qoph* section, verses 145 to 147: 'I call with all my heart; answer me, O LORD, and I will obey your decrees. I call out to you; save me and I will keep your statutes. I rise before dawn and cry for help; I have put my hope in your word.' Verse 148: 'My eyes stay open through the watches of the night.' Verse 149: 'Hear my voice in accordance with your love.'

Sleepless nights, early mornings, the language of despair and anxiety and longing, calling out to God.

What reason has he got to hope that God will answer him? Well, he gives us some clues. First of all, he recognises when his mind clears that actually God is as near to him as his troubles are. Look at verses 150 to 151. 'Those who devise wicked schemes are near' – they are getting near, my enemies, those who are against me, they are close, they are near. 'Yet you are near, O LORD, and all your commands are true.' They are near – but then, so are You.

There is indeed a lovely little ironical paradox there. '[The wicked] are near' – that is, 'they are near me', but they are actually 'far from your law', far from You. The troubles are near but God is nearer. The image is like that of a goalkeeper in the World Cup watching an attacker bearing down upon him. The attacker is near, but suddenly out of the blue comes a defender, the ball's away off to the touch-line, and the defender is nearer than the attacker. That is the kind of thought the psalmist is expressing. I love that expression, only once or twice used in this psalm but so common in many of the others: verse 114, 'You are my refuge and my shield.' The Lord God is a place to hide, a place to be sheltered where even the enemy can't find you.

At All Nations we are aware, as a place training people for Christian mission, that we are bound to be if not at the front line, then certainly pretty close to it, for satanic attention. What else does the devil want to attack, but people who are seeking to go out and do something for the kingdom of God? So we recognise that constantly we are under that attack of the evil one. Recently we were very much aware of it, and in my own life I was also conscious of the attack of the evil one. A few of us were praying together, some of my group of those in college who help to advise, guide and support me. One of them prayed, 'Lord, will You please hide Chris so that even the devil can't find him and won't know where he is.' That spoke to my heart! I lived on that for days. 'Hey, Lord, thanks for the angels! I know that the devil can't even find me. I know he's looking. But while that protection is there I'm in the refuge, in the hiding place, hidden in the cave where no one can find me.' I wonder if this psalmist was perhaps echoing something of the experience of David, who sometimes literally did shelter in caves away from his enemies, and knew that the Lord was that refuge, that hiding place, where the enemies couldn't reach him? And here is this psalmist saying, 'Lord, I know that the attackers are there but You are closer still and in You I find shelter. I am safe.' It's a tremendous feeling, to be safe with God.

That's the first reason why he thinks it's worth crying out to God, because God is actually there.

The second reason is that God is an exodus God. You may say, there's no exodus in this psalm; but the exodus imagery is there. Verses 153 and 154: 'Look upon my suffering and deliver me.' Look and save; that is the language of exodus, because that is exactly what it says in Exodus 2. Do you remember how God said to Moses, 'Moses, I have seen the suffering of my people'? In fact even in Exodus 1 it says that the Lord looked on His people and saw them and was concerned for them. And then He said to Moses, 'I am coming down to deliver them.'

The God who sees, and the God who knows, and the God who cares: that is the God that Israel worships. Other nations worshipped idols that had eyes but couldn't see. Israel worshipped the God who had no literal eyes but could see the whole earth and could see those who were suffering. He looks and He sees, and He will defend and He will redeem. Verse 154: 'Defend my cause and redeem me' – save me, lift me up as You did for the people of Israel at the exodus.

And again we ask the question, Where did the psalmist get all this? The answer, he tells us, is from the law, from the Torah, from the Scriptures. He personally had not been there at the exodus, just as we sometimes sing, 'Were you there when they crucified my Lord?' We have to say, 'Well no, actually in the literal, physical sense we weren't there at the cross. But yet in another sense yes I was there, because Jesus died for me. It was my sin put Him there, and He rescued me from my sin.'

In the same way this psalmist is saying, 'I wasn't actually there at the exodus, but I am the child of the same God who is the exodus God, who sees, who knows and who delivers. And so I can cry out to God, "God, will You please look, will You please see what is happening here and will You please do something about it."' That's where this psalmist gets it. We call out to the God who is not deaf and the God who is not blind.

He is determined to press ahead

I said his was a double reaction. And I want us to notice that as well as that crying out to God, there is also a determination to press on, no matter what. This psalm resonates with the sound of gritted teeth. It repeats again and again a sense of determination that no matter what happens, no matter what doesn't happen, no matter how great the opposition, whatever the cost, whatever God does or doesn't do, he is going to go on obeying God, trusting Him, serving and loving Him, and he will go on doing it and calling out at the same time.

Isn't that a contradiction? How can you at the same time ask God for help and also say, 'Right, now I've got to get on with it, I've got to struggle, I've got to work, I've got to put my own effort into it'? Isn't that to confuse grace and works?

Not at all. If it were, it wouldn't be in the Scriptures, would it?

Many of us will remember a song from, I think, the 1970s, which had the refrain, 'Do not strive.' 'Let Me have my way among you, do not strive, do not strive ... we'll not strive.' I know that it's saying, in a way, that we have to allow God to be God and to do what He wants to do. But somehow that suggests that God does what God will do, and all we've got to do is sit back and watch and not put any effort or work into our Christian lives.

If that's how we are thinking, I think the psalmist would not agree with us. This is a person who's saying, 'I will strive, and I will strive jolly hard. I am determined and committed to walk in the ways of the Lord and to go on with God in faithfulness.' In fact, in verse 32 he says, 'I run in the path of your commands.' He's not just going to crawl, he's not going to just struggle along in the dust, he's going to pick himself up and he's going to run on. In verse 81 we read, 'My soul faints with longing for your salvation, but I have put my hope in your word.' Verse 83: 'Though I am like a wineskin in the smoke, I do not forget your decrees.' He says that some of this affliction and suffering that he's been through has actually in God's providence been good for him. That is never an easy lesson to learn, and certainly not one to use in our pastoral ministry - 'It's wonderful that you are suffering so much, God will really bless you.' No, it's not somebody else that the psalmist talks about, but he does say in verse 67, 'Before I was afflicted I went astray, but now I obey your word.' And also in verse 71: 'It was good for me to be afflicted so that I might learn your decrees.' And in verse 75: '... in faithfulness you have afflicted me.' He knows what it is to struggle on with God in a determined way.

Do you remember the three friends of Daniel who were threatened with being put in the burning fiery furnace? In that wonderful response to Nebuchadnezzar they combined both of these responses beautifully. 'Nebuchadnezzar, you think you are some great king. But our God whom we serve is able to deliver us. Of course he is: He's the God of all power, and He will and He can deliver us.' And then come these wonderful words: 'Even if not – even if He doesn't, we want you to know that we are not going to bow down and serve you; because we will serve the living God even in the flames if necessary. We will not serve you' (cf Dan. 3).

It's the language of Job: 'Though he slay me, yet will I hope in him.' (Job 13:15).

It's the language of the disciples of Jesus, when He gave them the opportunity to go away. It was getting too tough for them, the pressure was building up; and they wanted to quit. But they said, 'Lord, to whom shall we go? You have the words of eternal life' (John 6:68)'

This is saying to God, 'Lord, I call out to You, I want, I long for You to act, I want You to sort out this mess, I want You to put things right. But Lord, I want You to know that no matter what You do, or no matter what You don't do, You are stuck with me. Because I am Your servant, and I love You and I am going to go on serving You no matter what happens in this life. For quite frankly I don't know what I could do, I don't know where else to go or what to do except to love, to serve, the living God.'

Is that your double response to the suffering and pain and struggle that life throws at us? 'Lord, will you please do something ... But Lord, while I'm waiting for You to do something, help me to walk on, to move forward, to be faithful in this struggle.'

And if the psalmist is not authority enough for us – don't we see something of this even in the Garden of Gethsemane itself? The personal struggle of the Son of God – 'Lord, please take this cup away from Me' – calling out to God in that moment for God to deliver Him. 'But nevertheless not what I want but what You want. Your will be done.' And then Jesus got up from His knees and walked forward to Calvary with God His Father.

That, I think, is the double response that God calls for from us. To hope in God, and to go on walking with Him. May that be the strength that the Lord gives us with the psalmist; that his experience, if it's ours, will lead us not to quitting, not to despair, but to renewal of our ho

pe and response to God and our determination to serve Him.

3. Personal Guidance and the Word of Light
Psalm 119:97-105

There's a song that we sing at All Nations Christian College, that comes from Africa. It begins, 'We are marching in the light of God.' It's the same wonderful picture that in the English cultural tradition is enshrined in the hymn 'Onward, Christian soldiers, marching as to war': a glorious army marching in step, in time, in a great organised, wonderful, beautiful procession.

Though it's certainly a biblical picture and is used sometimes of the people of God, it is actually more often used of God Himself, marching forth victorious. The Bible describes human life much more as a walk. Perhaps for some of us it's more like a confused wander through a maze, or a crawl up a mountainside, but the metaphor of walking is certainly a very biblical one. We are going to look at it quite a lot this morning.

We do long for a walk in life that will be clearly guided. We want to know we're going in the right direction. We long for understanding and insight, to know, 'Yes, this is where I should be going and I know why.' We want to know God's will, we want to know His plan for our lives – if indeed, we sometimes speculate, He has one.

As did this psalmist of Psalm 119. He didn't just want to avoid sin – the negative aspect, which we saw in our first study. He didn't just want to have help from God in his times of struggle, as we saw yesterday. He wanted, much more positively, that in everyday, ordinary, life and decisions, he would be living well and wisely; that he would be behaving in a godly way in his life.

So in this psalm he repeatedly asks God for two things. First, for light on his path, and second, for learning as a pupil. So we will be looking at personal guidance, with the word of God very much as the word of light.

Light for the path

Walking in the way of the Lord

Psalm 119 begins, 'Blessed are they whose ways are blameless [literally, 'those who are upright in their way'], who walk according to the law of the LORD.'

I'll give you a few further examples; there are many more. Verse 26: 'I recounted my ways and you answered me' – 'I told You, Lord, the ways I've been walking, how I've been moving with You.' Verse 29: 'Keep me from deceitful ways; be gracious to me through your law.' Verse 30: 'I have chosen the way of truth; I have set my heart on your laws.' Verse 32: 'I run' – well, it's a bit faster than walking, but it's still movement! – 'in the path of your commands.' And verse 59, 'I have considered my ways and have turned my steps to your statutes.'

So the vocabulary frequently used in this psalm is 'the path ... the feet ... the steps'. Perhaps the most familiar verse, and one that could almost be the key verse for this part of our reflection, is verse 105. Many of us knew it from our childhood. It is a key Scripture Union verse. 'Your word is a lamp to my feet and a light for my path.'

Life then is a journey, a process. We still use that metaphor in everyday conversation, even in English. For example, we talk about somebody 'leading a particular kind of life'. So let's think about this, because the psalmist uses it as a picture or metaphor so often that it's obviously something he's familiar with from his Scriptures and from his faith tradition. But we need to reflect on some other parts of the Old Testament to establish exactly what he's talking about. What does it mean, to be 'walking in the way of the Lord'?

GENESIS 18

One of the earliest examples of this expression is in Genesis 18:19. The context is of God on His way to bring judgement to Sodom and Gomorrah, which happens in chapter 19. He comes on a kind of fact-finding mission with two angels to warn that He's on His way. Verse 20: 'The outcry against Sodom and Gomorrah is so great and their sin so grievous that I will go down and see if what they have done is as bad as the outcry that has reached me. If not, I will know.' This is the wonderful way the Bible has of speaking of God in human language; it pictures God up in heaven saying, 'I'd better go down and see' – as if He can't see from heaven! But this is the human language of God. So He comes, and on His way to Sodom He stops off and has a meal with Abraham and Sarah. Perhaps the reputation of Sarah as a good cook had even reached the angels; they say, 'Come on Lord, let's have a meal with these two.' At first Abraham and Sarah think that they are just three men visiting; the fact that one of them is the Lord only becomes apparent as the story proceeds.

'When the men got up to leave, they looked down towards Sodom, and Abraham walked along with them to see them on their way. Then the LORD said, "Shall I hide from Abraham what I am about to do?"' (verse 16). The answer He gives to Himself is obviously 'No', because He says, 'Abraham will surely become a great and powerful nation, and all the nations on earth will be blessed through him.' (That's God reminding Himself of His great promise to bless the nations.) And then God says this about Abraham: 'For I have chosen him, so that he will direct his children and his household after him to keep the way of the LORD [there's that expression] by doing what is right and just, so that the LORD will bring about for Abraham what he has promised him' (verse 19).

God says to Himself, 'I can't keep back from Abraham what I'm going to do, because he is somebody whom I chose. I have called him with a purpose. And that purpose is that he should be the fountain-head of a community of people, his own household and his descendants – all of those who will come from him as their head, who will be committed to keeping and walking in the way of the Lord.' As distinct, of course, from Sodom and Gomorrah who are walking in the way of the world – in the way of evil, oppression, callousness, perversion and everything else that is described in Genesis and other parts of the Old Testament. So in contrast to the way of Sodom, where God was going to bring judgement, God says, 'I want Abraham and his people to be committed to the way of the Lord.'

I think that is the clearest expression you will find of what is called 'Old Testament ethics'. If you were to ask an average Israelite (as I wish I could have done when I was doing my doctoral dissertation) 'Excuse me, could you please tell me about Old Testament property ethics?' he would probably have replied, 'What are you talking about? "Ethics"?' But if you had asked, 'Excuse me, could you please explain to me about walking in the way of the Lord?', he would have replied, 'Ah! Now I know what you're talking about; because that is what we understand. That's what we are to do: to behave as God behaves, to look at His footprints and in them plant our own, to be imitators of the Lord God, to walk in His ways, to be like Him.'

And, just in case the reader of Genesis might have missed it, we are told that God immediately added, 'by doing righteousness and justice'. Those are two of the biggest words in the Hebrew Old Testament scriptures. It's the whole character of God in a nutshell. The Lord loves righteousness and justice; righteousness and justice are the foundation of His throne (cf Psalm 89:14).

So God says, 'To walk in My way, to walk in the way of the Lord, means to do what is right and just. That's why I called Abraham, so that he will be like that, and his people.' But then God says that there is another reason: 'so that the LORD will bring about for Abraham what he has promised him.' Now, what had God promised to Abraham? He had promised that through him He would bless all the nations and all the families of the world. That's God's mission, His concern for all the world and for all the nations – and that's God's agenda, vision and purpose.

So here in this little saying of the Lord Himself, He is actually binding together (to resort to theological language) election, ethics and mission. 'I have chosen him,' says God. That's God's election. 'So that he will live in a certain kind of way, be a certain kind of community, behave with certain values ... So that I can keep My promise to the nations' – that's God's agenda. And in between, there is a way of life, there is a moral agenda of righteousness and justice. If God's people will walk in God's ways, then God can get on with blessing the nations. If God's people do not walk in the ways of the Lord then His whole programme of blessing the nations is hindered, because the nations look at the people of God and say, 'What's the difference? They are no different from us. Why should we believe in any kind of God like that?' Or they look at the people of God, and as Deuteronomy said, they will say, 'Wow! What kind of God is this? What kind of laws are these?' (cf Deut. 4:32 ff).

DEUTERONOMY 10

Deuteronomy is one of my favourite books. In chapter 10 we have an example that the author of Psalm 119 would have had in mind when talking about 'the way of the Lord'. The psalmist tells us repeatedly that he wants us to do so 'according to God's law', so his mind would have been filled with texts like Deuteronomy 10:12.

Moses is approaching a climax in his sermon. Deuteronomy 10:12-13 has the flavour of a preacher coming to his main point. He says that the summary of the law is that all the Lord wants is for us to fear God, walk in His ways, love Him, serve Him and obey Him. Five simple words.

Notice that in these verses we find the expression 'to walk in all his ways'. Now, you might imagine the Israelites saying, 'That's wonderful, Moses; we want to do that. Can you please tell us what they are so that we can walk in them?' Later in the same chapter, Moses talks about the Lord explicitly. Verse 14: 'To the LORD your God belong the heavens, even the highest heavens, the earth and everything in it. Yet the LORD set his affection on your forefathers and loved them, and he chose you, their descendants, above all the nations, as it is today.'

'Yes, that is wonderful, Moses! We want to walk in the Lord's ways. How do we *do* it?'

Verse 16: 'Well, first of all you've got to circumcise your hearts and not be stiff-necked any longer. You've got to turn round from your rebellion and stubbornness, and start walking in the right direction. 'For the LORD your God is God of gods and Lord of lords, the great God, mighty and awesome.'

'Yes, yes, Moses – but please, what does it *mean* to walk in the ways of this God?'

And Moses replies, 'He is the God who shows no partiality and accepts no bribes. He defends the cause of the fatherless and the widow, and loves the alien, giving him food and clothing. And you want to walk in the ways of that God? Well then,' says verse 19, 'you are to love those who are aliens' – and presumably feed them, clothe them, care for the widow and the orphan and all the other things that God does. 'You want to walk in the ways of the Lord?' demands Moses. 'Then be like Him.'

'And you of all people,' he says in verse 19, 'ought to know this, because when I tell you the Lord is the God who loves aliens, you know it's true. Because that's why He loves you. He loved you when you were aliens in Egypt, when you were strangers, foreigners, oppressed, refugees, and you sought asylum in Egypt. The Lord loved you, preserved you and redeemed you. So: to walk in the way of the Lord is to follow His character of love that stoops down, of integrity, of impartiality, of incorruptibility. He accepts no bribes, He is not partial. He is the God of compassionate, loving justice. That is the way of the Lord – and you'd better be walking in it. It's the whole of life geared towards imitating the character of God.'

DEUTERONOMY 11
Very characteristically, Deuteronomy 10 – on which the psalmist may well have been meditating – about walking in the way of the Lord, obeying His character and being governed by His priorities in social and moral life, is followed in chapter 11 by the promise of blessing. There God says, 'If you will obey these laws, if you will walk in this way and not turn aside from it, then you will go on experiencing the blessing of being God's people, of being redeemed, of knowing the Lord as your God and being provided for by Him.' It's all there as you read through chapter 11.

That combination, of obediently walking in God's ways and experiencing God's continuing blessing as a result, is exactly the dynamic of Psalm 119. 'Blessed are they whose ways are blameless, who walk according to the law of the LORD,' reads verse 1, possibly echoing the familiar words of Psalm 1. There are only two ways to walk in the Bible. You don't stop at the sign-posts, you don't sit down and have a cup of tea; you are walking. And you are either walking in the way of the righteous under God's care and blessing, or you are walking in the way of the wicked, who, this psalm tells us, will ultimately perish.

Finding the way of the Lord

So how do we go about finding the way and staying in it?

The psalmist, as we have already seen, gives us the answer in verse 9: 'How can a young man keep his way pure?' The answer is, 'by living [or, by watching it] according to your word'. So we move from the theme of walking in the way of the Lord to that of watching your way in the light of God's word: the law of the Lord, the Scriptures.

This psalmist was possibly among the more fortunate generations of the human race. He lived before the great era of publications. He had the Scriptures and that's probably about all. In our day we are advantaged (or disadvantaged) by any number of books full of hints, tips, rules and guidance for a successful Christian life. Some of them are very helpful, I wouldn't want to deny that; and it's a great privilege to have so much Christian literature. But I would urge you to remember that your greatest, your primary and your most fundamental resource for walking in the way of the Lord is the Bible itself that you have in your hand.

In his wonderful challenge to the people of Israel to be sure they are paying attention to the word of God, Moses wants to move them on from any notion that the word of God is for the specialist few, the very clever or the very educated. He says to them,

> What I am commanding you today is not too difficult
> for you or beyond your reach. It is not up in heaven, so
> that you have to ask, 'Who will ascend to heaven to get
> it [this law] and proclaim it to us so that we may obey it?'
> Nor is it beyond the sea, so that you have to ask, 'Who
> will cross the sea to get it and proclaim it to us so that we
> may obey it?' (Deut. 30:11-13).

He is saying, 'Don't think that God's law and God's word are so complicated or so academically remote that you are going to have to get the experts to climb the mountains or cross the sea for you, to find the answers that you can't find out for yourself. It's not like that. It's not too difficult. It's not impossible.'

There is a false idea about, that God made His law so hard and His demands so rigorous that there was never any possibility of our keeping it; and it is because we fail so often that we are driven to the gospel. Well, we do fail, and Paul clearly explains that part of the function of the law is to expose our failure. And it does drive us to the gospel. But the reason we fail is not because God's law is so impossibly demanding that we could never have kept it in the first place. In fact a number of the psalmists, without arrogance or self-righteousness, are able to say to the Lord, 'Lord, I have kept Your law, I am seeking to live in obedience to You.' There is such a thing as a life lived in a way that is honouring and pleasing to God; a life of which God can say, 'I am pleased with you; I approve of the way you are living.'

We do not get the impression in such psalms as Psalm 119 that their authors were constantly oppressed: 'Oh, isn't it terrible? All this law that we can't keep – all these commands that we could never actually live up to, even if we tried!'

Moses cuts that argument off. 'No, it's not like that. The word is not in your hand, it is in your mouth and in your heart, it is near you so that you can obey it. Not so that you can be convicted because you can't keep it, but so that you *can* live it and obey it' (cf Deut. 30:14). And I want to tell you, this is your key to your guidance. This is where it begins. The word of God in your heart, in your mind, in your mouth, in your hands day by day as you read it.

How the Bible guides us

How do we use the Bible for guidance? Well, I hope we're all way past the stage of sticking a pin in the Bible to see what it's going to 'tell' us for today. We're all familiar, I expect, with the kind of absurd 'answers' that method can produce. I was told the probably apocryphal story of a young lady who was convinced that God had called her to South America. She had once prayed that God would show her, by the first thing she saw when she left home for the day, where He wanted her to serve Him. And the first thing she had seen was a big bag of Brazil nuts. David Hardy, the last principal of All Nations College, told me that story, adding that he wondered what the outcome would have been had she seen a Mars Bar ...

Another story is absolutely true. Shortly before I and my family went to India as missionaries, we were experiencing considerable anxiety about what it would mean and how our family would cope in a different country and its culture. I'm sure most missionaries have felt the same as they began. At a church house-party at Ashburnham we shared our fears in a morning prayer meeting. A dear brother gave my wife Liz a portion of Scripture as a word from the Lord especially for her. It was Genesis 46:3-4, where God says to Jacob, 'Do not be afraid to go down to Egypt, for ... I will go down to Egypt with you, and I will surely bring you back again.' It was 'a word of encouragement'. I waited until later in the weekend conference before I pointed out to Liz that the way Jacob came back from Egypt was in a coffin.

I'm sure the brother meant very well, and it *was* encouraging. Of course the Lord was going with us to India. But the idea that that particular verse was exactly the word that the Lord needed to guide us at that time was perhaps ... misguided.

What the Bible does do for us is, *it gives us access to the mind and the values of the Lord Himself.* It is His living word. So the more that we soak ourselves in the Scriptures, the more our whole way of thinking will be moved to the kind of preferences and priorities that God Himself has. The more you talk with someone and listen to them, the more time you spend in their company, the more like each other you get and the more you know how the other is thinking. And if it is in the Scriptures that God has poured out to us His heart, His mind, His word, His emotions, His feelings, His sense of priorities and what He's really interested in, the more our own thought processes and decision-making processes will be shaped by it.

Secondly, the Bible will guide us because *it is filled with stories and role models* that work, almost at a sub-conscious level, to shape our own sense of moral values and choices. Most of us have a good idea what makes a good driver, parent, or teacher. We have those mental models because our lives have been shaped by experiences and by stories and examples in which we can see what good driving is. Similarly if our own parents or teachers weren't particularly good ones, we are able to look to other parents and teachers whom we admire, to create our concept of good parenting. We are moulded a great deal by experience, by stories, by what happens in life.

And as we read the Bible's stories, as we learn them and as they are taught to us, as we reflect on them as children and later as we grow into adulthood, then they begin to make our whole world-view biblical. Our thinking and our priorities are shaped by the word of God.

Thirdly, *it sharpens our sense of sin and gives us some very clear 'government health warnings'*. We recognise that if we don't walk in God's ways, there can be very serious consequences. So again, our decisions, our choices, the things that we are going to have to do, this way or that, are being governed by how Scripture has shaped our thinking.

Fourthly, *it provides, within our lives and in our hearts, that good soil in which the Holy Spirit is able to plant His seeds* – seeds of ideas, of thoughts, of decisions that are going to actually help us to bear the fruit that He wants. The Holy Spirit is going to guide us, but He will have much more scope to do so if His word is already in our hearts and we already know a lot of what He's said before. So the Scriptures prepare the way for Him. We are fed on the Scriptures and therefore the Scriptures are able to guide us.

I want to say this as strongly as possible: if you want light on your path in life, get to know your Bible. If you want guidance in life, get to know your Bible. Paul says in Colossians 3:16, 'Let the word of Christ dwell in you richly.' There is no substitute for that.

There is also no short cut to it. It is a matter of regular (daily, if possible) reading, soaking up, learning, and enjoying the Scriptures that God has given us. We do not have time in this Bible Reading to go into all the details of how to read the Bible properly, to do more than just stick pins in its pages. Hugh Palmer will be covering that topic in his seminar later in the Convention. One of the results, I hope, will be that we won't sit in a convention gathering like this, being taught from the front by experts about the Bible, and respond, 'Isn't it wonderful all the things that they can see in the Bible? I would never know how to get that out of the Bible.' Because it's not true. Maybe it's not God's will for you to become a Keswick speaker, but there is nothing that I have done to prepare these Bible Readings that you could not do for yourself. I have read the Scriptures, I have thought about them, I have used commentaries, I have reflected, I have tried to analyse the passages, I have asked what they mean, I have looked them up. You can do that too, and the word of God can speak to you and teach and guide you in your life. Please don't think that Bible study is for the experts. It's far too important to be left to them! The Lord wants to teach you as well.

Staying with the theme of guidance and walking in the ways of the Lord, an interesting point in this psalm is that more often than not the psalmist refers to avoiding wrong paths rather than finding precisely the right one. In other words, he is quite often seeking 'negative guidance'. He wants God to keep him away from mistakes, from going down a wrong path, from falling into sin. He asks God to do that often: 'I hate wrong paths, I don't want to sin against you.' But nowhere in the psalm does he ask God for a detailed blueprint for every choice and decision he has to make. Yes, he's going to walk in the Lord's way; and it will be the way of the Lord that he wants to walk in. But he still talks about 'my steps', 'my feet', 'my path'. In other words, knowing that the Lord has a way for him doesn't take away the responsibility of his own choices and thought processes in deciding which way he's going to walk. I think that's significant, because we need to be careful in our theology of guidance. Sometimes we take more of our beliefs on the subject from popular Christian paperbacks and from various kinds of myths and traditions and stories that go around, than we actually do from the Scriptures.

A common notion in evangelical circles is, 'God has an absolutely perfect blueprint for your life, which began at least from the moment you were converted, if not before. It's all there in great detail. All you have to do is find it out each day.' It's like a game of hide and seek with God. If you miss one point in the blueprint, you're out of line for ever, because a small alteration will have increasingly large repercussions in the whole diary or programme. Miss Plan 'A', and you have to settle for Plan 'B' for the rest of your life.

That – perhaps somewhat caricatured – is 'blueprint theology'. At the other end of the scale is another view with which I disagree: 'Well – it's really up to you. God is there, He cares for you and He'll look after you, but basically He lets you get on with your life. It's up to you how you go and what you decide. God isn't particularly interested in everyday, ordinary things, is He? He's far too important for that.'

We need a biblical balance here. I would certainly want to affirm with the whole Scripture that yes, God is sovereign; yes, God does have a will and a purpose; and yes, that will and purpose includes you and me, sometimes in very specific, clear ways. God does lead, God does guide. The Scriptures promise us so. But I must say, I do find very little – if any – evidence for a perfect, detailed blueprint that exists somewhere, or that all we have to do is find it – especially if the result is a rather mechanistic view of guidance.

I remember George Verwer saying once, 'I used to believe in "Plan B guidance" until I got to at least plan D or E or F and G; and then I began to praise God that we've got an alphabet with twenty-six letters, because I'm on to at least X, Y and Z by now.' (The Hebrew alphabet's only got twenty-two letters, so maybe we've got even more chances of guidance than the psalmist!) Plan B guidance reduces God almost to a horoscope; somehow it's all fated, you've just got to find it. It often makes God a very mysterious God. He has a perfect plan hidden away that we never quite manage to find. The other problem is that it can seem to reduce the responsibility that the Bible clearly lays upon us: to think, to decide, to choose for ourselves.

'In your thinking be adults,' said Paul (1 Cor. 14:20). There is a time in our children's life when almost all their actions are chosen by their parents. We choose where we are going on holiday, what they will wear, and so on, in some case for several years. But we know that it would be quite wrong if parents tried to do that through their children's adult life. There comes a point when, although we have our opinions and preferences as to what our children ought to do, we nevertheless let them make their own choices. Mind you, it's lovely when they discuss those choices with us! My son Tim has consulted me several times in the past few years when he's had difficult decisions to make. We've talked each decision over together. But I won't make the decision for him. I may well know what I want him to choose, but he has to think things through and choose for himself.

Now, the Scriptures tell us that God is our Father. He's neither our horoscope, nor our tyrannical diary. He isn't like that. God is our Father, He is our light on the path, He shows us the direction in we are to move. But that doesn't mean He predetermines every step that we should be determining for ourselves, albeit with His help and under His sovereignty; so that our weaving of the tapestry fits in with the pattern that He is weaving for the world, and the two work together so that we are co-workers with God in His will and His purpose.

There is a mystery; of course there is; a mystery of how to combine the sovereignty of God and His word and guidance with our own human responsibility. So we need not only light on our path. We also need discernment, understanding, wisdom and enabling to think and act wisely in the light of the Scriptures that God has given us.

Learning for the pupil

And now the psalmist changes his metaphor from that of taking a lamp on a dark night as you walk along the path, to that of sitting with a teacher; learning, studying, absorbing, interacting, growing, memorising what the teacher says but also reflecting and applying it in everyday life; sitting under the teaching of God Himself.

A television advertisement currently being shown remarks that nobody forgets a good teacher. It's quite true. Most of us can remember the names of our teachers, even from our childhood, and the psalmist remembers his. In verse 102 he says, 'I have not departed from your laws, for you yourself have taught me.' I like that; here is not just an academic theologian saying, 'I've learned a lot from the Scripture.' He says, 'The Lord Himself, You were my teacher.' Yes, the Bible is our teacher – but it's God Himself who's teaching us through it.

Isn't that what Paul said to Timothy in that familiar verse 2 Timothy 3:14? 'As for you, continue in what you have learned and have become convinced of, because you know those from whom you learned it.' Yes, Timothy had been well taught, by his mother and his grandmother particularly. But Paul continues, 'From infancy you have known the holy Scriptures, which are able to make you wise for salvation through faith in Christ Jesus. All Scripture is God-breathed and is useful for teaching, rebuking, correcting and training in righteousness, so that the man of God may be thoroughly equipped for every good work' (3:15-17). Timothy was well taught by human parents, but it was God Himself through the Scriptures who had been his real teacher.

Indeed this psalmist reckons that having God as his teacher and the Scriptures as his textbook means that he actually has greater understanding, and deeper insight, than his human teachers and elders. Verse 98: 'Your commands make me wiser than my enemies.' Verses 99 to 100: 'I have more insight than all my teachers, for I meditate on your statutes. I have more understanding than the elders.'

I don't think he's being boastful. I don't think this is arrogance. I think it is a simple fact of life; a person who's got the word of God in their heart may actually have deeper insight and knowledge than somebody who's got all sorts of academic understanding that doesn't include God's word in the heart. A school child who knows the Lord and knows his or her Bible can actually understand God better than an R.E. teacher with a degree in religious studies.

It may sound rather arrogant, but some of us who were theological students thought that about our professors. In 1969 I was studying theology at Cambridge. I recently met again one of my fellow-students from those days, who told me that her abiding memory of me and our fellow-student Hugh Williamson is that we were constantly asking questions and challenging our professors. So often we thought they were talking rubbish; often they were. In our arrogance we thought we could put them right, because we knew the Scriptures and we knew that what was being taught was wrong. Maybe our approach was wrong – but that's what we did. (Hugh is now Regius Professor of Hebrew at Oxford, so perhaps he's getting the same treatment there!)

The expression 'Teach me Your precepts' or 'Your laws', and the similar expression 'Give me understanding in Your word', are just about the commonest expression that you will find this psalmist using. 'Teach me Your decrees' occurs at least eight times, 'Give me understanding' or 'Give me discernment' seven times. To prepare for this Bible Reading I made a list of all the occurrences and the verses in which they occur, to see if there was any pattern, or parallels with other expressions. Both are certainly true, and I want to show you now some of the ways the psalmist uses these expressions.

First, let's look at 'Teach me Your precepts', which occurs in a number of contexts.

TEACH ME YOUR PRECEPTS

I found that the expression 'Teach me Your decrees' in its first and its last occurrences in Psalm 119 relates to praise. Verse 12: 'Praise be to you, O LORD; teach me your decrees.' Then at the very end, as if to match and balance that, verse 171: 'May my lips overflow with praise, for you teach me your decrees.'

LEARNING AND PRAISE

Here obviously is a person who saw no dichotomy between his head and his heart, between his theology and his doxology, between what would be academic in the sense of something to be learned and thought about in his mind and his head as a matter of teaching and learning – and what was a spiritual response of his heart and his lips and his mouth in worship: 'Teach me your precepts so that I can praise You.'

That is such an important balance. Unfortunately, and tragically, Christians sometimes set these two things against each other. They seem to feel that learning and the use of the mind, the intellect and our study faculties are somehow in opposition to that which is spiritual and devotional. It's one of the battles that we constantly fight in the world of theological education. People sometimes accuse a Bible college like All Nations, 'Oh, you're becoming academic' – as if somehow that is in itself a bad thing, as if asking someone to think might somehow do them some damage! But actually the Lord tells us that we are to love the Lord our God with all our heart, all our mind and all our strength. We make no apology for making people think. Teaching and studying exercises the mind, and that's important, but it does not contradict wanting to be devoted to the Lord in our worship and our praise. The psalmist wants to be taught so that he can worship, and that is the balance he maintains.

In Nehemiah 8 we read that all the people gathered together to learn together, because the law of God was being read to them by Ezra, and some of the Levites were going out among the people teaching them, perhaps in languages with which they were more familiar. 'Then all the people went away ... to celebrate with great joy, because they now understood the words that had been made known to them' (Neh. 8:12). It was going into their minds, so they were rejoicing. And that of course is part of the wonderful

dynamics of a conference like Keswick: we are here to learn and we
are here to praise.

LEARNING AND PRACTICAL OBEDIENCE

There are two places where the expression, 'Teach me Your
precepts' links up with practical life and obedience. Verse 26: 'I
recounted my ways and you answered me; teach me your decrees.'
And verse 33: 'Teach me, O LORD, to follow your decrees; then I
will keep them to the end.'

So just as the psalmist sees no dichotomy between the
intellectual and the devotional, neither does he see any dichotomy
between the intellectual and the practical. 'I want to learn to study,
to be taught the precepts of God, so that I can go out and obey
them.' His practical obedience is linked to his Bible study. And
again, it is tragic if in our Christian communities, in churches,
universities or colleges, the academic study of God's word – the
theology – should come to be divorced from its practical
implications in terms of obedience of life, change of life,
commitment to the Lord and so on. These things are necessary. At
All Nations we have a slogan that describes what we are trying to
do: 'Heads, hearts and hands for the kingdom of God.' We want
to learn with our heads, we want to be committed in our hearts
and we want to obey with our hands and our lives.

LEARNING AND GOD'S CHARACTER

In four occurrences, 'Teach me your decrees' refers to God's
character and God's action.

Verse 64: 'The earth is filled with your love, O LORD; teach me
your decrees.' Again, the same thought in verse 124: 'Deal with
your servant according to your love and teach me your decrees.'
Verse 68 links it to God's goodness: 'You are good, and what you
do is good; teach me your decrees.' And in verse 135 we read,
'Make your face shine upon your servant and teach me your
decrees' (perhaps the psalmist had in mind the Aaronic blessing:
'May the Lord be gracious to us and bless us and lift up the light
of His countenance upon us.') In each case God's goodness, love,
gracious presence and blessing are linked to the desire that God
should teach us His laws, His decrees.

Again, what a shame it is that people so often imagine that

God's laws, precepts, statutes and all such concepts have nothing to do with God's love and God's grace. Here in this psalm, in these verses, they are paired together. 'Lord, it's because You are so good, it's because You are so loving, it's because You are so gracious that I want You to teach me Your precepts; I want to know more about You, I want to know Your law.' The Old Testament Israelites always thought of God's law as a gift of God's grace, embodying God's love and, therefore, the best guide to human life.

Give me understanding

This phrase also occurs seven or eight times. 'Understanding' is a word used very frequently in the book of Proverbs, where it means insight, discernment, the ability to see beneath the surface of things, to see behind what is being presented to you. It means practical wisdom that comes from experience and maturity but is something that can be learned. And it is the gift of God Himself. Indeed, the New Testament includes this amongst the gifts of the Spirit that we are to be given by God: the gifts of discernment, understanding and maturity of faith.

In Psalm 119:27 we read, 'Let me understand the teaching of your precepts; then I will meditate on your wonders.' The 'wonders' of God usually refers to His work in His creation. In verse 73 the creation idea comes through again: 'Your hands made me and formed me; give me understanding to learn your commands.' God is the creator of the wonders of creation, the world that we see around us, the beauty of Keswick. He is also our personal creator, who made our own individual body and mind and heart. It's because God is that, that He knows all there is to know. So we can turn to Him and ask for understanding from our creator.

In verse 34, the desire for understanding is again linked to obedience. 'Give me understanding, and I will keep your law and obey it with all my heart' – 'I can only obey You, Lord, if I really know what it means to obey You, if I understand the laws that You are giving me.' There's none of this business of blind faith – 'You don't need to understand it, just do it.' No. The psalmist says, 'Lord, I want to understand, I want to know, what Your law is, so that I can obey it and keep it and live by it.'

There are some other occurrences. Verse 125: 'I am your

servant; give me discernment that I may understand your statutes.' Because I am your servant and You are my Master, says the psalmist, let me know what it is I have to do. Verse 144: 'Your statutes are for ever right; give me understanding that I may live.' And verse 169: 'May my cry come before you, O LORD; give me understanding according to your word.' In other words, God is my Master, God is my life-giver, God is my helper. Therefore I can turn to Him in relationship and ask for understanding.

Desiring knowledge of God

So once more this psalmist asks for guidance, for wisdom, for learning, for understanding. Not because he wants a degree, not because he wants to be famous as a wise expert, but because he longs for God. He has a heartfelt desire to know God, and so he says, 'Lord, teach me.'

Indeed, if we combine the two emphases of light and of learning, he might well also have echoed the words of Psalm 27:1, 'The LORD is my light and my salvation.' And if he had known them he would certainly have echoed the words of Paul in 1 Corinthians 1:24 and also verse 30, where he says that Christ is our wisdom, our righteousness, our holiness and our redemption. He has become that for us. The Lord is our light, the Lord is our understanding, and it's knowledge of God that we want.

He may even have echoed – might even have known, depending on when he lived and wrote – the words of Jeremiah: 'This is what the LORD says: "Let not the wise man boast of his wisdom or the strong man boast of his strength or the rich man boast of his riches, but let him who boasts boast about this: that he understands and knows me, that I am the LORD, who exercises kindness, justice and righteousness on earth, for in these I delight," declares the LORD' (Jer. 9:23-24).

And the psalmist says, 'Lord, I want to know You, I want to delight in You, even in the midst of all this learning and understanding; I want to be wise, but that's not all I want. I want to be godly, I want to know you.'

I would say to any students here today, particularly if you are a student of theology or religious studies, 'Stay humble! Make sure that all that theology and learning about the word of God is all directed towards a guidance of life based on the Lord Himself.'

When I was starting out on the road of theological understanding and thinking, one of the ways in which I kept my mind in that direction was frequently to remember my own father. For I could say to myself, 'Maybe now I know more theology than he does. Maybe now, because of all this academic study, I know more of the Bible than he does. But I would never claim that I know the Lord more than he does. I would never claim to have that relationship with God in prayer, obedience and commitment that he has.' No matter what your head gets filled with, make sure that your heart is still in love with the Lord and is being guided by Him, so that, to quote that lovely Celtic prayer, God will be in your head and in your understanding.

Not just the word of God, but God Himself, in His guiding of our lives – may that be so for us, for His name's sake.

4. Personal Commitment and the Word of Love
Psalm 119:57-64

It's very obvious that the person who wrote this psalm is totally committed, heart and soul, body, mind and spirit, to God and to the ways of God. He loves the Lord. In fact it was that word 'love' – 'How I love your law!' – which gave me the clue to the subject for today when I was trying to divide the psalm up into themes.

The reason for his commitment is not hard to see. He has his entire world-view and understanding of reality shaped by the conviction that God's word is true and trustworthy, and that he can build his life safely on this foundation. Even when his life is tough, uncomfortable, depressing and dangerous he knows that he is basing it on something that will last. In other words, his commitment is based upon his core belief about God and about God's word.

One of the joys and constant challenges of training Christian people for mission is that you are dealing year after year (as people come, train and depart, and from time to time come back to visit) with people whose lives are filled with this commitment to serve God. And I've observed again and again that commitment flows out of ultimate beliefs, core values, reality as the centre of life in which those people passionately believe. That's why they go and do the things that they do.

There are all sorts of examples. You could visit people in Portugal, Kenya, France, Lebanon and elsewhere who are busy caring for God's non-human creation, caring for birds and plants because they have a core belief that that is a biblical thing to do; that we were commanded to care for the earth, and that a love and care for God's whole creation is a part of biblical Christian commitment; their particular behaviour and commitment proceeds from that core belief. And if Jesus says that not even a bird falls without our Heavenly Father knowing it and caring for it, then how much more should we do the same.

I can think of one student who came to college after having been in Central Asia. When he was asking us to pray for him he pulled out of his pocket a handful of bullets. 'If anyone wants to pray for me, take one of these bullets and it will remind you. I picked them,' he said quite casually, 'out of the lampshade of my bedside lamp, the curtains and the walls.' What keeps a person living in a war zone? Only a core belief that the people who are there are worth serving, and that their lives are worth helping and healing and restoring.

I recently read a book by another former student, a midwife who has given her life to working in some of the toughest parts of the world, in African famine areas, in war areas, among refugees and in other parts of that continent, simply seeking to deliver life, to help mothers. Out of her book flows the core belief that every single human life matters to God because it is made in the image of God, no matter what colour, religion or anything else. If it is a human life, God loves it and cares for it. That's a core belief of the Christian faith, a biblical affirmation not found in other religions. And it's because she is building her life on that core faith that she goes and does that.

One could ask, similarly, why people of my father's generation[1] went to the Amazonian jungles in the days before people cared about rain forests, to care about the people who lived in those forests? Christians who lived in Brazil told my father, 'You don't need to go to the Indians, they haven't got souls, they're not even human. So why are you going to live among them and evangelise

1. The Rev. J. C. Wright was a missionary with UFM in the Amazonian region of Brazil from 1926 to 1946.

them?' Well – why did he? Because he did believe they had souls, he did believe that they were human, and because he believed that they were lost without Christ. Out of that core belief flowed half an adult lifetime committed to seeking to bring Christ to them and bring them into the kingdom of God.

Commitment and behaviour flow from what you actually believe about life, the universe and everything. And I want us this morning to look at some of the ways in which this psalmist articulated his view of the word of God, the law of God, intellectually, emotionally, and behaviourally (or, if you want a longer word, 'volitionally') – how he actually put his choices into action.

And so we have three foci for our thinking this morning. First,

God's word as the focus of trust

My key verse for this section is verse 66, which begins with the same phrase we looked at in our last study: 'Teach me knowledge and good judgment, for I believe in your commands.'

'Believe' is quite a strong word in the Hebrew. It's the word from which we get 'Amen', and it means, 'I put my trust in, and give my whole mental assent, to what you have said.' It's the language of total commitment and faith. 'I understand and agree with Your word, I am committed to it. It's true and valid and I can depend upon it.' He says the same in verse 86: 'All your commands are trustworthy.' Why does he say this? He doesn't just affirm it once, he goes on to a whole chain of verses threaded through this psalm that make this kind of affirmation. And there are at least three distinct kind of affirmations that this psalmist makes about God's word that we can pull out and see.

First of all, there are a group of sayings that affirm,

The universality of God's word

They affirm that it is eternal; it is for ever; it covers the whole earth, and the heavens and the earth and all that there is; they affirm its eternal, universal nature. Listen to some of these words. Verses 89 to 91: 'Your word, O LORD, is eternal; it stands firm in the heavens. Your faithfulness continues through all generations; you established the earth, and it endures. Your laws endure to this day, for all things serve you.' Isaiah said, 'The heavens and the earth may pass away but your word endures for ever' (cf Isa. 40:8, 51:6), and I don't think this psalmist would disagree.

Verse 96: 'To all perfection I see a limit; but your commands are boundless.' In other words, even the best we humans can do and offer will always be limited. Even the most wonderful things we can achieve will come to an end or will wear out. 'But Your word is limitless, boundless, not flawed by contingency or partiality. It is infinite.'

And finally in this section, verse 152: 'Long ago I learned from your statutes that you established them to last for ever.' The word, the law of God, he says, is eternal. There is something universal about this word.

That does not mean that God simply stood up in heaven and spouted forth great timeless, meaningless abstractions, irrelevant to local and specific situations. The paradox is that God's word did come to the human race, to us, as the book of Hebrews tells us, in 'many and varied ways' (cf Heb. 1:1), through many different people, in many different historical periods, using different authors, different speakers, in order that that word of God could be – terrifyingly, sometimes – sharp and specific and personal in detail, all the way through the Bible.

Yet the remarkable truth is that through all of that, God has created a word that has an enduring quality that enables it to transcend particular times and places. We can read what God said in Jerusalem or Judea in the ninth or eighth century BC and it can cut right into our hearts today. We can read what comes in the law or the Gospels or Paul's letter to the Corinthians in the first century AD and it speaks to us because it comes from God. So it is His eternal word because it shares in His character of ultimacy and finality. It is God's word, God's law, God's promise. That's very relevant to our contemporary culture, as we shall see.

A second group of sayings about this focus of faith in God's word affirm,

The moral, righteous quality of God's word

The law not only shares in God's eternal transcendent universal nature; it reflects His moral character of righteousness and justice. We see that especially in the second half of this psalm. Verse 128: 'Because I consider all your precepts right, I hate every wrong path.' Verses 137 and 138: 'Righteous are you, O LORD, and your laws are right. The statutes you have laid down are righteous; they are fully trustworthy. Verse 144: 'Your statutes are for ever right.' And verse 172: 'May my tongue sing of your word, for all your commands are righteous' – he is speaking of the righteousness of God's law.

'Righteousness' is a word which in Hebrew has the basic idea of something that is straight, like a straight-edge or a measuring tape; something that is exactly what it should be, and against which everything else is measured. You don't ask the standard metre whether it is a metre. You ask whether everything else is a metre in comparison with it. It's a standard; it defines the norm. And that is what is meant here in terms of God's law; it provides the moral standard by which our behaviour and opinions are to be measured and judged.

The psalmist says again and again that the words that he's reading, the written law, have this quality of moral righteousness because they reflect God Himself. As verse 137 says: it's because You are righteous, O Lord, that all Your laws are right. Just as the law is eternal because God is, so it is righteous because God is.

And just as we saw earlier, the paradox is that that righteousness of God's word and law is revealed not in terms of some grand, universal, abstract assertion of religious philosophy, but in terms of the very specific particulars of the instructions, laws and guidance that God gave to Israel. He dealt with them as a particular people, living in that time of history, in that particular land, with that particular kind of culture, language, social structure and everything else. By dealing with that particular society God has given to us a light for the nations, a paradigm of righteousness that shows us what He wants and what His priorities and values are. And in some of the key sections of the law (as we saw in Deuteronomy 10, or in the Ten Commandments), we find these values of God reflected. So the law gives an objective nature to morality and righteousness.

The third little group of verses which make the law a focus of faith and affirmation speak about,

The reality and truthfulness of God's word

The psalmist says that God's word and law is not just eternal and not just righteous; it's also true. Verse 142: 'Your righteousness is

everlasting and your law is true.' Verse 151: 'Yet you are near, O
LORD, and all your commands are true.' Verse 160: 'All your words
are true; all your righteous laws are eternal.' In fact verse 160
literally says, 'The totality of Your word is true.' It's not just
speaking about every individual word but about the whole
package. God's word is truth.

Now, what is truth? – as Pilate famously asked. Well, truth is
what corresponds to reality. If a statement is to be true there has to
be something that makes it true. There has to be some existing
reality that makes it true or false, a faithful reflection of what is or
what isn't there. A statement can only be true if it relates to
something real. So, for example, if I say to you 'Daffodils are
yellow,' you can say 'That's true.' There is a biological reality, a
plant that we happen to call a daffodil, and when you see it in
daylight there are certain realities of the properties of light in the
spectrum that make us see it as yellow. It is an objective reality of
biology and physics that makes the statement 'daffodils are yellow'
a true statement.

But if I say to you, 'Tooth-fairies have wings,' and ask you if
that's true or false, you will respond that it's not so much true or
false as ultimately meaningless. It doesn't matter really because it's
a figment of the imagination. There is no reality to which it refers.
Thus when the psalmist says that the word of God is true, what he
means is that there is something to which it refers that is real, that
is there. God is there, a world is there, there is a universe that it
describes which is really and truthfully described. So when the
word of God talks about God it is true; when it talks about human
life made in the image of God it is true; when it says that the earth
is the Lord's and everything in it, that is a truthful description of
the way the world is; when it talks about righteousness, justice and
judgement at the end of the world, that is truth because there's a
reality to which it refers.

We need to get hold of this: that when we talk about truth and
falsehood, that's what we mean. It's not just a matter of accuracy,
it's a matter of reality, of what is actually there. And because it is
true, it is also trustworthy and you can rely on it.

So then, putting these three things together: when the psalmist
looks at the word of God, reads it and meditates on it, he focuses
on it as something solid, objective, dependable and real. It is

universal in its scope, because it is eternal and shares in God's transcendence. It is normative in its moral demands; it is the word of God that decides whether a thing is good or evil, right or wrong. And it is totally reliable in its truth-claims; it is ultimate in what it refers to. For the benefit of any philosophers present: the psalmist is making the word of God the foundation of his metaphysics, his ethics and his epistemology.

These are pretty vast claims. I really want us to get hold of how this psalm really cuts across, and is actually in stark conflict with, the culture and the ethos within which we happen to live. The world in which the psalmist lived was also a world of surrounding idolatry and pluralism, in which there were certainly other nations with other gods and all sorts of other truth-claims. He knew, I am sure, that to stand up and say, 'The earth belongs to Yahweh; the earth is the Lord's,' or 'The word, or law, of Yahweh is the truth,' would be to invite debate, at least in Babylon or in Egypt where a different world-view was held. But certainly he conflicts with any easy pluralism or relativism that says, 'It doesn't really matter what you believe, nothing is true anyway.'

That is very much the culture of post-modernity in which we live today. Let me give a brief definition. Modernity, which we've lived with for about 250 years now, is the view that through the application of science and technology and rational thought we can not only understand the world, but can manage and improve it. We can develop it, and we can control our environment and make our human lives better. Progress through science and technology is the whole heart of the modern world.

Post-modernity arises out of disillusionment with modernity. It says, 'Actually, things don't look like that. We haven't made the world any better. Science hasn't got all the answers. It looks as if the world is more mysterious than we thought; and in any case, we now live in a pluralist world, in which any culture has just as much right to claim to be "true" as any other.' So in the end, what the post-modern view says is that there is really no such thing as a transcendent reality, no such thing as a universal reality, no such thing as an absolute truth. There is no Truth with a capital 'T', there is nothing that is final or ultimate. If you try searching for such certainties in religion or in science, you are misguided. It's pointless. No culture or religion has any universal standing place, or any absolute truth, either in its narratives and the way it understands the world, or in its morality: everything is relative.

Life, according to this view, is a carnival. The floats go by, and you can observe all the wonderful spectacles. Look at this culture, that culture, this viewpoint, that viewpoint; they all pass you by and you can enjoy them all, you can even set up one of your own if you want. But basically it doesn't have any point, it's just a merry-go-round. So enjoy the plurality, enjoy the variety, but don't look for any depth or reality. Don't ask, 'Is it really *true*? Where is its heart and core?'

That sort of viewpoint even applies to personal identity in a post-modern world-view. Who is the real you? In post-modernism you don't have to bother to ask. You can be whatever you like to be. You can decide what you want to be, you can accept anything, you are what you eat, you are what you wear, you can change your mind and be what you want. But don't ever look for some kind of core reality, the real you. That's like looking for a real truth or a real religion.

I found a good illustration in the *Daily Mail*, where Ginger Spice, who had just left the pop group the Spice Girls, gave an interview. She said, 'Every day I can be somebody else. I can wear a slinky little number, or I can be chic, or I can be pretty and girlie. The future is all about my imagination.' In other words, 'It doesn't really matter who I am; I can change every day, depending on what I wear. I can just make myself up, reinvent myself as I go along.' Now, I never had the opportunity of meeting Ginger Spice, and I haven't lost a lot of sleep over that. But the question came to my mind when I read that: Who are you, when you come to the end of your wardrobe? When there are no clothes left to wear? It's a tragi-comic comment on life. And yet it is so real for us. Everything is just what you wear.

Of course what we wear has some importance. My wife and I do have discussions about whether my socks match my shirt and tie. But when I get sent upstairs to change my socks, I don't change my personality, it doesn't affect who I am as me. That's dependent upon something a bit deeper – ultimately, on the fact that I am a human being made in the image of God, loved by my Creator and redeemed by my Saviour. That's who I am. And that will be there, whatever I wear.

My point is, that this is all part of a world-view that says there is really no reality, only image. There's no morality, only opinion; no eternity, only the circus of the present. And that affects education, politics, philosophy – it is everywhere. Against that kind of thinking and world-view, this psalm says, 'There is an eternal transcendent reality: God, our creator. And we have access to Him through His word. He's not the great Unknowable, He's the God who's revealed Himself to us. There is a universally relevant moral standard with claims on all human beings, in every age and every culture.'

God realises that every age and culture will be different. But there are core fundamental realities of what it means to live as a human being in God's world, accountable to our creator. That reality goes back to the Garden of Eden and will be there in the new creation also. It is eternal and fundamental. The Scriptures give it to us; and we have access to it through the word of God. 'Your word is righteous.'

And there is an objective truth; an account, an explanation, a world-view that actually fits the way things are, says this psalm. To it we have access and much of it we can grasp by the word of God and by the exercise of our reason and our thought-processes under the authority of God and His word. That authority was certainly the origin of Western science: seeing the world as God's creation.

So all of this human knowledge, morality and understanding, says this psalm, is to be related to the biblical world-view of life, the universe and everything. The psalmist says that is a matter of faith and trust – not in a blind sense, but in the sense of a reasonable, rational, sensible understanding of the world based on a commitment: 'I believe in a God who made this world. I believe in those things, they are sensible, they make sense to me and God's word tells me so.'

That is the kind of faith that you can stand on, the kind of faith you can defend. Is that your conviction? And to those of the younger generation that may perhaps be more infected by the post-modernism, scepticism and relativism in our society, I would ask, 'Can you base your life on it? Can you live on a moving staircase? Or are you going to build on the rock of the word of God?'

Let's move on to some other points that need, I think, less comment.

God's word as the focus of love

We really can't ignore this, because the psalmist's response to the word of God and the law of God is not some kind of cold intellectual, metaphysical assent. He's not a philosopher or a professor writing the kind of books such people write. Here is somebody who just revels in the word of God. And once again, this is quite a shock to people who think of the Old Testament as all mere cold legalism.

First of all,

The law – a matter of joy and delight

Verse 14: 'I rejoice in following your statutes as one rejoices in great riches.' He says it's like winning the lottery. '*Wow!* – that's what I think about the law of God,' he says. Verse 162: 'I rejoice in your promise like one who finds great spoil.' The word 'delight' is used too; I won't read all the references, but look for examples, then read them through for yourself. Verse 16: 'I delight in your decrees.' Verse 24: 'Your statutes are my delight; they are my counsellors.' Verse 35: 'Direct me in the path of your commands, for there I find delight.' And so it goes on, about another ten times.

Do I need to comment on that? Here is someone who says, 'Lord, Your word is a pleasure to me, I love it.' What do you use 'delight' for in life? It's a common expression. You might say, that was delightful, that piece of music was a delight, that scenery overlooking the lake is delightful, it gives you such pleasure. Or you have a lovely meal, tasty, delicious, and you say, 'Wasn't that delightful?' That's the kind of language that this person is using about God's law. Delight and joy.

The law – an object of love

Now the language becomes even more emotional and expressive. In fact, and I don't think I need apologise for saying this for it's so elsewhere in the Bible, he is using almost erotic language of emotional, affectionate love. Verse 47: 'I delight in your commands because I love them.' Verse 48: 'I lift up my hands to your commands, which I love.' I've got outstretched arms, he says. Give me, give me, gimme the law of God! I want it, I love it.

Not the way most people treat the law of God, I think!

Verse 97: 'Oh, how I love your law! I meditate on it all day long.' Verse 131: 'I open my mouth and pant, longing for your commands.' He's gasping for it, wanting the love of God. If you love someone or something, it's constantly in your mind and you don't forget them. And, he says, even when he's far from home, even in the night, he still remembers the law of God. Verse 54: 'Your decrees are the theme of my song wherever I lodge.' Verse 55: 'In the night I remember your name, O LORD, and I will keep your law.' You don't forget what you love.

Just before coming here my wife spent a fortnight in Canada at a family wedding and I was on my own at home. It's quite unusual for her to be the one travelling, and a bit of an experience for me! Did we forget each other? Of course not. Last thing at night and first thing in the morning, I was conscious of her pillow there beside mine and I put my head on it, remembered her and prayed for her. You don't forget the one you love – though I can't say with the psalmist that I arose at midnight to give her thanks (verse 62)!

Delight, joy, love, remembering – this is the language of an emotional, affectionate relationship. So where is all this legalism stuff? Where is all this bondage to the law? In fact, quite contrary to the idea of bondage, this person finds that obedience to God's law is a perfect recipe for real freedom. There is a lovely paradox in verse 32: 'I run in the path of your commands, for you have set my heart free.' And verse 45: 'I will walk about in freedom, for I have sought out your precepts.' You see, far from obedience producing bondage, obedience (he says) actually produces freedom.

He also says that the law is superbly precious to him. It is so valuable, so endearing that the only way he can describe it is in superlatives. What's the richest thing you can think of? Gold, silver, lots of it? Verse 72: 'The law from your mouth is more precious to me than thousands of pieces of silver and gold.' What's the sweetest thing you can think of? Honey, perhaps? Verse 103: 'How sweet are your words to my taste, sweeter than honey to my mouth!' There's nothing more valuable than faithful obedience to God, nothing more satisfying than living for Him. God's word then is the focus of love, as well as of faith.

God's word as the focus of commitment

'Of course,' this psalmist would say, 'the word of God is for my intellectual assent. And yes, the word of God is for my emotional appreciation. But this word of God is also to be for my behavioural commitment. I am going to live it.'

Two expressions that seem to express this struck me particularly as I read through Psalm 119.

A total commitment

'With all my heart', or 'my heart is set on ...', occur eight or nine times. Here are some examples. Verse 2: 'Blessed are they who keep his statutes and seek him with all their heart.' Verse 10: 'I seek you with all my heart.' Verse 30: 'I have chosen the way of truth; I have set my heart on your laws.' Verse 34: 'Give me understanding, and I will keep your law and obey it with all my heart.' Verse 36: 'Turn my heart towards your statutes.' Verse 58: 'I have sought your face with all my heart.' Verse 112: 'My heart is set on keeping your decrees to the very end.' Verse 145: 'I call [to you] with all my heart.'

There's an echo here surely of that fundamental prayer and commitment in Deuteronomy 6:4-5, sometimes called the *Shema*, that great credal prayer of the Israelites and of the Jewish faith ever since: 'Hear, O Israel: the LORD our God, the LORD is one. Love the LORD your God with all your heart and with all your soul and with all your strength.' You might ask why I didn't included this in the last section, when I was talking about emotional commitment to God. Isn't that where love should be?

Actually it's not quite so, because in Hebrew the heart is the seat of the mind and of the will, much more than of the emotions. If you want to express emotions in Hebrew, you go a little bit lower down the body; you talk about your bowels or your kidneys or your stomach. That's what you emotionally love with. The heart is where you think. Remember the verse in Proverbs that the Authorised Version renders, 'As a man thinketh in his heart, so is he' (cf Prov. 23:7, AV). And Jesus, you remember, said that it's out of the heart come evil thoughts: anger, lust, pride and eventually murder and all the rest (cf Matt. 15:19).

So the psalmist here is not talking about emotional affectionate commitment, he's talking about deliberate, conscious, thought-out, intelligent commitment to the word of God; where a person has thought it through and said, 'I know what I'm doing, I've thought about it, and with the totality of my mind and intellect I want to obey God. I want to do it.' It's whole-hearted commitment to God.

He uses the words 'fully' and 'for ever' quite often. For example, verse 5: 'Oh, that my ways were steadfast in obeying your decrees!' Verse 20: 'My soul is consumed with longing for your laws at all times.' It's virtually the same in verse 40, 'How I long for your precepts!' And in verse 44, 'I will always obey your law, for ever and ever.' So here is a person who says, 'Yes, I want to be committed, but I'm not making a shallow or transient commitment. It's not just for this tent, this meeting or this week. It's something that I want to be, with the totality of what I am; and I want it to be for the whole of my life for ever.'

A present commitment

Also, he says, it should also be for now. Verse 60: 'I will hasten and not delay to obey your commands.' It's no good professing total commitment, if it is only going to start tomorrow or when you leave university or when something else happens. It's no good either having a kind of 'forever-ness' attitude – 'I'll love you for ever and ever and ever, but I'm not prepared to do anything today.' The psalmist is aware that this commitment he is making is with all his heart, fully, for ever, and for now.

A personal commitment

In conclusion, I want to challenge us about our personal commitment to the word of God as it impacts upon our lives, for that's what this psalm is leading to.

I trust that other generations represented here won't object if I address myself particularly to the younger generation. I certainly don't want you to miss out, because I am well aware that Joshua, for example, well into his eighties and forty years after the conquest, was still saying to his contemporaries, 'Choose you this day whom you will serve.' Commitment, choice and all of these things are lifelong challenges, so I am not excusing anybody from this.

I want to ask: What is the direction of the commitment that you make in life? And what is the world-view that underlies it? What is the basic core belief that you found your life upon, out of which flow your choices, your direction, your decisions, whether or not you are going to do this or that in life, and how you are going to follow God?

Here in this psalm we have somebody who was intellectually convinced about God's word, that it was transcendent, that it had moral value, and that it gave him ultimate access to truth and reality. Now, that is a fundamental world-view issue. Is the Bible at the core of your view of reality? Is it the word of the creator God for you – not just for you but for the whole world, the whole universe? And when the Bible says 'the earth is the Lord's and everything in it', do you say, 'Yes I believe that the earth belongs to God, the whole universe. He is God in heaven above and in the earth beneath. Everything comes from You, and of Your own do we give you'? The Bible gives us absolute statements about God and about the universe. Are we intellectually committed to them, so that our world-view, our philosophy, and our whole life are based upon an assent to that truth?

And here in this psalm we have a person who is emotionally excited about that truth. He loves it, he is delighted with it, he finds it beautiful. They tell me that one of the motivations for people to continue in the field of mathematics is that it is such a beautiful discipline. I have to take their word for that, but I can understand how they feel. I do know professional mathematicians, and they say it gives them great pleasure and a great joy and thrill, a great delight, to see how things work out – to see the mathematical beauties of the world. Here is someone who has that same feeling towards God's word: emotional delight, pleasure. There's something precious about it. Do you have that feeling when you open your Bible? When people say, 'Let's turn to such-and-such a passage,' do you respond, 'Right! Let's turn to it, let's see what's there! It's got to be something that's going to thrill me, because I'm emotionally committed to it.'

And thirdly in this psalm, we have somebody who is whole-heartedly, totally committed to this way of living. I want to say that all three of these characteristics are absolutely necessary, if we are going to get involved in any real, radical, committed discipleship and obedience to the Lord. Core commitment flows out of core beliefs and core affections in life. There has to be a combination of the head and the heart and the will, because if any of them are missing things will go wrong. If you only have intellectual commitment without the heart and without the will, then you will end up in academic sterility, dryness. If you only have emotional commitment without the assent of your mind and commitment of understanding, then you will end up with the froth of emotionalism, excitement and the spectacular without a depth of understanding and the balance that comes from the Scriptures.

And if you only have zeal – 'Yes, I'll go for it! I'll be there!' – that sort of zeal and commitment that Peter had, bless him, in the days of the gospel, then zeal without knowledge will become action without wisdom, and can end up being self-destructive.

So the question is: Will you respond, as the psalmist did, to God with obedience, because you are able to say to Him, 'Lord, I believe with all my heart that Your word is true, righteous and eternal; and because I love it and I want to run in the path of Your commands, with enthusiasm, with energy, with all that You have given to me in my personality and my temperament and my emotions and my affections and everything else'? And will you say, 'Lord, I set my heart to do this'?

Today is a day when this kind of challenge will be coming from this platform, I am sure, time and again. It is certainly a day when the Lord will, I am sure, be speaking to people about the issue of personal commitment to God in mission or ministry, or in any way that obedience is going to call them. Where is God calling you? What is God calling you to do? Where does God's mission impinge upon your agenda? Where does your life-choice fit, in God's vision for the universe and the new creation? Where do you fit, in all of that?

The answer will only come to you as you bow your head under the word of God with this psalmist and say, 'Lord, this is Your word, and You are the Lord of the universe.' It's not that I'm wanting to say 'Jesus is *my* Lord', but 'Jesus *is* Lord'; and because He is Lord, He is my Lord, and therefore I will obey Him because there is nobody else to obey. And therefore I am committed to the truth of His word and to obedience to the Master of the universe.

There is no other sensible thing to do, no other satisfying thing to do; and there is no other safe thing to do, but to be in that position, with this psalmist. May God give us grace to be so.

5. Personal Renewal and the Word of Life
Psalm 119:153-160

Now we come to the last of our sessions, and I would like you to
read Psalm 119:153-160, the section in which each line begins
with the Hebrew letter *resh*, 'R'. You will notice an expression or
prayer that occurs three times and will be the focus of our thinking
in this Bible reading.

I expect that if I were to ask you, 'Why did you come to
Keswick?', many of you would answer, 'Well, I came for
refreshment, I came for renewal, I came to try and get my life
together again because I wanted God to renew and restore and
refresh my life.' And that same desire for life is a very prominent
longing of this psalmist. In fact, it was the first thing that struck
me when I was reading this psalm again and again, deciding how
to divide it for these Bible Readings. I discovered that at least
fourteen times he prays this prayer: 'Renew ... restore ... preserve
my life ... give me life ... let me live,' or similar expressions.

In fact, all those English phrases are translations trying to
capture one single Hebrew word that the NIV translates in different
ways. It is *hayah*, which means 'to make alive, to cause to live'. The
psalmist uses the emphatic, causative form of the verb: 'to live, to
have life'. And he prays again and again, 'Lord, make me live, get
me life, let me live.'

Once more I am going to read from a whole chain of these verses, because I feel that doing so gives something of their cumulative effect. The first is verse 17: 'Do good to your servant, and I will live; I will obey your word.' Then verse 25: 'I am laid low in the dust; renew my life according to your word.'[1] Verse 37: 'Turn my eyes away from worthless things; renew my life according to your word.' Verse 40: 'How I long for your precepts! Renew my life in your righteousness.' Verse 50: 'My comfort in my suffering is this: Your promise renews my life.' Verse 77: 'Let your compassion come to me that I may live, for your law is my delight.' Verse 107: 'I have suffered much; renew my life, O LORD, according to your word.' Verse 116: 'Sustain me according to your promise, and I shall live; do not let my hopes be dashed.' Verse 144: 'Your statutes are for ever right; give me understanding that I may live.' Verse 149: 'Hear my voice in accordance with your love; renew my life, O LORD, according to your laws.' Verse 154: 'Defend my cause and redeem me; renew my life according to your promise.' Verse 156: 'Your compassion is great, O LORD; preserve my life according to your laws.' Verse 159: 'See how I love your precepts; preserve my life, O LORD, according to your love.' And finally, the very last but one verse: verse 175, 'Let me live that I may praise you, and may your laws sustain me.'

It seems to me that some of these verses do seem to arise out of a situation of threat or difficulty that was impinging upon his life and led him to say, 'Lord, please renew [or preserve] my life.' Secondly, almost all of them have the expression 'according to' in them – 'according to Your word ... Your law ... etc.', and seem to be suggesting to God, 'Lord, here's a reason why I want you to restore my life and a suggestion as to how you might go about doing it.' And thirdly, some of them supply a motivation – why God should renew his life; because something else will happen.

So I want to use that as a way of approaching our subject this morning.

1. Some versions of NIV read 'preserve' instead of 'renew' in several of the following verses. This is because some minor changes were made to the text in revisions during the 1980s. The Hebrew word allows both translations. Where my Bible quotations are different to those in your Bible, it is because I sometimes prefer the earlier NIV text's reading.

Threats to life

You may remember an old song with the refrain, 'Every time I say goodbye, I die a little.' It was Paul's testimony that every day we are dying a little. Many things in life are deadly; they spoil life, they pull life away, they are anti-life. And, of course, the great ultimate 'anti-life' is sin itself, as we know from the Garden of Eden: 'The day you eat, you will die', is the warning, and death enters and impinges upon human life from then on.

Some of the verses we have just read describe situations that we looked at mainly in our second study in this series, when we saw the struggles and difficulty that the psalmist is going through in life. And it's remarkable how often he asks for life: 'Lord please give me life, let me live, because something is threatening it; something is stopping me having the life that I know You want me to have.'

At least three things, I think, come into that category. First of all there is,

Depression and exhaustion

Look at verses 25 and 28 in the section beginning with *daleth*, 'D'. Verse 25: 'I am laid low in the dust; renew my life according to your word.' And verse 28: 'My soul is weary [or exhausted, shattered] with sorrow; strengthen me according to your word.' Even the word 'dust' in verse 25 suggests death. 'Dust you are and to dust you will return,' says God in Genesis 3:19. And in the book of Ecclesiastes, dust is often associated with death. So here is somebody who feels that already in life, because of depression and suffering and sorrow, death is invading.

Depression is a terrible thing, as I am quite sure some of you know either through personal experience or that of someone you love deeply. Depression can be very mild and just spoil life for a few days because you feel tired and things are going badly; or it can be much more serious. It can be a clinical illness, caused by physical factors, mental stress, emotional pressures, bereavement – all sorts of factors can cause it. But one of the things that seem to be most frequently expressed by those going through it is that life doesn't seem worth living any longer. All the point has gone out of it, there doesn't seem to be any hope, any joy; you no longer do the things that used to give you pleasure, everything seems dark and pointless. Is life worth living at all? In that sense depression is life-destroying. You don't have to be physically dead to feel dead, to feel that death has somehow impinged upon life.

Many of the other psalms give voice to such feelings, whether the depression is the result of sickness, opposition, or sin. You get it flowing through Psalm 102, for example, which is headed 'A prayer of an afflicted man, when he is faint and pours out his lament before the LORD.' Read verses 1 to 11. The psalmist speaks of loss of appetite (verse 4), weight loss (verse 5), sleeplessness (verse 7), and oppression by human and spiritual enemies (verse 8). It's about depression, sickness, weariness – life-threatening matters. And the psalmist says, 'That's why I have to ask God to give me life.'

The temptation of selfishness and obsession with worthless things

This is the second, death-impinging, life-threatening element. It's interesting that in verse 36 and verse 37 they are put together. 'Turn my heart towards your statutes and not towards selfish gain.' Then, immediately: 'Turn my eyes away from worthless things; renew my life according to your word' – as if the psalmist were saying, 'Lord, I know that when I get all turned in on myself and become obsessed by greed, selfishness or the things I want for myself, it ends up wasting my life. I feel that despite all I've managed to get for myself, at the end of the day I'm not living at all. Life has lost its meaning even though I'm gaining so much.'

As Jesus said, what's the point, if you gain the whole world and lose your own soul (cf Matt. 16:26)? If you haven't got a life worth living, it doesn't matter how much you own. I think the psalmist is aware of that temptation, so he says to the Lord, 'Lord, don't let me be obsessed with myself and with selfish gain and worthless things, because that's deathly, it's a waste of life. I want you to renew and restore my life, and not let me become obsessed.'

Perhaps the sharpest example of this in the Bible is the rich young ruler who asked Jesus, 'Teacher, what must I do to inherit eternal life?' (Luke 10:25). He wanted to be among those who on the last day would be among the redeemed people of God and would be with Him, inheriting the life of the age to come and that new life in the kingdom of God, about which Jesus was talking and about which all believing Jews knew. Jesus didn't give him a tract.

He pointed to what was actually dealing in death in his life – his obsession with wealth and his refusal to let it go, and his covetousness. And having been pointed to the way of life he walked away sad and returned to the ways of death, because he was not going to allow Jesus to turn his heart away from selfish gain and worthless things in order to renew his life according to the word of the Lord.

So depression and exhaustion will be death-dealing, and so will the temptation to selfishness and worthlessness.

Hostility and opposition

And so too will suffering under the opposition and attack of others. Three verses give a hint of that. Verse 50: 'My comfort in my suffering if this: Your promise renews my life.' Verse 107: 'I have suffered much; renew my life, O LORD, according to your word.' And verse 154: 'Defend my cause and redeem me; renew my life according to your promise.' He means, 'Redeem me, save me, deliver me from those who are attacking me.' He needed to be delivered from hostility, from all that would enter his heart and soul and produce bitterness, vengeance and negativity. They too can be life-destroying.

It's a terrible thing to live with constant criticism or opposition, or the attacks of people who, whether or not they should know better, are always making life a misery for you. It can crush the spirit and squeeze all the life and energy and enthusiasm out of you. It can squeeze God's vision out of you, because you feel, 'It's not worth it, if that's what they think all the time.' Life can be threatened by that kind of suffering and oppression whether the source is human, satanic or a combination of both.

Our psalmist was not the only psalmist to think of these things.

> Listen to my prayer, O God, do not ignore my plea;
>   hear me and answer me.
> My thoughts trouble me and I am distraught
>   at the voice of the enemy,
>   at the stares of the wicked;
> for they bring down suffering upon me
>   and revile me in their anger.
> My heart is in anguish within me;

the terrors of death assail me ...
I said, 'Oh, that I had the wings of a dove!
    I would fly away and be at rest –
I would flee far away
    and stay in the desert' (Psa. 55:1-4, 6-7).

He wants to be away from them all with the Lord. That's the feeling of somebody who knows this oppression of his enemies. Psalm 56 says the same kind of thing. Verses 2 to 4: 'My slanderers pursue me all day long; many are attacking me in their pride. When I am afraid, I will trust in you. In God, whose word I praise, in God I trust; I will not be afraid. What can mortal man do to me?'

That kind of language comes from people who are experiencing what is almost putting them to death. They are being killed by criticism and opposition. Maybe you experience that; maybe, God help you, you deal some of it out. Can I urge you to be careful about how you oppose those who are in spiritual leadership? Maybe you do it out of good motives. Make sure that you do it before the Lord and in the Lord's sight, and that it is constructive and not destructive, life-giving and not death-giving, if you are called upon to speak words to those who are in Christian leadership.

What then is eating away at your life? It could be any of those things: depression, exhaustion, selfishness, opposition. It could be unconfessed sin, as the psalmists also discover: remember Psalm 32. When the psalmist didn't confess his sin, his bones were withering away, he groaned, his strength was sapped. A pretty deathly experience.

It could be your stubbornness and pride. It could be your disobedience. It could be anything. But whatever it is, recognise it as a threat to your life and say the prayers of this psalmist: 'Lord, renew my life, restore my life, let me live, let me come back to You.'

Sources of Life

Out of his weakness, out of all those things, the psalmist turns to God and says, 'Make me live.' But how and why should God do that?

Let's look at a number of verses in this psalm that speak about, first, the character of God as the source of life, and second, the words of God as the source of life.

The character of God

Verse 40: 'How I long for your precepts! Renew my life in your righteousness.' The righteousness of God here is seen by the psalmist as the source of life, not the cause of judgement and death, wrath and punishment. That may be something of a surprise, because in the Bible, and certainly in the Old Testament, God's righteousness is much more frequently associated with salvation and deliverance than it is with judgement. Of course it is associated with judgement; it is because God is righteous that also He will punish the wicked. He is the righteous judge and He will do what is right. But it's much more common, as you will find if you follow this up with a concordance, for the righteousness of God to be associated with the fact that God is the God who vindicates, who delivers, who saves and who rescues people. As Isaiah 45:21 says, He is 'a righteous God and a Saviour'. Not 'a righteous God but on a good day a Saviour too'. He is a righteous God and *therefore* a Saviour.

Some of the psalmists are particularly keen on reminding God of His righteousness as a reason for His salvation. For example, Psalm 35:24: 'Vindicate me' – that is, 'show me to be innocent when accused' – 'in your righteousness, O Lord my God; do not let them gloat over me.' Or Psalm 36:5-7: 'Your love, O Lord, reaches to the heavens, your faithfulness to the skies. Your righteousness is like the mighty mountains, your justice like the great deep ... How priceless is your unfailing love!' God's righteousness is paired with love and faithfulness, and the idea of God as a refuge and a deliverer.

Or Psalm 40:9-10: 'I proclaim,' says this psalmist, after some experience of great deliverance, 'righteousness in the great assembly'. That doesn't mean he's become a preacher of hellfire and judgement. 'I do not seal my lips, as you know, O Lord. I do not hide your righteousness in my heart; I speak of your faithfulness and salvation ... your love and your truth.' It is the righteousness of God as a source of salvation.

Now why is that? Well, because fundamentally, in the Old Testament, 'God's righteousness' means 'God putting things right'.

That's why, when the psalmist in Psalms 96 and 98 looks forward to that great day when God will put everything right, the whole of creation is called to rejoice. The mountains clap their hands, the trees are rejoicing, the whole world is rejoicing before the Lord, for He comes – to do what? – 'to judge the world in righteousness'. And that is a matter of joy, because when God comes to judge He will put things right, not only by punishing the wicked, but also by vindicating, restoring and renewing the faithful.

So the psalmist says, 'Will you please make me live? Because You are righteous – not because I deserve it and can claim to have earned it, but because Lord, You are the God whose righteousness is a matter of good news.' That, of course, is why the apostle Paul could say those famous words, 'I am not ashamed of the gospel [the good news], because it is the power of God for the salvation of everyone who believes: first for the Jew, then for the Gentile. For in the gospel a righteousness from God is revealed, a righteousness that is by faith from first to last' (Rom. 1:16-17).

It took Martin Luther quite a few months lecturing on the Psalms before he came to recognise that what Paul meant in Romans 1 was that the righteousness of God in the gospel was salvation, not judgement. It was the beginning of Luther's great turnaround in his understanding of the meaning of justification by grace through faith. In fact, it was while he was lecturing on the Psalms that he began to discover it.

The compassion of God

Verse 77: 'Let your compassion come to me that I may live, for your law is my delight.' These are beautiful words in Hebrew, that speak of the tender emotion that you feel in your bowels, deep down inside you – that tender, compassionate pity felt for something that is lost and needy, when you are moved to love out of mercy and compassion.

That, as we have been discovering all week, is part of the Old Testament's definition of God. It was first heard by Moses, at Mount Sinai of all places, when he was confronted with the reality of the presence of God. Passing in front of him, God proclaimed, 'The LORD, the LORD, the compassionate and gracious God, slow to anger, abounding in love and faithfulness' (Exod. 34:6). 'Compassionate' is the same Hebrew word used here in Psalm 119.

It was the revelation of God that the Israelites needed at that particular point, because they had just committed that awful apostasy, the sin of the golden calf, and it was only by God's compassion and mercy that they were able to move forward from that place at all.

Or, back in the book of Psalms, the wonderful words of Psalm 103: 'The LORD is compassionate and gracious, slow to anger, abounding in love ... He does not treat us as our sins deserve or repay us according to our iniquities' (Psa.103:8,10). How I thank God for that! And how my heart echoed what Tom Bathgate said in his address the other night, when he quoted those wonderful words, 'If you, O LORD, kept a record of sins, O LORD, who could stand?' (Psa. 130:3). If He were to pay attention, to count our iniquities, who could stand before Him? Not one of us; there would be nobody in this tent or reading this book, let alone on this platform. 'But with you there is forgiveness; therefore you are feared' (130:4).

So it is out of the compassion of God that this psalmist can say, 'Lord, restore my life; I can live, I can be restored, not just because You are righteous, but also because You are compassionate.'

God's love

Verse 159: 'See how I love your precepts; preserve my life, O LORD, according to your love.' It's a lovely balance, isn't it. 'My love for Your law ... therefore give me life.' The word is *hesed,* which means covenant, promise-keeping love; the defining character of God again. He is the God who consistently, faithfully fulfils that love for us.

Graham Kendrick's well-known song says, 'Such love / springs from eternity, / streaming through history, / such love, / fountain of life to me.' Love is life-giving, as we know from our human relationships. When you know somebody loves you, it makes life better. People have been loved back to life and wholeness. Love supports people, gives life to people, lifts people up out of depression, out of illness, out of whatever it is; love lifts us and gives us life.

Ultimately it is the love of God that does it. Psalm 63:3: 'Because your love' – Your loving kindness, it's the same word – 'is better than life, my lips will glorify you.' And it's the very essence

of the gospel: 'For God so loved the world that he gave his one and
only Son, that whoever believes in him shall not perish but have
eternal life' (John 3:16). Love gives life.

So when the psalmist wants God to give him life, he doesn't just
say, 'O Lord, pity me, isn't it awful the way I am?' He says, 'I want
You to give me life because of who You are. You are righteous and
You are compassionate, and You are love. Therefore please renew
and restore my life.' But he doesn't only think of God's character,
he thinks of God's words. At least eight times the psalmist links his
cry for life with the phrase 'according to Your ...' Several times,
'according to Your word'; twice, 'according to Your promise', and
three times, 'according to Your law'.

If I had been this psalmist, how would I have expected the word
of God, the promise of God and the law of God to be life-restoring
to me? I know that as a Christian I can go to the cross, I can think
of the resurrection, I can think of the Holy Spirit poured out at
Pentecost, I can think of all those wonderful New Testament
promises. But this psalmist is living before all of that. What was it
that he would have turned to?

ACCORDING TO YOUR WORD

First of all let's just look at where the word occurs. Verse 25: 'I am
laid low in the dust; renew my life according to your word.' Verse
37: 'Turn my eyes away from worthless things; renew my life
according to your word.' And verse 107: 'I have suffered much;
renew my life, O LORD, according to your word.'

I wish I could have asked him what the word of God meant to
him. I would love to hear an Old Testament believer expounding
'the word of the Lord', because they loved it. They could say that
all life in the universe comes from the word of God, so how much
more does my little life? Psalm 33:4-7 says, 'For the word of the
LORD is right and true ... By the word of the LORD were the
heavens made, their starry host by the breath of his mouth. He
gathers the waters of the sea into jars.' Verse 9: 'For he spoke, and
it came to be; he commanded, and it stood firm.' Wow! Why don't
we say those words? We read them in Genesis 1:3: 'And God said,
"Let there be light," and there was light.' It's great – and we just
pass over it.

We've got a wonderful picture on the wall of our library at All

Nations. At the top is written, 'And God said – '. Below that, are all the equations of electro-magnetism, very complicated equations of wave energy and particle energy and so on, which is what light is. And then at the bottom it says, 'And there was light.' But actually the key to the picture is not the equations but the words 'God said'. It's taken the human race a few thousand years to discover the workings of light, and we think we are wonderfully clever. But God didn't say, 'It did occur to me some time ago that that's what I needed to get light going.' He said it, and it was there. By the word of the Lord, the heavens were made. All the galaxies, stars, light, energy, matter, anti-matter, everything that's there, is there because God put into it all the information, all the parameters, all the equations, all that was needed for it to happen in the first place, and for it to expand to the point where it is now.

We have eyes to see it and lips to talk about it. God said it, it is His word that did it. There is only life because God speaks the word of life. There is only the energy of the universe, there is only the biological life of this planet, there is only animal life, there is only human life, there is only spiritual life – because of the word of God. So when this psalmist says, renew my life according to Your word, he is saying something pretty big. So can you, if you say it: 'according to Your word'.

ACCORDING TO YOUR PROMISES

But he goes on to say, 'Renew my life according to Your promises.' Verse 50: 'My comfort in my suffering is this: Your promise renews my life.' Verse 116: 'Sustain me according to your promise, and I shall live.' Verse 154, 'Renew my life according to your promise.'

The Hebrew word means literally 'your sayings'. But just as we say, 'I give you my word', it has come to mean 'promise' also. A person's word is what they have promised to do. And this Hebrew expression has the same flavour. 'Lord, because You've said it and promised it, You are going to renew my life.'

So again: ask an Old Testament believer, 'What do you mean, "according to your promises"? What promises have you got in your Scriptures?' He could list them. Isaiah 43:1-2: 'Fear not ... When you pass through the waters, I will be with you;' – promising deliverance, protection – 'and when you pass through the rivers, they will not sweep over you' – promises of blessing, of life itself.

Like the promise that Moses heard, when at Mount Sinai he was appealing to the Lord to rescue his people and the people had done everything they could to deserve destruction (cf Exod. 32). God said to him, 'Get out of my way, I'm going to destroy these people because of their sin.' And Moses replied, 'Excuse me God, You can't do that, I'm sorry; because these are Your people, it was You who brought them out of Egypt and You have promised to be their God. And Lord, would You please remember Abraham and how You promised to Abraham that You would make this a great and mighty nation through these people? You are going to bless all the nations of the world – so Lord, if You wipe them all out now what's going to happen to Your promise, to Your word, to Your oath? What's going to happen to You, Lord, if You go back on Your promise? You can't.'

And so Moses is saying effectively, 'Lord, restore, preserve the life of these people according to Your promise, as You are a promise-keeping God, and that is Your very nature.'

ACCORDING TO YOUR LAWS

Verses 149 and 156 may seem paradoxical. Those who are in the unlikely situation of having been brought up solely on Paul's theology in Romans, Galatians and elsewhere, may have thought that the only thing to know about the law is that it's an agent of death. Of course in the context in which Paul was writing, and in the context of people seeking some kind of righteousness according to the obedience of the law, not based on a faithful and grateful response to God as their Saviour, then yes, in that sense the law became an agent for the exposure of sin and the recognition of death that sin brings. Please don't misunderstand me, I don't want to have an argument with the apostle Paul at this point.

But here in the Scriptures that Paul knew and loved is a psalmist praying for life 'according to God's law'. And we have to stop and think, 'What does he mean by wanting life in, and according to, the laws of God?'

As so often in Hebrew poetry, verses 149 and 156 use the device of parallel construction. Hebrew poetry is a kind of stereo, it always gives you something through both ears, there's a three-dimensional sound. And in both of these verses something is put parallel to law: in verse 149 it is love, and in verse 156 it is compassion.

We've had those words already. The psalmist has already told us that he wants God to renew his life out of love and compassion. But we have to ask again, 'Where did he learn about God's love and God's compassion?' The answer is, 'In the law.' It was in the laws of God, back there – in those books of Exodus, Leviticus and Deuteronomy, including some bits of the Bible that we hardly ever read – that the Israelites were confronted with the compassion and love of God that they were to imitate and live out in their own social relationships; to give life and restore life to one another, through social compassion and social love in reality and in practice.

Here are a few examples.

In Deuteronomy 23:15-16, God's law gives instructions on what to do if a slave runs away and takes refuge with you. In every other society in the world that has condoned slavery (including our own until not so very long ago), a runaway slave is in danger of being put to death and anyone who harbours one is going to end up with a severe penalty. But in contrast to all other slavery legislation, this law says that if a slave runs away, you are to let him live among you wherever he chooses. Don't send him back! You are to give him life in your community out of compassion, compassion in which his human need is to take priority over the slave-owner's legal rights. (It is an interesting feature of Old Testament law that it quite often elevates needs above rights. Jesus did the same in the Gospels.)

Deuteronomy 24:6 says that if you are taking security for a loan, 'Do not take a pair of millstones ... for a debt.' That is, the grinder that you use to grind your daily bread. 'Don't take that away from your debtor, because that would be stealing a life. If somebody's going to live they've got to eat, so your behaviour must be compassionate towards them.' The jubilee law, by which people were to be released and restored to their land after fifty years, was laid down 'so that your countryman may continue to live among you' (Lev. 25:36). The laws of the tithes and the debt release in Deuteronomy 14 and 15 talk about how 'the fatherless and the widows who live in your towns may come and eat and be satisfied' (Deut. 14:29). The Israelites learned from God's law that they were to live with compassion and with love towards one another, because that's what God is like. And quite frequently, the example is God Himself.

So this psalmist can say, 'Lord, I want You to restore my life just as I have learned from Your laws that that's what You want to happen. You want life restored. I am poor, I am needy, I feel like an alien on the earth, but Your law tells me that You are the God who cares for the alien and the needy and who wants to restore the poor and the suffering. So, Lord, will you please renew my life, just as You say in Your law?' That's why He founded the law. It's the Scriptures that teach the psalmist about the God he worships, and therefore enable him to cry out to Him.

So I would ask us all: Where will your renewal of life come from? I trust that as you come to Keswick (and to other conventions, services, revival meetings or whatever it might be), as you look to leaders and speakers, and to the books that we read – please take from this psalm the knowledge that the renewal of life comes ultimately from the Lord Himself. 'Lord, it's Your righteousness, Your compassion, Your love, Your word, Your promise, Your law. That's where I will find my refreshment, in the Lord Himself.'

We don't know who wrote this psalm. It may have been David. In any case, David is a particularly good example of this. There are two lovely passages in 1 Samuel that came to our attention at All Nations recently when we were going through the life of David in our Wednesday morning worship times. One is 1 Samuel 23:16. David is on his own in the desert of Ziph and he has just learned that Saul has come out to take his life. So here is a man like the psalmist: under threat, death staring him in the face (he's already been dodging Saul's javelins). And now, he's on his own and he is really in for it. Saul is coming to get him. And then we read, 'And Saul's son Jonathan went to David at Horesh and helped him to find strength in God.'

What a friend Jonathan was! We all know about Jonathan and David's friendship. This was its quality. He helped David find strength, refreshment, life in God. And David was a good learner, because just a few chapters later, in 1 Samuel 30:6, David is up against it again. This time he's not on his own. He probably wishes he were; it's after the defeat at Ziklag, and with a great crowd of people who wanted to kill him. 'David was greatly distressed because the men were talking of stoning him; each one was bitter in spirit,' because their sons and daughters had been captured and carried off. Then come these lovely words: 'But David found strength in the LORD his God.' Or, as the RSV translates it, 'David refreshed himself in the LORD his God.' He didn't have time to go up to Keswick, or go off on a retreat, or go anywhere in fact. He was in the midst of a crowd of people who were after his blood. And somehow or other he was able in his heart and his mind to say, 'Lord, I need You here, I need Your strength, I need to be refreshed, I need Your life' – in God, not anywhere else.

You can be a Jonathan for somebody else or you can be a David for yourself, or both as the case might be. You don't have to be a trained counsellor in order to be able to direct other people to God, to God's character and to His word so that they can find renewal in that. Again, please don't misunderstand me. I'm not in any way minimising the role of counsellors, of skills and caring people. It's a very important ministry. But all of us, if we have the Scriptures, can minister life to people through God's word.

Not very long ago I went through a crisis in my own life and feelings. It was actually a friend on the phone who spoke to me a word of Scripture that gave me back hope and made me feel there was life again. Just one word of Scripture; I then went and found many more. But that friend was a Jonathan to me at that moment, helped me to find strength in the Lord.

Finally, thirdly,

The effects of renewal

Something is going to happen if he is renewed, either for himself, or for God. For himself, he hopes that as he prays, as God renews his life, he will find that there will be sustaining strength and energy to carry on.

Strength, comfort and hope

Verse 28: 'My soul is weary with sorrow; strengthen me according to your word.' How weak we sometimes feel, don't we? We just can't go on. And at that moment, we need that strengthening life of God within us. Look at verse 116: 'Sustain me according to your promise, and I shall live' – 'Sustain me, hold me, lift me; I can't hold on any longer, but You can hold on to me.' Verse 175: 'Let me live that I might praise you, and may your laws sustain me.' I hope that one of the effects of walking through this psalm will at the very least be a strengthening experience for us; that it will refresh us, will nourish us, will be like that moment when we are on a long walk in the hills and you get to the point where you can't go any further. So you sit down with your flask of tea and some food and you are strengthened; you are given energy to carry on. That's what he says: 'Lord, give me strength, give me energy to keep going.'

Also, he expects to find comfort and hope. I know there are many here for whom that is deeply personal. Verse 50: 'My comfort in my suffering is this: Your promise renews my life.' Verse 49, immediately before it: 'You have given me hope.' And verse 116 again: 'Sustain me ... and I shall live; do not let my hopes be dashed.' You can't live without hope. When people have totally lost any sense of a future, of a life that is there to be lived, they are in a dangerous condition. But there is hope, because God is a God of hope, who renews life.

Renewed obedience and amplified praise

If God answers his prayer and restores his life, then – to put it bluntly – what's in it for God? The psalmists are not averse to thinking that way. They sometimes say, 'Well, Lord, You've got to restore me because there's something in it for You as well.' And two things are going to be in this for God, if God will hear this prayer.

OBEDIENCE

The first is obedience. Actually this is the substance of the psalmist's first prayer for restoration: 'Do good to your servant and I will live; I will obey your word' (verse 17). I don't think he is trying to strike a bargain. It isn't some sort of wrong attitude to God. He is saying, 'Lord, how can I obey You if I'm not alive? You'd better keep me alive, and then, if I'm spared to live at all, then I want to live for You and I want to obey You.'

There's a wonderful cycle in the Old Testament: God has blessed us, therefore we want to obey Him, out of gratitude. But when we obey Him, God gives us life and gives us blessing. So because God has restored our life, we'll go on obeying Him. It's not that you earn God's blessing by obeying Him. God blesses you and you want to obey Him. But as you obey Him He goes on blessing you

... it's a constant cycle of blessing and obedience. And this is what this psalmist says first of all: 'Lord, let me live, restore my life, so that I can go out and obey You.'

PRAISE

Secondly – and it's virtually the last thing he says – in verse 175 he says, 'Let me live that I may praise you.' Obedience and praise! It's a wonderful way to begin this psalm and a wonderful way to end it. He prays for life so that he can praise God.

Again I think there is a wonderful earthiness in this Old Testament, pre-resurrection context; when people weren't obsessed with what would come after death, or getting to heaven, or all those things we now know concerning the Lord Jesus Christ and His resurrection. There's a lovely 'down-to-earthiness' about these sayings in the Psalms. What they say (and in fact one of them says explicitly, Psa. 30:9), is, 'Lord, if I die, if I go down to the grave, then who's going to praise You? Will the dust praise You, will the worms praise You? Of course not. There's not going to be much praise coming up from my grave, Lord. So please let me live, because if I'm alive I'll praise You, and while I've got breath in my body I'll praise You.'

Praise doesn't mean just happy-clappy cheerfulness. This psalmist has still got struggles and needs. In fact the very last verse, 176, reminds us that he still feels like a lost sheep. So praise doesn't rule out lament. In fact, in the Old Testament psalms it's part of praise; praise means that you acknowledge the reality of God in every aspect of life, saying that 'No matter what happens down here, Lord, You are still God, and I will praise You because You are God, no matter what's happening to me.' So praise is even more praise-y, in Old Testament terms, when you bring God into your troubles.

One of the things that sometimes annoys me in worship (it hasn't happened at Keswick, I'm glad to say) is when people say, 'Well now; let's leave behind all our troubles, let's forget everything that we're worried about, and let's just all come into the presence of God and forget all that's bothering us.' But what happens then? All that happens is that you praise God and then you go back to your troubles. They are waiting for you at the door as you go out, but you haven't brought them into the presence of God. No, praise with the psalmist is when you come into the presence of God and you say, 'God, I am hurting and life is tough. But I'm still going to praise You, because You are still God and You are still on the throne.'

So this psalmist is not saying, 'Restore my life and I'll be happy ever after.' It's not a fairy story. He says, 'Restore my life and I will praise You, even when I feel like a lost sheep.'

Renewal of life

'Renewal' is a mis-used word today. It's a bit twisted and distorted. People talk about 'renewal meetings', 'renewed churches', about 'getting renewal' this way and that. And sometimes, you know, it means little more than spiritual narcissicism: 'Look at me, look at how I got blessed.'

People want blessing. They want renewal. But they are not often so willing to obey and to praise God who gives it to them. That's why, sometimes, meetings that tell you how to be renewed and be filled in the Holy Spirit are packed to the doors, while meetings that tell you how to go out in mission, obedient to the word of God, to disciple the nations, get a handful attending. It's a reality, isn't it? We want the blessing, but we don't want the obedience.

But renewal without obedience to God is a fake, no matter how spectacular it is. Remember Simon the sorcerer? He wanted all the spectacular signs of the Holy Spirit, but his heart was not committed to obedience. Renewal without obedience is a fake, and renewal without praise – well, I would say it's frankly impossible. But if it were to happen it would be nothing more than self-focused idolatry.

I expect, I hope, I trust, that many of us will go back from Keswick this year and say, 'Wasn't that a wonderful time of renewal of life, of refreshment?' But if that's what it has been, then do make sure that it leads to obedience, to whatever it is that God has been saying to you that He wants you to be doing. And make sure that it leads also to a primary expression of praise, to the God who has brought you here.

So we have walked a long way with this psalmist. Let me finish reading again the closing words of this psalm. May this be our prayer, as we close our sessions together.

> May my cry come before you, O LORD;
>   give me understanding according to your word.
> May my supplication come before you;
>   deliver me according to your promise.
> May my lips overflow with praise,
>   for you teach me your decrees.
> May my tongue sing of your word,
>   for all your commands are righteous.
> May your hand be ready to help me,
>   for I have chosen your precepts.
> I long for your salvation, O LORD,
> and your law is my delight.
> Let me live that I may praise you,
>   and may your laws sustain me.
> I have strayed like a lost sheep
>   Seek your servant,
>   for I have not forgotten your commands.

Isn't it a comfort that at the end of the day, as at the end of this psalm, it is the responsibility of the shepherd to seek and find his stray sheep, and not the responsibility of the sheep to find the shepherd? God is looking for you, as much as, and more than, you are looking for Him.

So may God bless you and may God find you as you seek Him with all your heart. For His name's sake. Amen.

Studies in 2 Timothy

by Rev. Alistair Begg

2 Timothy 1:1-14

Probably nothing clarifies the issues of life so much as the prospect of death does. Some of us have come close to it, for example when we have received a very difficult diagnosis for ourselves, or have sat with loved ones or friends as they faced the end of their lives. It is quickly apparent that people in such situations, provided that they are still possessed of their faculties, have a great desire to communicate what is most on their hearts and what they believe to be most crucial for us to know who are being left behind. If we were in that situation ourselves, and we were given the opportunity to write a final letter, we would surely try to convey the strongest and deepest longings of our hearts – especially so, if we were writing to those close to us and dear to us. And we would also try to make sure that, at the same time, we passed on those things that we believed to be of the greatest, most vital importance.

That is exactly the context in which Paul finds himself as he writes his second letter to Timothy. He recognises (4:6) that his life is ebbing away. The time has come for his departure. He realises that he is probably writing his last will and testament to Timothy, the young man who has been his colleague in ministry and also his son in the faith.

This letter is generally regarded as the third of the three

'pastoral' epistles – a designation that goes back to the eighteenth century. They were called 'pastoral' because they are written to specific individuals; two to Timothy and one to Titus. The other epistles were written to churches; but swan-song, if you like, is a letter to a young man, to whom Paul is handing on the baton of faith to be carried on into a subsequent generation.

But Paul wrote at a time when the church was facing a variety of threats. Some came from the inside, others from the outside. The devastating consequence of those threats for the church was that the very prospect of the church surviving as a Christian community into a subsequent generation, even a few years on, seems to have been called into question by those viewing the matter from a human perspective and the point of view of a realistic observer. Years ago, Bishop Handley Moule, describing the context of this letter, said, 'Christianity ... trembled, *humanly speaking*, on the verge of annihilation' (*The Second Epistle to Timothy*, 1905, p. 18). So it wasn't that everybody felt good about everything and the church was in fine form. They weren't making great gains. Society was not being dramatically impacted, nor were people coming to Christ in droves. They were being persecuted by Nero. In the province of Asia large numbers of people were turning away from the things of Christ. And the apostle himself, who was such a strategic instrument of God's purposes, was sitting in prison under the shadow of execution.

He writes, therefore, with a passionate concern. He wants to ensure that the gospel of the Lord Jesus Christ will be guarded and then passed on, without disguise or distortion, to a subsequent generation. As we shall see, he wants to entrust the gospel to Timothy and to other faithful men and women, who will herald it and proclaim it in all of its fullness.

You don't have to be very smart to recognise, even from that sketchy introduction, that there are some obvious and direct parallels to the church in our own day. I would suggest to you that once again the church in our generation trembles; not, I believe, before the threat of annihilation, but before the prospect of capitulation. It is a double capitulation. It is *a theological capitulation* that imbibes the spirit of the age in all of its syncretism and pluralism. And it is *a methodological capitulation* that imbibes the spirit of the age in relationship to its methodology – a failing, at least in certain areas, to recognise the call to be radically different. The prevailing climate of our generation is one in which being unsure and vague is far more acceptable than being clear and certain. Indeed, those who have conviction and appear in any sense to be dogmatic are regarded as the most suspect and most to be wary of. The only thing that we can be certain of is that we can be certain of absolutely nothing.

That spirit is also abroad in the church of the Lord Jesus Christ. The notion of an unequivocal voice, of a trumpet giving a certain sound, is not as obvious as it was in previous generations. That is why I think that those who have chosen the second letter to Timothy for our studies have chosen very well, prayerfully and purposefully. We are without question living in a time when people are greatly confused as to how they ought to behave; and they are certainly confused concerning what they ought to believe.

That is very easily illustrated from the newspapers. Yesterday's *Times* titled its editorial about the Lambeth Conference, 'The Lambeth Way'. However else you describe it, it is definitely confused. Let me give you just a taste. 'The deliberations this year,' the writer said, 'run some risk of being overshadowed by demands by lesbian and gay Christian movements for the ordination of practising homosexuals.'

I don't believe it's possible to speak of 'lesbian and gay' alongside 'Christian movements'. The fact that *The Times* does merely highlights the confusion. The Lambeth method, however, has been to surmount differences by emphasising what a report before the conference describes as 'the creative fusion of provincial autonomy and inter-dependence'. Now, there's a wonderful phrase that we could spend the rest of the morning trying to understand! The editorial goes on, 'Pluralism has an obvious place in this far-flung church of 80,000,000.' The only thing that the 1998 Lambeth Conference has any prospect of adopting a unified stance on, according to the editorial, is the cancellation of Third World debt.

Such situations point to the need for the pressing, urgent declaration of the message of 2 Timothy.

Underpinning all I shall be saying is the conviction that there is a crying need among the people of God for a solid experiential grasp of basic Christian doctrine; doctrine on fire, yes, but nevertheless solid and experientially grasped.

You wouldn't want a carpenter to come to your house and start crashing around with his tools with no indication that he knew why he was there or what he was going to do. Yet in the realm of theology, there are people who are crashing around with all kinds of tools and no obvious indication of what in the world they are trying to do. They will be able to go on doing so. Why? Because there is a generation growing up right alongside us that is clueless. Sinclair Ferguson has said that it is one of the enigmas of our day that, in a world of great opportunities, many adult Christians have less knowledge of doctrine than children had in Sunday school in previous centuries. That may also be a reason for the difference between the quality of Christian character of previous eras, and the relatively poor standard of our own Christian lives today.

The greetings (1:1-2)

With all of that by way of background, look at the greetings in verses 1 and 2. Paul, as he usually does, introduces himself and introduces the one to whom he writes. Notice, he describes himself in striking terms: 'an apostle of Christ Jesus by the will of God, according to the promise of life that is in Christ Jesus.' Isn't that a little surprising, when you think that he is writing to someone with whom he is so familiar – a friend and colleague in the ministry? Well, we have to recognise that while the letter was read initially by Timothy, Paul was aware that it would have a much wider hearing. It was imperative, especially since Timothy was taking up where Paul was leaving off, that those who became the hearers of the letter with Timothy understood the credentials of the mighty apostle. And etched indelibly in his mind was that encounter on the Damascus road, when he was not only converted but commissioned. Years later, before the Roman authorities, he recalled how he had heard a voice saying, 'Now get up and stand on your feet. I have appeared to appoint you as a servant and as a witness of what you have seen of Me and what I will show you' (cf Acts 22:6-21).

'*Ego ekapostelo* – I "apostle" you,' said God (cf Acts 22:21). 'I bring you to Myself and I send you for Myself.' The wonder of that truth was at the very heart of all that Paul did and consequently of all that he wrote. He recognised that his appointment was not the result of human ingenuity but of divine initiative. He was added to the unique group of apostles – an unrepeatable group in the foundation of the church – who shared a sight of the risen Lord, a divine commission from that Lord, and the inspiration of God's Spirit. From that starting point he was then to go out to proclaim 'the promised life which we have in union with Christ Jesus' (TEV).

In other words, Paul's concern is to formulate the gospel and to communicate it. He identifies this in introducing his letter to young Timothy. As he faces the prospect of death, his concern is the promise of life.

How wonderful that this letter does not begin with a great whining and groaning, a moaning dissertation on the dreadful predicament in which he finds himself! Instead he is consumed by the wonder of what God has done in redeeming and commissioning him; he is passionately concerned with this issue of the gospel; he wants this young man, whom he loves, to know that even in the shadow of execution he is committed to the news of the promise of life, and to Jesus who said, 'I am come that you might have life.' He is the one about whom Paul is going to say, 'He has brought life and immortality to light through the gospel.'

Verse 2 moves the focus from Paul to Timothy, 'my dear son'. The lovely way in which Paul refers to this young man throughout his letters is striking. In 1 Corinthians 4:17 he describes him as 'my son whom I love'. In Romans 16:21 he is his 'fellow-worker'. In Philippians 2:20 he says, 'I have no-one else like him.' There is an intimacy between them. In just the same way, at this moment I have in my Bible a postcard that was left for me last week by a gentleman who means everything to me in the faith. I wasn't surprised to receive this card, but I was stirred. If I didn't have it in my Bible I would have it in my inside pocket; I would keep it close to my heart because frankly, it means absolutely everything to me.

Those are the relationships that God establishes in the gospel! And you yourselves will be able to identify similar things: notes and quotes, anecdotes, telephone calls and dimensions of relationships that are precious to you. Such relationships are not apostolic, but they are meaningful in the gospel. It is that kind of wonderful intimacy that is conveyed not only in the greeting, 'my dear son', but throughout the whole letter.

What makes it so amazing to me is that Timothy was not an

obvious choice as recipient of this letter or of this charge – at least, not humanly speaking. When you piece together the Identikit portrait of Timothy that is to be found in the various letters of the New Testament, you discover that he was comparatively young (which is why Paul told him, 'Don't let anyone look down on you because you are young' (1 Tim. 4:12). Added to that, he was physically frail (which is why he was to take a wee drop of wine for his tummy's sake, 1 Tim. 5:23). Also he was naturally timid (which is why Paul asks the Corinthians to put Timothy at ease when he arrives in Corinth, 1 Cor. 16:10).

So we aren't shown some strong, mature individual, able to walk into circumstances and just take control. Instead we are shown a rather diffident chap who looks too young for what he's doing. We are told he has a weak tummy, and that's probably due to his diffidence and timidity. And yet, he's the man. The man whom God has chosen is somebody who would be hard-pressed to get his name in front of the average vacancy committee.

He was a young man. In his journal, George Whitefield describes how, as a young man himself, he was asked to preach at the chapel of the Tower of London. He says that he went there reticent and fearful, overawed by the prospect of what he had to do. But was there tremendous encouragement, as he made his way there? Not at all.

> As I passed along the streets, many came out of their shops to see so young a person in a gown and cassock. One I remember in particular, cried out, 'There's a boy parson.' ... As I went up the stairs almost all seemed to sneer at me on account of my youth; but they soon grew serious and exceedingly attentive. (*Journal*, 1736, aged 21).

Why? Because he was God's man. And God delights to pick men and women – comparatively young, naturally weak, physically frail, obviously diffident. He says, 'Here, you're My girl, you're My fellow, for the task to which I have appointed you.' And so it is to a young man, more prone to lean than he is to lead, that God entrusts this wonderful task. How Timothy must have drunk in Paul's greeting, which provided him with a reminder of his resources!

'God the Father and Christ Jesus our Lord' – together, says John Stott, these words 'constitute the one spring from which this threefold stream flows forth'. Don't you wish you could write a sentence like that just once in your life? If you come to me after I've preached and say, 'That last paragraph was remarkable,' I probably got it from John Stott's commentary on 2 Timothy. And you'll be able to find it there too![1]

Grace for the trials, mercy for the failures, peace in the face of the dangers and doubts. There it all is for us this morning. What do we need? Grace, mercy and peace – the exact things that Timothy needed – in every generation.

Spiritual foundations (1:3-5)

After his greeting Paul reminds himself and his readers of the spiritual foundations which were Timothy's. Again, the opening phrase in verse 3 is a wonderful illustration of his selflessness. No complaining and no groaning; just concern for this young man.

Consider his care for Timothy, in the light of what he tells him in verses 3 and 4: 'I constantly remember you in my prayers' – it's good to know that others pray for us – 'I long to see you.' That doesn't mean 'Maybe I'll see you' or 'Perhaps I'll catch up with you.' It is the longing that I have to see my loved ones when I get the chance to return across the ocean. Paul is 'possessed of a homesick yearning', which is the phrase he uses.

Verse 5: 'I have been reminded of your sincere faith' – he adds, 'By the way, let me encourage you to stir up the gift that is in you' (cf 1:6). Does that mean that we have the necessary ingredients for discipleship, for helping each other along on the journey of faith? Well, I believe that we couldn't say we have everything, but we are given some helpful pointers here. All of us in the journey of life are being helped on by those of us who are ahead, and presumably we are encouraging others alongside and behind us. Fred Mitchell, who preached at Keswick years ago, said memorably: 'You can never lead souls heavenward unless climbing yourself. You need not be very high up, but you must be climbing.' And as Paul continues

1. John Stott, *The Message of 2 Timothy* (IVP: The Bible Speaks Today series, 1973).

to climb, he encourages Timothy to climb along with him.

What are the elements that make up Paul's urging of Timothy onwards on the path of faith? Let me suggest to you that there are four.

First, verse 3, *faithfulness in prayer*. 'I constantly remember you ...' Second, verse 4, *warmth in friendship*. 'I long to see you.' Third, verse 5, *encouragement in his words*. 'I have been reminded of your sincere faith.' He doesn't say to Timothy, 'Now, I know you are a bit of a disaster; I know that you are far too young and are making a hash of things generally. So I thought I'd write and tell you how dreadful you are. I'm sure that you are encouraged to know that I know and that everyone else knows ...' No. Many of us have the capacity to make people's hearts sink; do you remember Caleb's reminiscences in Joshua 14:8, of the twelve coming back from checking out the promised land? Caleb and Joshua stood out because they encouraged the people. It says of the other ten that 'they made the hearts of the people sink'. It's easy to do it. May the Lord save us and forgive us for those times when we do.

Fourth, verse 6, *purposefulness in exhortation*. 'For this reason I remind you to fan into flame the gift of God, which is in you...' These verses contain a wonderful, necessary reminder of the benefits and blessings of a Christian heritage. From infancy Timothy had been acquainted with the Scriptures, as we see in 3:15. And I testify this morning of the immense privilege and benefit that it is to have been reared in that kind of environment. Years ago as a teenager, somewhere in West Yorkshire, I was given the opportunity to speak to a gathering of people at some majestic affair like a 'daffodil tea' or something like that. I made the observation in passing that I had the privilege (I didn't even say 'privilege', in fact) of being brought up in a Christian home. Then I paused and added, 'Frankly, I don't know whether that's a plus or a minus.' Then I continued with what I was saying.

A man who seemed very elderly to me at the time (he was probably the same age as I am now!) grabbed me firmly by the scruff of the neck and ushered me round the bookstall. He said, 'Now listen here, lad. Thou may not know now – thou may be too daft now – to understand. But one day thou'll know that it is a grand privilege. And never forget that.'

I've never forgotten it. I was stupid to say what I said. I had the benefit of a godly grandmother from the Highlands of Scotland who prayed for me from, or even before, conception; a mother who loved Christ and nurtured me; a father, too.

I want to say a word to you godly grannies. You're at the forefront, the very knife-edge of things, laying hold of God's throne for your grandchildren who are growing up in an age of confusion. Many of them are taking on board great chunks of confused thinking and bizarre lifestyles. Eternity will reveal the impact of your prayers, even if you don't see it within time. So – praying grandmothers and praying mothers, pray on!

Spiritual gifts (1:6-7)

Not only has Timothy been reared in a godly environment and been befriended by a mighty apostle, he has also been endowed with spiritual gifts. That's why Paul gives him an exhortation: 'Fan into flame the gift of God, which is in you.' I'm inclined to agree with those who say that what Paul is referring to here is simply the authority and power to be a minister of Christ. It may be more than that; I certainly do not believe that it is less than that.

What is this 'gift of God, which is in you through the laying on of my hands'?

The average home Bible study group can spend a fortnight on this as everybody debates it and nobody knows what it is. My best shot at it is, that it is the authority and power of Christ to be a minister of Christ. But this, you see, was the necessary reminder. Timothy is frail, Timothy is timid. Therefore it seems only right to encourage him to fan this into a flame. Note the wonderful balance between what God does and what we do! The power necessary to fulfil the exhortations of Scripture is supplied to us in the Spirit: 'Work out your salvation with fear and trembling, for it is God who works in you to will and to act according to his good purpose' (Phil. 2:12-13). Fan into flame the gift of God in you – 'For God did not give us a spirit of timidity, but a spirit of power, of love and self-discipline' (1:7).

You see, if the sentence ended with 'the gift of God', Timothy might have responded, 'You know I've been trying to do that. I haven't been making much of a go of it. What am I supposed to do? After all, look at me.'

Then comes a reminder of the resources.

Power

We have to be very careful of the notion of power. Verse 7 is speaking not about power of personality, persuasive speech or human boldness. Paul writes in his second letter to the Corinthians, 'We have this treasure in earthen vessels' (2 Cor. 4:7, AV), so that the glorious power might be seen to be from God and not from us. But in his first letter to them he is very anxious not to press home his abilities and his background. His desire for them in this matter is 'so that your faith might not rest on men's wisdom, but on God's power' (1 Cor. 2:5).

And in our generation, in another time, when there is so much made of being powerful and useful and so on, let us remind ourselves that it is axiomatic throughout all Scripture that an awareness of our inadequacy, our frailty and often our fearfulness is the environment in which we make the discovery of God's enduement. So the very trials we run from are the means of God's blessing. The thing we try to cover up – our weakness, diffidence, lack of giftedness – is the very foundation God uses to magnify His Son. Our endeavour to make much of ourselves, or to let people know how powerful or useful we might be, is the denial of the experience of that which God longs to give to His children.

Love

Love is a vital prerequisite in a servant of the Lord Jesus Christ. Hopefully, the older we get the more we understand this, as we minister to one another. There are more flies caught by a jar of honey, as C. H. Spurgeon said, than by a bottle of vinegar. Some of us have a vinegar face and a vinegar ministry. We wouldn't be described as 'honey-pots' – certainly not by our wives.

If you are a pastor, do your people know you love them? I don't mean some 'buy-yourself-a-teddy-bear', squishy sentimentality. Do your folks know that you love them by your self-giving to them, by your opening up of the Scriptures to them, by your life among them?

For that's what God has entrusted to His servants. Not only power so that we can be useful, but love so that we can be approachable and self-disciplined, so that we can fulfil all the duties of our ministry.

Self-discipline

The missing element in many of our lives is simply self-discipline. We're chaotic. We might make jokes about the state of the average pastor's study – but it's unacceptable, and it's often a reflection of the individual's life.

Paul's application (1:8-10)

In verse 8 we come to the word 'so'. Incidentally, pastors, in our preparation we should always have two words written up beside our Bibles: 'So what?' Because that's what our people are asking. 'So what, in the light of my recent bereavement? So what, in the light of the challenges of my employment? So what, in relationship to my teenage children? So what, in relationship to my singleness?'

What are the implications of verses 1 to 7 for Timothy?

'Do not be ashamed'

You would think after he had written all this that the last thing in the world Paul would write is this. He's just told Timothy, 'You've got power, you've got love, you've got self-discipline, you've got a godly heritage, you've got good friends, you've got me going for you' – you might have thought he would have said, 'So preach the word.' But he says, 'So do not be ashamed.'

I don't know about you, but that's a great encouragement to me. It is so easy to be ashamed: to be ashamed of the Master, to be ashamed of the Master's men, and to be ashamed of the Master's message. 'Do not be ashamed to testify about our Lord,' he says, 'or ashamed of me his prisoner.' You see, vague talk about religion, about God, about spirituality, is largely tolerable in a pluralistic culture. What is unacceptable is a clear, humble, unequivocal declaration that there is salvation in no-one other than Jesus Christ, for there is no other name under heaven, given among men, by which we must be saved.

Let me tell you what you *can* say in a pluralistic culture. You can say what John 14:6 says: 'I am the way and the truth and the life.' That's not a problem. Just don't add the second part of the verse – 'No-one comes to the Father except through me.' In our generation we can make all kinds of big and sentimental statements that are loosely akin to the gospel, without them being the forceful declaration that the gospel truly is.

'Join with me in suffering for the gospel'

When we are prepared to be unashamed and unequivocal, the word of Paul to Timothy will be a word for us. What a word this is, and what a strange word to our day! Yet Jesus says in Mark 8:38,

> If anyone is ashamed of me and my words in this adulterous and sinful generation, the Son of Man will be ashamed of him when he comes in his Father's glory with the holy angels.

We are going to have to work this out, it seems to me. The invitation that Paul extends here to join in the privilege of suffering for the gospel is not an invitation that will be responded to quickly by the faint-hearted. Frankly, it is an invitation that is troubling to contemporary triumphalism that always seeks to present the Christian life in glowing colours and in powerful and transcendent ways. One of the missing elements in evangelicalism, I fear, is a well thought-out theology of suffering.

In the words of the old hymn, 'I am the Lord that healeth thee.' We want to confirm and affirm the fact of God's power to heal. But both the Bible and human experience tell me that in the vast majority of cases – setting aside death as the ultimate healing – God, to whom we have continued to pray and from whom we have claimed, sometimes in outlandish ways, all kinds of promises, will by no means always heal a sick person. Christians and those for whom they pray still suffer from multiple sclerosis, still see through a glass darkly, still are devastated by emotional concerns, and still live in the midst of difficult days. And it is a failure on our part to realise what the Bible says concerning the nature of suffering that leaves us dumbfounded before the questions of our generation. Our triumphalism isn't true and we are left with nothing to say. We write few songs about heaven these days because nobody's apparently anxious to go there. We like it too much down here, and if truth be told we have apparently brought all that is going to be up there, down here. So why go? Why not just stay? We don't tell the truth. As John Newton wrote in 'Amazing Grace',

> Through many dangers, toils, and snares
> I have already come.

That's the truth! And there are still more to come. But –

> 'Tis grace has brought me safe thus far,
> and grace will lead me home.

That's how we can speak with conviction under the shadow of the gallows. There's no silly talk from Paul, no bizarre unrealistic claims; just theological substance that stirs the heart and transforms one's life.

The only way that we will be able to join in the suffering of the gospel is by the power of God. So now we come to a wonderful section.

'By the power of God who has saved us'

We have been saved, not on account of anything desirable in us but on the basis of God's 'own purpose and grace ... given us in Christ Jesus before the beginning of time'. The undeserved favour of God reaches into the eternal councils of His will. Stay up late, drink a lot of coffee and try and work that out!

> I've found a Friend, O such a Friend!
> He loved me ere I knew Him;
> He drew me with the cords of love
> And thus He bound me to Him:
> And round my heart still closely twine
> Those ties which naught can sever,
> For I am His, and He is mine,
> For ever and for ever. *(James Small)*

And where did that begin? In the eternal councils of His will. 'What is that?' That is the doctrine of election. 'And where did you get it?' Out of the Bible. 'And how are you to use it?' As Eric Alexander explained: 'Not as a bomb to be dropped, not as a banner to be waved, but as a bastion for the soul in the midst of difficult and sometimes doubting days.' I could never keep my hold. He will hold me fast. What a wonderful truth! And what a necessary truth for a young man, facing such a prospect in his day.

Now lest any of this should seem to be merely rarefied theology Paul shows that the purposes of God are 'given us in Christ Jesus' (verse 9). That might remind us of Titus 2:11, which in the Anglican Lectionary is one of the selected readings for Christmas Day: 'For the grace of God that brings salvation has appeared to all men' – the epiphany. What is this grace? How does this grace come to me? If it is in this mysterious way that God has ordained it, how do I meet it, how do I greet it? It comes to us in the person of the Lord Jesus Christ. He is the one who has destroyed death and has brought life and immortality to light through the gospel.

What a word for our day!

The only pornography left at the end of the twentieth century, the only dirty word you are not allowed to say, is death. It's the only subject you mustn't introduce at a party. But the statistics are known: one out of one dies. People try to distance themselves from it, and nowhere more so than in America, where people often look a lot better dead than they did when they were alive. The undertakers have cleaned their spectacles for them, there's a big fountain pen in their breast pocket. What are they saying? They're saying, 'He's not really gone away.' But he *has* gone away. And you will go away too. So it's better to go to a house of mourning than to a house of laughter, because in a house of mourning we will reflect upon this. And who has anything to say to a society that is consumed with death and has no answer?

The Christian has. The Christian who knows Christ, who knows that in Jesus there is life and immortality, that it has been brought to light. We are not simply going to have some kind of 'soul existence'. We are going to have the whole bang shooting match. 'When I get to heaven I'm going to put on my shoes, I'm going to walk all over God's heaven' – isn't that what the negro spiritual says?

Go out and tell people, God is not dead. He is alive!

Paul's testimony (1:11-14)

Paul writes, 'And of this gospel I was appointed a herald' – bringing the king's announcement – 'and an apostle' – as we have seen – 'and a teacher' – to explain and apply the truth. 'And incidentally,' he says, 'if you think that I am living in a Holiday Inn and getting picked up in a big swanky car and being driven everywhere, I've got news for you. That is why I'm suffering as I am. I am a preacher and teacher of the gospel, and you'll find me in the jail.'

For us, this is history. God knows whether it will become a reality to a subsequent generation. I do believe that as we are prepared to stand firm on the issues of human sexuality and on the issues of the absolute particularity of the person of Jesus Christ, pluralism will eventually do to us what it did to the Christians in the Roman empire. For pluralism only accepts pluralists. As long as we are prepared to put our Christ into the pantheon alongside the other gods, they will tolerate us. But to the degree that we are prepared to stand up and say that 'At the name of Jesus every knee should bow, in heaven and on earth and under the earth, and every tongue confess that Jesus Christ is Lord, to the glory of God the Father' (Phil. 2:10-11), they will say, 'Put your head on the block, we'll set fire to you, we'll pour tar on you.'

'I am suffering,' says Paul. It is for the offence of the cross. 'I am not ashamed, because I know whom I have believed.' I might be a prisoner, he says, but I'm not imprisoned for fraud, manipulation, worming my way into people's homes or seeing godliness as a means to financial gain. No! I am here on account of the gospel. So Timothy, Paul says in verse 13, I want you to keep what I have been telling you as 'the pattern'; let it be the model to you. Don't fiddle with it, don't try to reconfigure it. This is it. Guard it; it's a good, a beautiful deposit. How should you guard it? Not in a bombastic way, but 'with faith and love'. Some of us are good at guarding it in a very obnoxious, unattractive way. Paul says to Timothy, 'Make the gospel of the Lord Jesus attractive in a generation that doesn't believe.'

So when we guard it, let us do so with faith and with love. And the means provided is: 'with the help of the Holy Spirit who lives in us'.

2 Timothy 1:15-2:13

At the end of our last Bible Reading we noted Paul's exhortation in 1:13-14 to Timothy, to keep the pattern which he had received and to 'guard the good deposit'. The urgency of this is underscored by the reminder, in 1:15, of those who had defected in the province of Asia.

Introduction: three portraits

You may remember that in Acts 19 Luke mentions a great awakening in Asia. Everybody, he says, heard the news and many of them believed. Now, within a relatively short period of time, there is wholesale sell-out by these same people in Asia; those who had heard the word of God, those who had listened to it, had now departed from it. That is why Bishop Moule, whose commentary I mentioned in yesterday's Bible Reading, says that to every eye but that of faith, it must have appeared as if the gospel were on the eve of extinction.

Phygelus and Hermogenes (1:15)

The letter comes not at a time of great encouragement, but of great confusion. People are unsure what they believe, there is doctrinal confusion; they are unsure how to behave, there is moral confusion. In the midst of all of these nameless people, Phygelus and Hermogenes rise to the top of the list. Whether they were the ring-leaders we cannot say with certainty, but nevertheless they were well enough known to be mentioned by Paul in this letter.

What a sad thing it would be to have only one line in the Bible where your name appeared – and for that line to say you were a deserter. We are all leaving a legacy; every day of our lives we are creating, for good or ill, the recollections that our children, friends, neighbours and loved ones will have of us. We are building a reputation, we are making a name for ourselves. If you or I were only to be given one line in the record of Holy Scripture, what would they put against your name or mine to indicate what contribution we have made so far to the kingdom? For most of us the best we can hope for is that on our tombstone someone will say something nice about us. Isn't it a shame that you have to wait till you die before people say nice things about you? It's amazing. Just like when a pastor moves church – they've criticised him for years, and when he leaves they tell him all the things they really loved about him. If they'd told him while he was there, he might have stayed a little longer.

Most of us are only immortalised in a line or two on a tombstone. But Phygelus and Hermogenes have left their obituaries in this letter. We know what kind of people they were.

Onesiphorus (1:16-18)

In contrast to the desertion of these characters and their cohorts, we have recorded for us the devotion of Onesiphorus. His name means 'the bringer of profit', or colloquially 'the refresher'. You can see how well he lived up to his name, because he was profitable to the apostle. 'He often refreshed me and was not ashamed of my chains ... he searched hard for me until he found me ... You know very well in how many ways he helped me in Ephesus' (1:16-18). So his inclusion in the letter is justified not only because Paul can thereby honour his memory, reflect upon him and pray for him and his household; but because the example of Onesiphorus can be a stimulus to the young Timothy. Paul reminds him, surrounded as he is by so many who are defecting, of one who was devoted. The clear implication is, 'Don't go with the crowd, with Phygelus and Hermogenes. Follow in the track of this lovely man Onesiphorus, who refreshed me.' When I was a child, I remember, there was (and maybe still is) a brand of sweet called 'Refreshers'. They were supposed to jazz up your mouth! That was the impact of Onesiphorus. He made an impact for good.

There are individuals who sap our energies. You see them coming towards you when they're still a long way off, and even on your best days you find yourself thinking, 'Oh, no! Here we go again!' But there are other people who bring with them the prospect of invigorating us, bringing to our lives and our ministry just the right word of encouragement or spirit of refreshment. And we are so grateful to them.

May I say, in the Christian pilgrimage we don't really need any more Smarties, but we do need a few more Refreshers! You know the Smarties – the people who write to you taking the sermon apart, introducing you to things you never even knew yourself. They think they're refreshing you somehow, but in fact they're just Smarties – 'smarty-pants' – and we don't need any more of them. Are you a Refresher, or are you just a Smartie? Mental cleverness may live on in the printed page; eloquence, I guarantee, will be quickly forgotten; but genuine kindness will live on in the hearts of men and women for many a generation.

In Edinburgh we used to visit an old people's home where a very elderly man called Mr Blair lived. Sometimes when I called he was out, so I took the opportunity to speak to some of the other residents, including his close friends and mere acquaintances. They all gave Mr Blair the same unsolicited testimonial: 'Oh, Mr Blair! He's such a *good* man.' It was his goodness that stood out. Not his eloquence, nor his striking giftedness, nor the forcefulness of his personality, but the impact of his goodness. Paul wrote to Titus,

> Jesus Christ ... gave himself for us to redeem us from all wickedness and to purify for himself a people that are his very own, eager to do what is good. (Tit. 2:13-14)

Onesiphorus had obviously grasped this fact and had been just that kind of person to the apostle Paul. Consequently Paul prays for him at the beginning of verse 16, and later for Onesiphorus' household that they might be the beneficiaries of God's mercy, and 'that he will find mercy from the Lord on that day' (verse 18).

The task defined (2:1-2)

Now he returns to exhort Timothy, his young lieutenant in the faith. 'Come on now, Timothy,' he says – 'You then' (2:1). There are several 'you' or 'you therefore' phrases that occur throughout the pastoral epistles as Paul describes the prevailing circumstances. He calls Timothy here to live in contrast to the consensus of his day. He's essentially picking up verses 13 and 14. He is urging Timothy to be a man of conviction, even though the consensus may be overwhelmingly opposed to him. In other words, 'Be a man of conviction in a sea of consensus.'

This is the great longing where politics are concerned, is it not? People want to hear people who have conviction, even if their convictions are wrong. They think it would be refreshing to hear somebody say what they believed, just for a moment or two, even if they disagreed with them; instead of a constant political licking of the fingers, to find the direction the wind is blowing, so that we might move again in that direction.

Be strong

There's a wonderful story in Margaret Thatcher's *The Downing Street Years*. She was participating in an EEC summit for the first time, and was determined to get the controversial matter of Britain's financial contribution to the EEC tabled for discussion. She was told that topics for discussion the following day must be raised before business ended that evening. She was the only lady at the talks.

During a lunchtime stroll she said to the French prime minister, who was chairing the summit, that she planned to raise the question. 'Oh yes,' he said deferentially. 'I'm sure we'll get to that.' But he clearly had no intention of doing so. As the meeting wore on, the fragrance of the evening meal cooking began to emerge from the kitchens. The French prime minister began to look at his watch, and finally said, 'Time has gone by. I think it's important to wrap this up. Dinner is beckoning, and if nobody has more to say I suggest we adjourn.'

And Margaret Thatcher said, 'I do have something to say.'

He didn't appreciate that, and the others were annoyed because they wanted their dinner. But the result was that everybody agreed that the matter should be added to the next day's agenda. And as the group left the room, one foreign aide was heard to remark to another, 'Britain is back.'

That's just a political illustration, but it's an example of conviction in a sea of consensus. It is the spirit of Caleb, returning as one of the twelve from surveying the land. As we saw yesterday, ten of the twelve made the hearts of the people sink. But in Joshua 14:7 Caleb records, 'I brought him back a report according to my convictions.' Right or wrong, he says, these are my convictions. Yes, there are giants; and yes, there are grapes that fall in clusters; yes, there are all these things. 'It's my conviction,' says Caleb, 'that by God's enabling we can certainly go up and take the land.' And Moses says, 'I like this, Caleb. And I'm glad to hear from you, Joshua. The other ten of you – you sit down over there and I'll talk to you in a minute or two.'

Hand on the faith

That is the spirit to which Paul is calling Timothy – timid Timothy, the most unlikely fellow for such a challenge. 'Come on, Timothy, be strong!'

You might as well tell a snail to fly as tell someone like this to be strong. How is he going to take the stand needed in a situation where the prevailing drift is in the opposite direction? See the wonderful balance of Scripture. 'You then, my son, be strong' – how? – 'in the grace that is in Christ Jesus.' The activity demanded is more than matched by the grace provided. It was God's grace that had redeemed Timothy. He had been saved by grace, he had been called into service, and he was going to be able to exercise his continued service – as a result of God's grace to him.

The issue here, of course, is not the reception of the gospel, but its transmission. It is imperative that the gospel be passed, like a baton in a relay race, safely into the hands of those who will hold it tightly, proclaim it boldly and suffer for it bravely.

What is it that is to be passed on? Verse 2: 'the things you have heard me say in the presence of many witnesses'. I don't think this refers to a single instance, but rather to all that Timothy had been on the receiving end of, as he walked and talked with Paul through these past years. He had understood what Paul had made so perfectly clear; that the gospel that Paul was conveying was not a gospel he – or anyone else, for that matter – had concocted.

Indeed, when writing to the Galatians about his concern over the defections from the gospel, he makes it perfectly plain that they must understand the nature of this gospel.

> I want you to know, brothers, that the gospel I preached is not something that man made up. I did not receive it from any man, nor was I taught it; rather, I received it by revelation from Jesus Christ. (Gal. 1:11-12)

So, says Paul to Timothy, it is imperative that what he convey is that which Paul received from Christ by revelation. 'You heard me say it and you understood it. It's a beautiful deposit, it's a good model, it's a real pattern. It's not to be tampered with, diluted, disfigured or fiddled with in any way. Do what I'm asking you to do. We've got good news to pass on, and you're my man. You've heard me say it in the presence of many witnesses, I received it from Christ, it's not some secretive thing. It's not special information for initiates, nor one of the gnostic heresies currently abroad.' We've declared this out in the open, says Paul. There are many people who are witnesses to what has been said.

This is a reminder to us that the continual work of the gospel, unlike the activities of the cults, is to declare the gospel. There's nothing secretive about it. We are prepared to do it openly, and, I trust, boldly. We'll let the whole world believe! We'll preach it in the high street, we'll seize the opportunity in the media, we'll preach it from the rooftops. As Billy Bray said, 'If you put me in a barrel I'll shout glory to God through the bung-hole.'

This is quite unlike Scientology, for example. They have high street premises. You are invited inside to find out about your life, but it's not open, in the presence of many witnesses. Not so the gospel. 'Let the whole world know,' says Paul. I declared it to you 'in the presence of many witnesses'.

Be able and qualified to teach

From Christ to Paul, from Paul to Timothy, and from Timothy (and I think this is the real apostolic succession) to 'reliable men'. What are these men to do? They are to 'be qualified to teach others'. They are to be teachers of the word, ensuring, like the elders of Israel, that the truth of God is preserved in its entirety and conveyed in all of its authority.

I want us to pay careful attention to Paul's exhortation in 1 Timothy 1:3-7, where he describes people who have an unhealthy interest in controversy. I certainly don't want to be among them, but I do want to say, in the light of Paul's earlier statement in 1 Timothy 2:12 and in 2 Timothy 2:2, that I believe both passages are in accordance with the biblical pattern. The role to which 2 Timothy 2:2 refers is a role given uniquely to men – and not just any men: faithful men. And without any kind of prejudice – and with gratitude to God for all of our sisters in Christ and for all the ministry that God has entrusted to them – I want to say, on the authority of God's word, that it is surely long past the time for reliable, able and qualified men to stand up and be counted in the place of responsibility and opportunity.

All of that enabling, reliability and qualifying comes from God Himself. The reason there is such an indifference towards preaching today is largely because there is so much bad preaching. The fact that some poor souls have stumbled into a pulpit is a sadness to all concerned. 'Oh, he's a lovely man,' they say, 'and he's a nice pastor.' Well that's good. Why not let him just pastor, and get somebody else who is able, who is qualified, to teach? But he doesn't care to do that. So his congregation sits there looking for tapes and books to try to feed their souls. Why does that happen? Because we don't pay attention to what the Bible says. You don't send just anybody into battle. You don't send just anyone to fly an aeroplane. You don't give just anybody the responsibility of performing cardiac surgery. So why would you throw just anybody into the task of ensuring that the gospel is faithfully transmitted from one generation to another?

That's the challenge. It was the challenge then, and I believe it is the challenge today. Donald Guthrie says in his commentary, 'The torch of heavenly light must be transmitted unquenched from one generation to another.' And in these grievous and perilous times, as we'll see in chapter 3, that will call for men of the calibre of John Knox. Even ladies threw stools at him. But it was said of John Knox that he feared the face of God so much that he never feared the face of man.

The friends of Athanasius came to him and said, 'Athanasius, the whole world is against you.' 'Then,' he replied, 'I am against the whole world.' As Frank Houghton wrote in his hymn, 'Facing a task unfinished':

> We bear the torch that flaming
> Fell from the hands of those
> Who gave their lives proclaiming
> That Jesus died and rose.
> Ours is the same commission,
> The same glad message ours,
> Fired by the same ambition,
> To Thee we yield our powers.

Virtually every photograph of the Clubhouse at St Andrews' Royal and Ancient golf course includes the monument that stands nearby. Once in a while, my American friends ask me what 'that old stone' is. I tell them about the Covenanters to whom it is a memorial, and the heritage of people who gave their lives believing that Jesus died and rose.

Thirty years ago nobody could have imagined the extent of the present defection, within the framework of conservative evangelicalism, from truths that were then regarded as central and are now considered peripheral. Of course, if we are right now then we were wrong then, but we were not right both times.

The task illustrated (2:3-8)

This man-sized task is underscored by the pictures that Paul employs.

The good soldier

'Endure hardship with us like a good soldier of Christ Jesus.' That means total commitment, total concentration. I've never been a soldier, though I would like to have been one. The closest I came to it was on Stirling Castle esplanade when I was a youngster. There were still soldiers stationed there. I used to go there sometimes and march on the cobbles while the soldiers marched on the esplanade. I imagined myself to be a soldier; but I wasn't one, and I'm not sure I would have been a very good one.

Recently I attended the induction of 1,200 young people at a US military academy. The commanding officer made perfectly clear to them the hardship they would face and the focus they would require. They all had their heads shaved and they all looked immaculate and they all looked scared to death. I stood on the sideline and thought, 'My, I'm glad I'm up here and not out there.' I was told by some of the officers that out of that 1,200, by the end of the summer 300 will have gone home. Why? Because they can't take the commitment, and they are not prepared to make the concentrated focus.

My father tells a story against himself. He received his call-up papers to serve in the Second World War. He reported to Mary Hill Barracks in Glasgow, and they put him through the standard admission procedure – haircut, uniform and so on. Around 4.30 in the afternoon he was making his way out of the barracks gate. A sergeant shouted to him, 'Hello, where do you think you're going?'

'I'm going home for my tea,' replied my father.

I'm not sure how gentle the sergeant was, but he made it perfectly plain that having donned the uniform, signed the forms and made the commitment, my father would go home for tea when the Army said he could. It was going to be tough; he was in the Army now. And the sergeant looked him in the eye and said, in effect, 'You're mine, you're all mine.'

That's what Jesus does. He looks us in the eyes and says, 'You're all mine. Don't get entangled with civilian pursuits.'

The disciplined athlete

In Paul's day there were strict rules not only for competing, but also for training. If you didn't compete according to the rules you were flunked, if you did not train according to the rules you couldn't even compete. Consequently an athlete would never stand triumphant on the dais unless he had competed and trained according to the rules.

The short-lived victory of Ben Johnson in the 1988 Olympics is a classic illustration of that. For a time it appeared that he had outstripped all the field and had run to victory. But eventually they stripped him of his gold medal. Why? Because he had not competed according to the rules. The rules of entry and competing are external. They complement the internal discipline that marks out an athlete. Athletes go to bed early, choose their food with great care, maintain an exercise regimen. They are driven by something inside them that is consumed with the prospect of finishing the race, breasting the tape and receiving the crown.

Paul says to Timothy, 'Let these things be in your focus. Submit to your commanding officer. Get crouched down and ready for the fire of the pistol and run the straight race through God's good grace. But remember, you must do so according to the rules.' That is not particularly acceptable in our day either. In our lawless generation we have still to reaffirm the fact that the Christian is under obligation to keep the rules, to obey God's moral law. It's not that by our law-abiding we are justified, we know that. But without our law-abiding, we give no evidence of having been justified.

The hard-working farmer

Some of you are farmers. And you have come to Keswick leaving behind you all kinds of responsibilities in the hands of others. Farmers work while others are still asleep. They can be seen on their combine harvesters still working long after the time when others have decided that they are going to go to sleep again. Farmers know there are no quick results, that patience is vital, that they will only enjoy that which is as a result of their disciplined commitment to their responsibility.

Lazy people will never experience this. The writer of Ecclesiastes says, 'Whoever watches the wind will not plant; whoever looks at the clouds will not reap' (Eccles. 11:4). Solomon says, 'A sluggard does not plough in season; so at harvest time he looks but finds nothing' (Prov. 20:4). Where did we get the notion that somehow or other we are going to be spiritually useful, useful to the Master, without an emphasis on a serious commitment of disciplined living in the framework of Christian life?

We are breeding a Generation X. I prefer to call it Generation Shrug. Ask people, 'How are you?' and they just shrug. 'Did you enjoy that?' Shrug. 'Are you excited about your holidays?' Shrug. Maybe it's a particularly American thing, and you may say I am being very hard; but if so you obviously don't have teenagers. I have a nineteen-year-old, a seventeen-year-old and a fifteen-year-old.

We are breeding a generation of experts in unfinished business. They don't finish their vegetables, they don't finish cleaning their room, they don't finish their homework and the chances are they won't finish their marriages. But nobody harvests souls or holiness without an all-pervasive diligence.

I was recently at a well-known Christian college in the United States. I said, 'How many of you know J. C. Ryle's book, *Holiness*? I was just met by 2,500 blank stares. Then I said, 'How many of you know who J. C. Ryle was?' Equally blank. There is a great need here. Listen to Ryle:

> I will never shrink from declaring my belief that there are no spiritual gains without pains. I should as soon expect a farmer to prosper in business who contented himself with sowing his fields and never looking at them until harvest, as to expect a believer to obtain much holiness who was not diligent about their Bible reading, their prayers and their use of a Sunday. (J. C. Ryle, *Holiness*)

We won't go down that road. Our God is a God who works by means, and He will never bless the soul of that individual who pretends to be so high and spiritual that he can get on without them.

Time to reflect

Small wonder then that in verse 7 Paul suggests that Timothy should reflect and give due consideration to his illustrations. He says, 'The Lord will give you insight into all this.' That's the key to the reading and understanding of the Bible: our commitment to consideration and our dependence on the Lord for illumination; it is both, not either–or. If you read your Bibles like a kind of treasure trove, a promise book to dip into and pull anything out, if you seek a blessed thought, a funny feeling in your tummy as direction for your life – it's very dangerous. You mustn't do it. It's as if somehow you have been illuminated without the use of your brain. On the other hand, if you sit around trying to manufacture your understanding of everything and have forgotten the need for the illuminating power of the Holy Spirit, all of your study will yield you very little. It is our consideration, it is God's illumination; and He illumines it, as we bring our minds to a consideration to what He has said in His book.

Suffering and the gospel (2:9-10)

Each of Paul's illustrations involves a measure of suffering. This is the link with what follows, because in verse 8 he returns to this theme. He begins the verse, 'Remember Jesus Christ...' Jesus is the suffering servant. He is 'descended from David', which is a reminder of His humanity. He has been 'raised from the dead', which reminds us of His divinity.

The reminder of the Lord Jesus comes not only in Paul's words to Timothy but throughout the New Testament. When we are tempted to avoid pain, humiliation and suffering and we flinch in the face of death, then, as the writer to the Hebrews says we must, we 'consider him who endured such opposition from sinful men, so that you will not grow weary and lose heart' (Heb. 12:3).

Note again the link between the gospel and suffering. 'This is my gospel, for which I am suffering even to the point of being chained like a criminal.' He says 'like', not 'as'. He's not being chained as a criminal. He hasn't been selling non-existent time-share apartments, he hasn't been bilking women of their money, he hasn't developed a telephone scam to fleece people of their resources. He's been chained like a criminal but he hasn't been chained as a criminal. But there is no dungeon, he says, that is deep enough, there are no bars strong enough to contain the word of God. Don't you love that sentence at the end of verse 9? 'But God's word is not chained.' We should wear those words as a tattoo, I think! Charles Spurgeon was asked how he would defend the Bible. 'I would as soon defend a lion,' he replied. What do you do with a lion? You let it out of its cage. Paul writes to the Philippian church in a similar vein: 'What has happened to me has really served to advance the gospel' (Phil. 1:12). He's chained to a soldier, and every eight hours the soldier is replaced by another. And I'm sure Paul seized the opportunity to explain why it was that he was in chains.

'The grass withers and the flowers fall, but the word of our God stands for ever' (Isa. 40:8). This, I believe, is something that we need to have the Holy Spirit affirm in our thinking again and again. We are at the end of perhaps a quarter of a century in which the word of God and all its authority has been significantly undermined, not least in the hearts of God's people. And if Paul in writing to Timothy affirms anything, he affirms the absolute sufficiency and authority of the word of God, upon which this whole Convention finds its foundations.

Andrew Melville was an early herald of the Scottish Reformation. He was once denounced by a man named Regent Morton, who suggested publicly that if a few of Melville's type were hanged, it would silence their proclamation of the gospel once and for all. Melville looked Morton in the eye and said, 'It is the same to me whether I rot in the air or in the ground. The earth is the Lord's, my fatherland is wherever well-doing is. I've been ready to give my life when it was not half as well worn at the pleasure of my God, yet God be glorified, it will not lie in your power to hang or exile this truth.'

According to verse 10, Paul recognised that his sufferings had an evangelistic purpose. 'I endure everything for the sake of the elect, that they too may obtain the salvation that is in Christ Jesus.' In other words, his life, his preaching, his writing and his suffering were the means whereby God was redeeming for Himself a people that are His very own. And what an encouragement it must have been to Timothy as a young man, to have this seasoned campaigner – separated from him, under the shadow of execution – not whining and groaning, not writing about the glory days back at Lystra. He wasn't saying, 'Oh Timothy, you should have been around in the early days when it was really going well, when everybody in Asia was hearing and everybody in Asia was believing! And now everybody in Asia is deserting, and I'm a miserable soul down here in this dungeon ...'

No. He says, 'Come on! I'm chained – but the word isn't chained. People are defecting but there are always souls like Onesiphorus. Timothy, get up in the morning and pledge yourself to be a soldier and an athlete and a farmer, and [as we will see] a student of the word.'

Living for Christ (2:11-13)

Paul ends by quoting what are actually fragments of a hymn, and prefaces them with the assurance that this is a trustworthy saying. Verse 11: 'If we died with him, we will also live with him.' (Jesus said, 'Whoever loses his life for my sake will find it', Matt. 10:39). Verses 12-13: 'If we endure, we will also reign with him. If we disown him, he will also disown us; if we are faithless, he will remain faithful.' There is some debate as to whether John Stott is right in suggesting that in the final phrase in verse 13 we have a word of warning, in that 'faithful' means that God will faithfully carry out his threats to punish the wicked. George Knight on the other hand takes the opposite position, suggesting that what we have here is a word of encouragement. It is like the predicament of the prodigal son, who, having made a hash of things, returns home and is welcomed by the faithfulness of his father – in spite of the faithlessness of his journey.

So what can we say with confidence? With confidence we can affirm that 'God cannot disown himself' (verse 13). He does not, can not, act contrary to His will. His omnipotence is such that He can do anything He chooses to do, but He chooses only to do what is good and only to act according to the perfection of His character and His will. 'Will not the Judge of all the earth do right?' (Gen. 18:25).

We began with the faithlessness of Phygelus and Hermogenes; we conclude with a reminder of the faithfulness of God. In between, we've pondered the suffering of Paul, a call to disciplined endurance, a call to suffer for the gospel. Whoever conceived of this Christianity that was all smiles and strolls? People with empty heads and closed Bibles, I fear. Because if you read your Bible, you realise that to live for Christ is both demanding and rewarding. It must have been in consideration of these things, I think, that Jim Elliott wrote in his diary that he wanted to graduate from Wheaton College with an 'A. U. G.' ('Approved Unto God' – 2 Tim. 2:15, AV). And it was perhaps in consideration of the call to be the kind of soldier, athlete and farmer Paul describes, that he wrote in his diary one evening before going to bed, 'He is no fool who gives what he cannot keep, to gain what he cannot lose.'

'If we died with him, we will also live with him.'

Or think of C. T. Studd, turning his back on all that represented security, heading out in the firm conviction that if Jesus Christ is God and died for him, then no sacrifice he could ever make for Him could ever be too great. This was Studd's fundamental conviction: that if Jesus Christ is worth serving, He is worth serving well.

2 Timothy 2:14-26

Paul's great emphasis lies in the opening verse of our passage: 'Keep reminding them of these things' (2:14). One of the great dangers in pastoral ministry, perhaps especially for young people in ministry, is the notion that to be useful in nurturing God's people and seeing unbelievers become committed followers of Jesus Christ, it is imperative to be constantly at the cutting edge, thinking up new ways of doing things. Even worse is the danger of tampering with the very gospel itself, as if somehow or another by innovation we might be able to make it more useful.

'Remind them' (2:14 – 19)

It's quite striking how often the Bible reminds pastors in particular of the crucial responsibility that they have, to remind their people that the key to usefulness in Christian living lies largely in being enabled to do the basics well most of the time. The Christian life is not an easy life, but it's a straightforward life. The role of pastoral ministry is so much one of reminding God's people, 'Now come on! Make sure that you are continuing to believe this, to hope this, to do this and to live this.'

That is true not only of Paul but also of Peter when he writes his second letter.

I will always remind you [there's that word again!] of these things, even though you know them and are firmly established in the truth you now have. I think it is right to refresh your memory as long as I live in the tent of this body, because I know that I will soon put it aside, as our Lord Jesus Christ has made clear to me. [You see, the prospect of death is clarifying his vision and determining his priorities.] And I will make every effort to see that after my departure you will always be able to remember these things. (2 Pet. 1:12-15

Timothy, in the midst of widespread confusion both moral and doctrinal, is, says Paul, to labour to ensure that those under his care in Ephesus will understand that the main things are the plain things and the plain things are the main things. This of course is a matter of great concern for us, at a time when there is so much that swirls around us and can draw people in all kinds of directions.

A warning against arguments

Part of the ministry of reminder is to exercise a word of warning. And the warning is clear; it is reiterated in the verses before us. 'Warn them before God against quarrelling about words. Why? Because those quarrels are ultimately absolutely worthless to the people who engage in them; and they ruin those who listen. The picture here is that Mr Levi and Mr Simeon of the community in Ephesus are talking with each other and they get into a major discussion over some extraneous peripheral matter. As they do so, it becomes apparent that it's a futile exercise. At the same time there are others – perhaps young believers, maybe unbelievers – who are listening to the discussion. And frankly it may become the ruination of them. Warn them, says Paul, about quarrelling over words and issues that are not of the essence of things.

Probably all of us can remember similar situations when we have been guilty of engaging in this kind of dialogue or can vividly remember overhearing such dialogues. I can remember a Sunday school outing years ago, a trip down the Clyde from Glasgow. As we gathered at the starting point I became aware of a theological controversy going on near me. There were furtive glances and huddled conversations; the men were becoming increasingly distressed, and some of the women were getting involved. And then I saw the problem, coming towards me. It was a lady wearing trousers. In those days it was a very big issue. The problem actually seemed to be not that she was wearing trousers, but the fact that (according to the men who were arguing) she was wearing *men's* trousers. I wanted to know how they knew they were men's trousers, but even more I was struck by one glaring inconsistency that seemed to have been overlooked. At least one of those men with angry faces was wearing a kilt ...

But a great quarrel ensued, and it marred the outing for some.

One of the sorry features of post-war evangelicalism, both in Britain and in America where I have lived for fifteen years, is that more than any other branch of Christendom it has become adept at making the peripheral central and making the central peripheral. We engage in discussions and dialogue about issues that must be set aside if we would take seriously the instruction of Paul here, to Timothy as a young man: 'Be clear, Timothy, about what you're aiming towards – and also about what it is you are avoiding.'

A warning not to be ashamed

Verse 15 reads, in the Authorised Version rendering that was inscribed in a Bible given to me when I left Glasgow for Yorkshire at fifteen, 'Study to shew thyself approved unto God, a workman that needeth not to be ashamed, rightly dividing the word of truth.' When I took that Bible as a fifteen-year-old, I would never in my wildest dreams have imagined that some thirty-one years later this responsibility would fall to me. Here at Keswick I take seriously both the privilege and the responsibility. I must endeavour to do what verse 15 says and, in doing so, encourage you to do that in your lives and in your ministries.

What is this work that the workman is doing in verse 15? He is correctly handling the word of truth. It's imperative that the Lord's servant goes about the task with a genuine desire to work in relationship to the word, so that he will never be ashamed when the work is opened up to scrutiny.

I had an art teacher called Mr Lumsden who taught us pottery. My interest in pottery was right up there with my interest in the periodic table of the elements! He introduced us first of all to thumb pots. We had to take pieces of clay and mould them into beautiful little pots. I confess that I wasn't particularly excited about it all, and decided to make mine a little more avant-garde than the rest. It seemed a bright idea – until he brought them out of the kiln. I remember him saying, 'And whose is *this* one?' What had seemed a great idea when I was clowning around two Thursdays previously made me smart with shame when I saw the sorry thing coming out of the oven.

With that picture in mind consider the nerve-jangling statement of the apostle Paul, when he says of his understanding of ministry and its responsibilities: 'If any man builds on this foundation using gold, silver, costly stones, wood, hay or straw, his work will be shown for what it is, because the Day will bring it to light. It will be revealed with fire, and the fire will test the quality of each man's work' (1 Cor. 3:12-13). Not the quantity of his work, nor how well known was his work, nor how apparently influential was his work – but the quality of his work. I think that is one of the most stirring, striking statements in the New Testament. Frankly, if you knew my heart you'd never listen to me preach, and if I knew yours I'm not sure I would want to talk to you. But the God who searches our hearts and knows us completely knows that what people may regard as gold and silver and precious jewels, is actually in fact wood, hay and stubble. And the day will bring it to light.

A warning to seek God's approval

Therefore the exhortation 'Make sure that you are a good workman, Timothy' is no arm's-length theology, it is no superficial exhortation. It is at the very heart of the matter. And Timothy's life, his destiny and influence upon the church in Ephesus, rests upon the fact that, under God, he takes these issues seriously. Are you and I aiming for God's approval, in the light of the fact that we move towards a day when it will be obvious, in the light, just exactly what it was we were doing?

The word for 'handle' in verse 15 is, in Greek, *orthotomeo*. It has been translated in various ways. It means 'to cut a straight line'. Imagine there's some shrubbery in your garden separating one little patch of grass from another. You go out on a Saturday morning to deal with it so that you can get your lawn mower from A to B unimpeded. Unless you are planning on creating a maze, you will take the shortest point between the two little patches of grass and there you will cut a straight line. And that, says Paul to Timothy, is how it is when you open up the Scriptures. You need to cut that kind of straight line. It's a call to clarity, to accuracy, to simplicity: the good workman in handling the Bible does not seek to bamboozle the people or to impress them with his knowledge of the word. For we cannot make people impressed with ourselves, and at the same time make much of Jesus and His word. We must make a choice. 'Timothy, handle it like a good workman, with clarity, yes; with authority, with accuracy, with humility, with simplicity.'

Professor William Barclay of Glasgow University made a superb contribution in the realm of historical background and textual matters, though many of his theological assertions need to be treated with care. He left university with great success and began in his first parish ministry in the Church of Scotland down the Clyde. Having a Ph.D. and being a learned man, he began to teach his congregation. He records in his biography how he was walking down the High Street one day, soon after he had arrived, and met an elderly lady from his congregation. She said to him, 'Mr Barclay, I think you are a very nice man; but you need to know I can't understand a word you're saying.' It was because of that encounter, he said, that he wrote *The Plain Man's Guide to Prayer* and *The Plain Man's Guide to the Gospel*. He decided that if he was that clever, he'd be able to make it that simple. Anyone can make something sound difficult. You really have to be smart to take difficult material and make it simple enough to be understood.

That is part of the charge. And you will notice that in verses 17and 18 it is contrasted with bad workmen. 'Do your best to present yourself to God as one approved, a workman...'

'What's your dad?' they asked the pastor's son.

'He's a workman.'

'And what does he do?'

'He works in the word.'

You're a workman. The question is, are you a good workman, as Timothy is exhorted to be? Or are you a bad workman, like Hymenaeus and Philetus? They are all workmen, the distinguishing factor is the way in which they are handling the word of truth. That is the test.

In contrast to the idea of cutting a straight line, the individuals in verse 18 have 'wandered away from the truth'; they have missed the target. The verb used here for wandering from the target comes from a Greek noun which essentially denotes a bull's-eye. Whether Hymenaeus and Philetus started out aiming for the bull's-eye or not we cannot say; but we do know that they ended up missing the target altogether. It may have been by small degrees, an initial enthusiasm becoming a total lack of interest in firing at the target at all. But however it happened, they had diverted from their objective.

The implicit warning is this. 'Timothy, make sure that *you* stay on target. Don't be like these individuals who have missed it.'

For example, in his first letter to Timothy he talks again about those who have 'an unhealthy interest in controversies and quarrels about words' – those words again! And what is the result? 'Envy, strife, malicious talk, evil suspicions and constant friction between men of corrupt mind, who have been robbed of the truth and who think that godliness is a means to financial gain' (1 Tim. 6:4-5). At the end of the same chapter he talks of those who once professed the faith and have 'wandered from the faith'.

Again, how sad to find your name in the record of Holy Scripture as someone who missed the mark and was a hindrance to the church! I say again, we are all leaving a legacy behind us. People are keeping notes. They are remembering your contributions at the deacons' meeting, they are going to remember you when your seat is empty at the PCC. They are going to remember if all you ever had to say is, 'I want my disagreement with this recorded in the Minutes ... I am abstaining in this vote ...' When people go through the Minute Books, they'll find the legacy we left; largely disagreeable, largely cantankerous, and marked more by a concern about words and trivialities than with an over-arching concern for the well-being of God's people and for the advance of the gospel.

A warning not to undermine faith

Hymenaeus and Philetus had been guilty of robbing some people of their early beginnings in faith. The reason was that they had claimed that the resurrection had already taken place. People's faith had been unsettled. And still, at the end of the twentieth century and at the beginning of the twenty-first, the cornerstone of

Christian conviction is this same matter of the resurrection. It doesn't matter where we choose to begin with our post-modern people. You can start as Paul did in Athens, on the fringes, and say, 'I can see you are very religious, because I notice that you are interested in angels and in reincarnation. And I've been reading some of your contemporary writers, so I know that you have an interest in deity and spirituality, or in God.' If we choose to start there and quote the poets and the pop songs, eventually we can move to the point that Paul reached: 'He has set a day when he will judge the world with justice by the man he has appointed. He has given proof of this to all men by raising him from the dead' (Acts 17:31).

The historicity of our faith is crucial. Certainly, it is good to be able to affirm our personal experience of Christ: 'Well, Jesus has changed my life, I was once darkness but now I am light in the Lord.' But be very careful about using that as your ace-in-the-hole. 'You asked me how I know He lives? He lives within my heart. So there! *Nah nana nah nah...*' Because the person on the other side of the coffee table may well say, 'Funnily enough, Buddha lives within my heart. So there! *Nah nana nah nah.*' Where do you go then? You are left in a sea of subjectivism, unless you are able to articulate and affirm the verities, the historical truths of our Christian faith.

That is why those who undermine the matter of the resurrection pull apart the very cornerstone of that which underpins Paul's life and ministry. If Christ is not risen, he says, then those who have died are dead in their sins. Their faith is futile. There is nothing to look forward to at all. 'But,' he says, 'Christ has indeed been raised from the dead' (1 Cor. 15:20). To be prepared to give an answer to those who ask you for a reason for the faith that you have, you need to do some studying. Study to be prepared, so that you are not reduced to merely proclaiming your subjective experience.

You see, the undermining of conviction about the resurrection was not coming from people outside the church, it was coming from people who were naming the name of Christ and pulling apart the fabric within it. That's why Paul's warning is so crucial. It's an ugly warning. 'Their teaching will spread like gangrene' (verse 17). Do you like that picture? God forbid that any of us would ever experience it. I have visited people in hospital who were being eaten away by gangrene. It is a distasteful picture that Paul is using, like blood poisoning, or the sepsis that oozes from a wound and makes us wear masks and plastic gloves when treating the patient. Not because we want to be disdainful of the one who has the condition, but because we want to prevent the condition from spreading.

That's what Paul is saying. 'Don't muck around with this stuff. Don't play with it. You're not going to put the effulgence from seeping wounds on your toast, are you? No, you're going to stay as far away from it as possible.' You must consider the implications of this for you as an individual, in your life and in your ministry. You are sensible people; examine the Scriptures and work out your own salvation with fear and trembling.

It is Timothy's responsibility, as a young man in pastoral ministry, to ensure that people aren't quarrelling; that he's correctly handling the word of truth – that he's not allowing himself or his people to become preoccupied with this concern. It is possible for us to have our heads turned, and for a good pastor to find that all he ends up doing is constantly pointing out this and that and the next thing; and he never nurtures his people in the truth of the word of God. All he gives them is a long litany of who's doing everything wrong. That doesn't build the church, it doesn't stir within people a longing after Christ. So yes, we do warn and we do watch out; but we do also lead and we do also feed. That is the balance of pastoral ministry.

Verse 19: Timothy needs to remind himself that the solid foundation of God stands firm.

> When all around is sinking sand,
> On Christ the solid rock I stand.

The allusion here seems to be that of engraving inscriptions on buildings, to indicate either their date or their purpose. Paul imagines the construction of the framework of the church, and an inscription being written on the church fabric: 'Number one: the Lord knows those who are His.'

In other words, let's be clear – especially when we are dealing with error and confusion around us – that it is only the Lord who knows the genuine from the spurious, for it is ultimately only the Lord who sees the heart. However, there is a visible factor.

Everyone who confesses the name of the Lord must turn away from wickedness. And by the observation first of our own lives, and then in part of the lives of others, we can see that it is by our departing from wickedness that we bear testimony to the condition of our hearts. Isn't that the story of Bunyan's Pilgrim?

> 'Where are you going, Christian?'
> 'I'm going to the Celestial City.'
> 'Do you see yonder wicket gate? Do you see yonder shining
>   light? Why are you going there, Christian, and where are
>   you coming from?'
> 'I'm coming from the City of Destruction.'
> 'Why have you left it behind?'
> 'Because it has been made aware to me that there is no
>   hope here.'

The fact that Christian is making his journey declares, by his departure from wickedness, that he is one of the Lord's very own.

A domestic illustration (2:20-21)

Having already used illustrations from the worlds of the military, athletics and farming, Paul now uses a domestic illustration. He pictures a large house, but now he is concerned not with inscriptions on the outside but with what's going in the inside. The picture of the bad versus the good runs through this illustration too: he has already said, you can be a good workman, don't be a bad workman. Now he says, there are different kinds of china. Be the noble china, don't be the ignoble china. And in verse 21 he introduces the idea of service: be a good servant, don't be a bad servant. So the picture runs all the way through.

This reminds me of occasions like the ladies' 'daffodil teas' in Dalkeith, which I have already mentioned. I was a young minister invited to the daffodil tea, and I was embarrassed at being sat at a table with a large rotund lady, away from the other tables, in a position of honour. It was bad enough to be so marked out; it was bad enough to be sitting with her at that table; it was bad enough to be isolated from everybody else. But it was worst of all to be drinking out of the 'noble china' while everyone else had to make do with the ignoble china. I've always held that all should have noble stuff, or all should have ignoble; but don't sit me down in splendour drinking out of the noble china, while all my friends have the cheap mugs!

The condition of usefulness

Let me bring you back to Scripture now. What is Paul saying here? Well, the key is that he is identifying the condition of usefulness. And you will notice in the opening phrase of verse 21 that the condition is not giftedness, background, prominence or influence. What is it? It is purity.

'Timothy, you're going to be a good workman? You're going to warn, watch, lead and feed the people of God? Timothy, you are going to finish the course, you are going to take the baton from my hand and run the next 440 metres with all your might? Then, Timothy, let me remind you [as John Stott puts it so helpfully] the master of a house lays down only one condition. The vessels which he uses must be clean.' So the distinction between noble and ignoble is not aesthetic or a matter of sophistication. It has to do with the purity of what we drink from or eat off – or, in this case, the life which, and through which, we minister.

Now it is in the light of that that we have to go back and ask: What then are we to do with the contaminating influence of people like Hymenaeus and Philetus? Does this not at least suggest the possibility that we need to disassociate ourselves from their ilk? Is it not somehow akin to the final words in verse 5 of the next chapter, where Paul has described people who are religious hucksters, who are shams, who have a form of godliness and deny its power, who say the right thing, who quote the right creeds, who affirm the right articles and live in total denial of what they proclaim? What does he say there? 'Have nothing to do with them.'

Now you don't need to be a rocket scientist to understand that sentence. Every child knows what his mother means when she says, 'I don't want you going with those kids down behind the shed behind the playing field.'

'Oh but mum, I'm not really ...'

'Have nothing to do with them!'

Let me leave it there, because we must all must work out our own salvation with fear and trembling.

Separation

Does this mean physical or ecclesiastical separation from these individuals? John Stott is again very helpful in pointing out that what we are to avoid is not so much contact with these men as involvement in their error and their evil. In the context of our ministry, we must not allow their falsehoods a place in our thinking, nor their wickedness a place in our hearts and our lives.

In all this the imperatives are striking. The sense of responsibility, certainly energised by God's Holy Spirit, is undeniable. Look again at the opening phrase of verse 21: 'If a man cleanses himself ...' In other words, what we do is we take ourselves in hand, we think the issues out, we ask the Spirit of God to bring the word of God to bear upon our minds in such a way that we might be men and women of the book. We are not to be pushed to and fro by all the influences, unable to disengage ourselves from them so that we are not responsible for where we end up – so that our people say to us, 'You know, if you lived in the real world, vicar, pastor, then you would know that it's not as easy as you think.' Believe me, I don't think it's easy.

But I love a story told in Derek Brown's commentary on James, about a Portsmouth navy chaplain. He gets into conversation with the sailors in the cafeteria, and challenges them about their walk with God and the need to avoid what is evil and cling to what is good. They say to him what we have just been thinking about: 'All the influences are so strong upon us, Padre.' So he takes them outside and standing on the seafront they watch the sailboats plying back and forth. And the chaplain says,

> One boat goes east and one boat goes west
> by the self-same winds that blow.
> It's the set of the sails and not the gales
> that determine which way they go.

That is why it is so imperative for a young man in pastoral ministry to be nurtured and surrounded by people like Paul who will say to him, 'The wind is blowing all over the place. It's imperative that you set your sails, that you set your course by the pole star of Scripture and all of its sufficiency. Set your course with deep conviction in the absolute sufficiency of the atoning sacrifice of

Christ. Lay hold on all these things, young man, and write them into the very tablets of your heart. And then you will be "useful to the Master and prepared to do any good work".'

Wouldn't it be wonderful to be useful to the master? In our first Bible Reading we talked about epitaphs or things on your tombstone. It would be nice just to have 'She was useful to the Master', or 'He was ready for anything. He was so thrilled to be on the team. He was Your man, ready to play any position, ready for any good work.' Charles Wesley wrote in his hymn, 'Jesus! The name high over all',

> Happy, if with my latest breath
> I might but gasp His name;
> Preach Him to all, and cry in death:
> 'Behold, behold the Lamb!'

Timothy – come on now, son! – this is the kind of fellow that you need to be.

'Flee evil desires' (2:22-26)

Now for the key, and with this we come to our conclusion. Notice that the domestic illustration we have been considering in verses 20 and 21 nestles between the recognition in verse 19 that 'everyone who confesses the name of the Lord must turn away from wickedness', and the same point picked up in verse 22: 'Flee the evil desires of youth...'

So the matter of personal holiness and purity is not a sideline. The central conviction of the message of Keswick, the desire to inculcate in God's people a concern for, and commitment to, a life of practical holiness, is the very call that Paul is issuing here to Timothy as a young man. 'The key to your usefulness,' he tells him, 'lies in what you are running from, what you are running to, and who you are running with.' I tell my teenage children that all the time. I can sketch the rest of your life, just seeing you run.

He says, 'Flee the evil desires of youth.' Do you remember when you were young? The Beatles, in their song 'Help', sang of how when young they needed nobody's help; but now they were older they found they had changed their mind. 'Help me if you can, I'm feeling down ... Please, please help me.' It remains one of the most grievous cries of my heart to this day that that cry from Lennon's young heart in 1965 was never answered by anybody who had anything good to say about the Lord Jesus, or about what it would mean to find the life that is truly life. Still in our generation we drive searching, hopeless, drug-imbued young men and women into the arms of New Age mysticism, because our churches so often sit arguing about words which these people don't really appreciate or understand or want to have anything to do with.

Flee pride

One of the proclivities of youth is pride. Every pastor wishes he could start again, and most congregations wish their pastors could start again. Young people want power, they desire to be number one, they think it is so important. They think, 'It's our voice that needs always to be heard, our voice that comes last in the conversation, our notions that should become central.' Run away from your desire for power and for pleasure, from making yourself and how things are going the yardstick and criterion of everything. Run away from the real danger, Timothy; from thinking that the amassing of possessions is what it's all about, especially when you see people around you who are making a lot of money from their way of doing ministry. 'They think that godliness is a means to financial gain' – and you as a young man, Timothy, you could get stuck into that and begin to believe that too. You could start to preach for cash, you could start this or that, in the hope that this would generate that. Don't do that, Paul said. Run away from it!

I love this passage. It's so realistic. It's not a case of, 'Well I would never ever consider this.' It's, 'Timothy, I know your mind. Man, flee the evil desires of youth.'

Cultivate scepticism

If you're going to be a successful Christian you need to have a healthy dose of scepticism (though not of cynicism), because we live in a fallen world. You don't need to be sceptical about your next-door neighbour, just about yourself. It's a good place to start. Why did I carry the lady's shopping bag across the street? Was it because I really wanted to help her – or was it because I wanted her to say, 'There's a fine fellow'? Scepticism says, 'It was probably because I wanted the accolade.'

Shun sin

The reason we need to be ruthless in these matters is because, as Genesis 4:7 says, 'sin is crouching at your door; it desires to have you, but you must master it.' Every sin is an inside job. That's what Ronald Dunn said at Keswick many years ago. He used the illustration of somebody robbing a post office who had an accomplice hiding inside. At the prescribed time the thief knocked on the door from the outside and the man inside let him in. Ronald Dunn said, 'Every sin is an inside job. That's how it happens.'

That's why we bombed the runway in Port Stanley during the Falklands War. Why would we do that? Port Stanley was ours. But Margaret Thatcher said, 'Bomb the runway.' Why? To prevent enemy aircraft from landing. That's the key. Bomb the runway of power, pleasure, passion, possessions and prominence. If you don't, all kinds of people will descend on them and permeate your life, your ministry and your church. They will wreak absolute havoc. 'When should I bomb the runway?' Immediately. 'Right now while I'm sitting here?' Absolutely. If God reminds you of something, drop a bomb on it. How do we deal with sin? Immediately, ruthlessly, consistently.

As a young man newly arrived in the church I went on pastoral visitation to the home of a very large member of our congregation, whom I had not met yet because he had been ill. He was an interesting gentleman, and I enjoyed every visit I made to him. On that first visit, he had a large stick next to his seat, which worried me. He stressed that he was going to support me in my ministry; but he added, 'I must warn you, if you come away with any funny stuff, if you miss the target, if you get off the track – I'll take this stick here and I'll rattle it against the pews and I'll shout "Heresy!"'

I said, 'Thank you for sharing that with me.'

Back at home Sue asked, 'How was your day?' I said, 'Very interesting. There's a big guy I need to warn you about. He has a stick.'

I'll never forget a sermon he preached to the church congregation. In the same direct way, he spoke to the young people about the inroads of temptation and sin. 'Some of you are out there having prayer meetings about whether you should or should not do this or that. I'm telling you – don't pray about it, chuck it.'

Some of us are playing around with sin. And I'm telling you, chuck it.

Last night we had with us a dear brother from Korea. What should we pray for the church in Korea? Pray for purity for the church in Korea. What should we pray for the church in the West? Purity. What should we pray for in our local church? Purity. What should we pray for in our pastor? Purity. What should we pray for in ourselves? Purity.

Run away from these things. Run towards this lovely quartet: righteousness, faith, love and peace. Run along with those who love the Lord and call on Him out of a pure heart. In other words, just make sure you're in a good fellowship, make sure you're establishing good friendships, make sure that you are endeavouring to walk the walk.

> Blessed is the man who does not walk in the counsel of the wicked or stand in the way of sinners or sit in the seat of mockers. But his delight is in the law of the LORD, and on his law he meditates day and night. He is like a tree planted by streams of water, which yields its fruit in season and whose leaf does not wither. Whatever he does prospers. Not so the wicked! They are like chaff that the wind blows away. Therefore the wicked will not stand in the judgement ...' (Psa. 1:1-5)

Remember that. For 'without holiness no-one will see the Lord' (Heb. 12:14)

2 Timothy 3

Paul is very realistic. In no way does he seek to hide from Timothy the hard facts that relate to the commission he has received. Any notion that serving the Lord Jesus Christ in the cause of the gospel is an invitation to tranquillity cannot be taught from 2 Timothy; indeed, it cannot be taught from the Bible. And he is clearly aware of the hostility of the times in which Timothy is ministering. At the same time, he is aware of the timidity of Timothy in the midst of those times, and his great concern is that Timothy and others like him will be marked by stability grounded in the truth of the gospel of the Lord Jesus Christ.

In the light of this it's obviously essential that the Lord's servant should not be caught off-guard by the difficulties of his day, and in particular by the terrible times that Paul says will mark the last days. The opening phrase of verse 1, up until the colon there in the NIV, is striking, and purposefully so. 'Get a hold of this! Pay attention to what I'm saying! Mark this, because what I'm about to tell you, Timothy, is not simply a possibility, it's an absolute certainty. There will be seasons or spells that are painful and perilous.'

The reason is that opposition to the truth is not a passive fancy but a permanent fixture. The truth has been and will always be

opposed, at some times more intensely than others and with
different facets to the opposition. Nevertheless it will be impossible
to live life in any generation without the truth being opposed. And
the terrible nature of these spells is borne out in the word Paul uses.
A knowledge of the original Greek is helpful to our understanding
here. The same word, *chalepos*, is used in Matthew 8:28 to describe
the two demoniacs, whose 'violence' was such that people were
afraid to walk past them down the street. That is the word
translated 'terrible' in the opening verse of this chapter. In classical
Greek, it was the word you would use to describe the raging of the
sea or the untamable fierceness of wild animals.

So in case anybody should be left with the lingering notion that
we will be 'carried to the skies on flowery beds of ease', the answer
is, absolutely not. Or – to move from the sentimental hymn writer
to the sentimental song writer – 'I beg your pardon; I never
promised you a rose garden.' And that is exactly the kind of clarity
that the Bible demands that we have.

The phrase 'the last days' has set many a home Bible study off
on a lengthy tangent, and it is one of the favourite phrases of
certain people I meet as I travel around. They have their whole
Bible underlined in a variety of colours all relating to the phrase
'the last days'. And indeed, many of them have to conclude that the
reference here that Paul is giving to Timothy is somehow
hypothetical, because after all, according to their reckoning,
Timothy wasn't living in the last days. So when Paul gave him this
instruction, it was for the future, for a time yet to come – and of
course a few people have decided when it is.

The fact is, this is not hypothetical. We know that, because Paul
immediately applies it in relation to what Timothy is supposed to
do. He's not talking about something that is in the remote future,
he's talking about something that is in the immediate present.

The last days (3:1-5)

Hebrews 1 begins, 'In the past God spoke to our forefathers
through the prophets ... but in these last days he has spoken to us
by his Son.' When Peter preached on the day of Pentecost and
responded to those who, surprised at what was happening, claimed
that perhaps the people displaying these miraculous manifestations
might have been out on the bottle, he said, 'These men are not

drunk, as you suggest, after all it's nine o'clock in the morning. In point of fact this is what was spoken of by the prophets. You are in the last days. God says, "I will pour out my Spirit."' (cf Acts 2:15-17). So it's important for us to understand that 'the last days', according to New Testament parlance, were ushered in by the coming of Christ and will be consummated by the return of Christ. Clearly there will be last days before the last days, culminating in the revelation of the man of lawlessness (2 Thess. 2:3), but that is not the issue here. It is not the single event of the Second Coming which is in discussion here, as speculated upon by John Napier, for example. Napier, the inventor of logarithms, used his logarithmic method to calculate a date for the return of Jesus Christ, concerning which he seems to have had very forceful views. His books sold fairly well up until the day he had predicted as that when Christ would return, but it hasn't been in the Keswick bookshop for some time.

The notion here is rather that of epochs that recur throughout history – perilous, terrible times or periods that will inevitably increase in intensity, in clarification between light and darkness and truth and error, before the appearing of the Lord Jesus Christ. What are these terrible times marked by? Well, that is exactly what he goes on to identify.

The characteristics of the terrible times

The conduct that he exposes in 3:2-5 is as classic a description of moral decadence as can be found anywhere in the Bible, with the possible exception of Romans 1:21-32. Were we this morning to consider the whole catalogue of nineteen vices item by item, allocating two minutes to each, there'd be no prospect of ever finishing these studies. So I want to look at the passage in more general terms.

Some of us tend to think that these things are evidence of an idolatry that you can only find when you go abroad. Go to Hong Kong and see the shrines with their bits of apple and orange and gaily coloured tissue paper and you go away thinking, 'My, these people *are* idolatrous.' What are not so obvious are the shrines to self and to pleasure that are all round us, whether in Washington, Sydney or London. Whenever an individual or a culture begins to worship at the shrine of itself, then that person or culture is in deep trouble. And it is this kind of activity – for it is all largely idolatry with various faces – that is before us now.

Now how are we to view these nineteen characteristics? Donald Guthrie, who taught me New Testament or at least endeavoured to at London Bible College, suggests that the first two supply the key to understanding the remaining seventeen. In other words, he says, when people love themselves and love money, all of this ugly list will inevitably follow.

Another way to view them is to take the first characteristic, 'people will be lovers of themselves', then the last, 'rather than lovers of God', and to see the remaining seventeen characteristics as the filling of what is a very distasteful sandwich.

John Stott (as you will find, when you go to read the commentaries so that you can follow up on these studies!) divides these vices into three groups. I don't think he gives them the heading I give them, but it's a helpful analysis. He says that if you look at the list you can see how people reveal themselves. First,

INDIVIDUALS

'People will be lovers of themselves, lovers of money, boastful, proud and abusive.' In other words, when I love myself I am preoccupied with who I am and/or with what I have financially. And it will almost inevitably be accompanied by self-assertion, and that self-assertion will manifest itself in boastful, proud and abusive behaviour. It's a very ugly and unseemly picture.

Oscar Wilde, on entering the United States, was asked by customs officials, 'Do you have anything to declare?' He replied, 'Only my genius.' Some of us fight battles in this area. We want to write a book called *Humility and How I Attained It*. Or we'd be prepared to suggest to people, 'No, I am not conceited, although I have every right to be so.' Or, in the words of the Country and Western song, 'Oh Lord, it's hard to be humble, when you're perfect in every way.'

I want to point out something crucial here. I don't know if it is the case in the United Kingdom, but it is certainly so in the United States, that what Paul describes here as a disease is offered there as a cure. Paul is saying, 'At the very heart of this ugly list you have a problem – *philautoi* – people love themselves too much.' And when they love themselves inordinately then all these things will follow. From pillar to post, from couch to pulpit, all across America, the answer to everything from juvenile to pre-senile dementia is offered in terms of 'you need simply to love yourself'. But any time a disease is identified in the Bible as a disease and then offered in modern culture as a cure, you know we've got dreadful troubles. It is one of the evidences of the manifold confusion that abounds.

Of course a right self-esteem is necessary. But the opposite of self-love is not self-hate; it is love for God. 'Do not think of yourself', says Paul, 'more highly than you ought, but think of yourself with sober judgement with a due understanding of the way in which God has put you together' (cf Rom. 12:3). J. B. Phillips paraphrases it, 'Have a thin estimate of your own capabilities.' There is a great difference between that and an approach to life which consists of getting up in the morning and immediately beginning to congratulate oneself on how wonderful one really is; and how everybody from the breakfast table onwards is surely waiting with bated breath to see and hear from one again. Those people are dangerous, to themselves and everyone they come in contact with.

FAMILIES

Next 'disobedient to their parents, ungrateful, unholy, without love, unforgiving, slanderous' and so on. It's not nice at all. What is he saying? In these times, youth loses all respect for age, it fails to recognise the debt and duty that it owes to those who gave it life. Youth fails to stand up on the bus for an elderly gentleman or a more mature lady. Youth no longer stands when a teacher enters the classroom. Youth no longer removes its hat inside buildings because it's just too dense to understand the implications of propriety. And the implacable nature of this rebellious streak in a culture is identified in the words that Paul uses. These individuals, he says, when these times are bad, are utterly lacking in gratitude, they lack in purity and they lack in normal human affection.

You don't have to search very far for evidence of this. Time has passed, but surely the memory has not dimmed, of those boys taking the small boy away from his push-chair outside the Bootle shopping centre, and the little boy being found later mangled under the wheels of an express train. What in the world possesses youngsters to do such a thing? And what do they do when they've finished?

In a similar situation in the United States a group of teenagers planned to run away to Florida. One of the girls got cold feet and said she was going to tell their parents. The rest of them took her into the woods, beat her with stones and finally hanged her from a tree – her body was found a week later. Afterwards, the other teenagers went off to McDonald's and bought milk shakes. You say, How can this possibly be? You listen to the high-sounding nonsense: 'Well, you know, the Social Services just need to do a little bit more ... the educators just need to try a little harder ... she came from a bad house, you know, she lived up a close, his granny put him in a box when he was ten ...'

But there's only one explanation of the endemic nature of sin. And there's only one answer for it: the transforming power of the Lord Jesus Christ. When we identify the condition, we will declare the answer. When we fudge on the condition we will have no answer to give, and we will be left as a church mumbling and bumbling in our cereal with the rest of them. It's time to stand up and say, 'You may not like the answer, but we have an answer. You may not like the diagnosis, but we believe we have a diagnosis.' Let the voice be heard.

SOCIETY

I have already touched upon this. These individuals do not have the power necessary to control either their tongue or their appetites; they are like brutal savages: 'treacherous, rash, conceited' (3:4) – no self-control. They hate good, and they conduct their treachery with a recklessness which fills them with conceit rather than with shame. The final sentence (3:5) and verse 6, by use of the present tense, make it clear again that Paul has not been describing something in the remote future for Timothy.

Paul is obviously not calling for a total avoidance of sinners. The only way that we can totally avoid sin is to die. But the staggering thing, to my mind, is that the individuals from whom we are told to turn away are those, you will notice, who have a religious side to them (3:5). This is not a comment about the fallen culture out there, but about individuals who have religious faces. They are not outright pagans. They are marked by these characteristics, but if we saw them they would be involved in some kind of religious framework. They have a 'form of godliness', but their lifestyles deny the professions that they are prepared to make. Their religion is a shell and their lives are a sham.

All the way through the prophets, God is addressing such individuals. I did a series some time ago on Amos. In that book you cannot evade the staggering judgements of God on His people. For example in Amos 2: 'This is what the LORD says: "For three sins of Israel, even for four, I will not turn back my wrath. They sell the righteous for silver, and the needy for a pair of sandals. They trample on the heads of the poor as upon the dust of the ground and deny justice to the oppressed."' Morally, it's chaos. '"Father and son use the same girl and so profane my holy name. They lie down beside every altar on garments taken in pledge. In the house of their god they drink wine taken as fines' (Amos 2:6-8).

In other words, they are the forerunners of the Pharisees whom Jesus condemned. He looked at them and He said, 'You know you like to make sure that the outside of your cup is so very, very clean – what a tragedy it is that you stole the utensils that you are so concerned to have clean' (cf Matt. 23, Luke 11).

While the mercy of God extends to the penitent sinner, always prepared to cleanse, to restore and to forgive, the most stinging condemnations of Scripture are reserved for religious con men. They are reserved for those who have an external approach to religion, and yet their lives are like dead men's bones. If you get underneath them and begin to see what they are really like, then they will reveal in their lifestyle their denial of the things that they proclaim.

The Anglican Prayer Book mentions the case of 'an open and notorious evil liver'. It's hard in a post-modern culture to know who this might be, since there's no absolute standard by which we may judge evil, or tell who is notorious. They had no such difficulty when they penned the Prayer Book – they just said, 'What does the Bible say? That's good enough for us. Things haven't changed.' And what was supposed to happen to the evil and notorious evil liver? He was to be disciplined by the congregation, and if he remained impenitent and unrepentant, he was to be excommunicated from the congregation. And that is exactly what is supposed to happen today in our churches.

I wonder, in this vast congregation, when was the last time, in all of the congregations that are represented here, that any of you have been witnesses to any process of church discipline that has identified and dealt with open and notorious livers? I would suggest that the answer is: very few. It's not because of an absence of open and notorious livers. It's because of confusion and compromise and weak-kneed leadership.

Any mum or dad knows that you have to do this. You sit around the breakfast table with your children, and one of them demonstrates the fact that this morning they've got up as an open and notorious evil liver. Now you can either tolerate it and let it wreck the whole meal; or you can send them back to their room. When you do that it gives the opportunity to the remaining group to reflect, 'Hey! I may be the next going up the stairs! I may be the next for the pow-wow!' That's the whole principle of Matthew 18: the warning, the inter-personal relationships, the accountability, ensuring that these things do not run rampant. First you get a warning, then you get a yellow card, then you get a red card. You can read about it in Titus 3:10-11 – warning; yellow card; red card. 'Warn a divisive person once, and then warn him a second time. After that, have nothing to do with him.' I don't see that as difficult to understand. Yet our churches are divided by people who are cantankerous rascals with whom nobody has the guts to deal.

The strategy of infiltration (3:6-9)

Now, what is their strategy? What did these people do? Verse 6: they are the kind of individuals who worm their way into homes. The verb is *enduno* which means 'to creep'. Who creeps? Creeps do! That's what these individuals are. And their approach is insidious, and they inveigle their way into the homes of a particular kind of women.

Let me make myself absolutely clear. Paul does not use the standard term for a woman here, which is *gune*; he uses a diminutive form, *gunaikarion*. I think he does this to make his point most forcefully, that there is no derogation of women implying that 'weak-willed' is an appropriate adjective to describe the whole female sex. He is saying that there is a certain type of woman who is weak-willed. She displays an intellectual incapacity combined with a moral incapacity. These are women who are burdened by their own sins. They are consumed with a sense of guilt. They have filled their minds with deceitful lies. They are susceptible to sensational news, they long for a knowledge of the truth; they get snippets here and there, but they never seem able to put it all together.

Paul says that those described in verses 2 to 5 tend to come around the homes of women. It's interesting how much the approach of a cult has always been along those lines throughout the ages. Of course, today they don't need to come up the garden path, they come via the television screens. We have varieties of them, gargantuan, of dreadful proportions, that fill the screens in the United States.

These people are rejecting God's truth in a very subtle and dangerous way. They use the right kind of language. They simply distort its meaning. Their minds are corrupt, the condition of their lives is actually reprobate. They are depraved; and in relationship to the faith, Paul says, tragically they are rejected.

In 3:9 he adds encouragingly, 'But they will not get very far because, as in the case of those men,' – here a backward glance to the magicians in the time of Moses, identified in verse 8 as Jannes and Jambres – 'their folly will be clear to everyone.' All the things that have come against the church over the years eventually become antiques. And they don't become the antiques that people want to keep in their homes. I understand that Erich von Daniken has published a follow-up to *Chariots of the Gods?* Just when I thought that that nonsense had been put to bed, it has reappeared. But it will last for a moment or two and go away. Therefore it is important for us not to immediately rush to deal with all these things. You remember the Hare Krishna people, with their shaved heads and their jangling bells and long robes in the city streets? They've cleaned up their act amazingly. In America, they wear khaki slacks and golf shirts, they have a new style. But eventually the khakis and golf shirts will have to go as well, because they have nothing to say that is of substance.

So don't get your head spun off your shoulders, says Paul to Timothy. Make sure you stay on track. Be concerned about those issues, don't scramble to the defence of the faith but declare the faith, because their folly will eventually become clear to everyone.

The rising influences from outside (3:10-17)

Now as we come to verse 10 and move towards a conclusion, let us understand that we can expect the experience concerning which Paul alerted the elders when he left them in Ephesus (Acts 20). He took his leave of them on the beach and they wept when he said, 'None of you ... will ever see me again' (Acts 20:25). And he tells them, 'I know that after I leave ... even from your own number men will arise and distort the truth in order to draw away disciples after them. So be on your guard! Remember that for three years I never stopped warning each of you night and day with tears' (Acts 20:29-31).

In other words, this is not simply on the fringes. It may find itself in the very heart of the local fellowship – the rising influence of those whose morality is as bad as their theology, and yet remain largely influential. What is to be done by the likes of Timothy in these circumstances? Should he become a debater? Should he cease from the proclamation of the gospel, should he simply become an analyst of the error of his day? No, says Paul in 3:10. And here we have another of these 'You, however' phrases. 'In contrast to all of this,' he says, 'you know all about my teaching and all the rest. And in the light of the things that you know about, Timothy, I want to urge you to keep going. Continue in the faith. Don't concentrate on the newest deviations. Continue instead in the basic truths that you have been taught.'

Now this simply reinforces what we've said earlier in the week, that the role of the pastor is not largely a role of innovation but of affirmation. It is surely striking that Paul says here, 'You, however, know all about ...', so that the guiding and strengthening principles of Timothy's life are not to be in the discoveries of new information or of new ideas, but substantially in being able to do the basics well most of the time. It is a lesson for our age, when believers scurry for the latest notions, grabbing for the newest gimmicks in the forlorn hope that they have at last found a means to usefulness. And that itself is merely an extension of our generation's approach to so many things. People have made themselves very rich cashing in on the notion that there is an easy way to do things, a readily obtainable mechanism for self-transformation.

Did 'abdominisers' ever reach Britain? They were little plastic seats with two handles on their sides. It was claimed that buying one got you a flat stomach. People bought them by the thousand. I can just see someone unpacking one and laying it down on the floor, and his wife saying, 'Okay, go ahead.' So he sits in the plastic pail and waits. 'Could you get me a measuring tape? I'm not sure if it's kicked in yet.'

'You're not so stupid as to think you can just sit there and get a flat stomach, surely? You're supposed to go up and down – like this.'

'Oh, but that's sit-ups!'

'Yes,' says the wife, 'exactly.'

And across the Christian community people run around looking for plastic pails and mechanisms, to try to know what it is to live in the fullness of God's Spirit and in the power of God's word in obedience to God's truth. There is nothing new. It all goes back to your Sunday school, you know.

> Read your Bible, pray every day
> if you want to grow
> and you'll grow, grow, grow
> you'll grow, grow, grow.

Remember that? And now you're fifty-eight or eighty-five, and what's the key? Read your Bible, pray every day. You say, that's a very simplistic approach to things. Well, it's certainly simple.

Read the list in 3:10-11. Is Paul boasting? No. Paul said that he would never boast, save in the cross of Christ (cf Gal. 6:14). So what is he doing here? Well, remember he's a veteran soldier, an old man in jail. He's not trying to impress anyone. He's simply stating the facts. 'Timothy, you were around, you know what happened; you were there.'

And isn't it interesting that at the very head of the list he said, 'You ... know all about my teaching.' His life could not be separated from his instruction. Timothy was absolutely aware of this. He also knew that Paul practised what he taught. That's why Paul is able to say, 'my teaching, my way of life'. What he was in private concurred with what he was in public. Timothy had been with him, had slept close to him, had seen him in the silence of the night, had seen him in the unguarded moments, had watched his life. So if anybody was in a position to say, 'That's not true,'

Timothy was. But as he read the letter he must have thought, 'That's right, Paul. I do remember your teaching and I do remember your way of life.' So he was willing to respond to the exhortation: 'Guard your doctrine and your life closely, because if you do you will save both yourself and your hearers.'

You will find in Acts 13 and 14 the historical background of his Paul's reference to Antioch, Iconium and Lystra in verse 11. As you read them, you realise that Paul was a classic illustration of Psalm 34:4 – 'I sought the LORD, and he answered me; he delivered me from all my fears.'

Paraphrasing the end of verse 12, J. B. Phillips says, 'Persecution is inevitable for those who are determined to live really Christian lives.' Can I ask you, do you want to live a godly life in Christ Jesus? Do you begin the day, do I begin the day, saying, 'Lord, help me not to sin' – or, 'Help me not to sin very much'? Can you imagine hearing the pilot of passenger aircraft in which you were travelling announce just after take-off, 'Good morning! We will be heading south to our destination – and I just want you to know, my strategy as a pilot is not to crash very much'? It wouldn't have a very reassuring ring to it, would it? But that is how some of us approach our lives. Anyone who wants to live a godly life in Christ Jesus doesn't begin the day saying, 'Help me not to sin very much', but 'Help me not to sin.' I end the day saying, 'I didn't get 100%, I'm not even sure I got 70%,' but at least it doesn't stop me from beginning the day with a good challenge.

In Greek, 'godly' in verse 12 is a word that could equally be translated 'pious': 'Everyone who wants to live a pious life'. When was the last time you heard the word 'piety' used with any positive connotation? It's often used of dour people who are so heavenly-minded that they're of no earthly use. Now be honest, have you met many of those people lately? I have not, but I have met many who are the opposite. I meet one regularly in my shaving mirror as I begin the day; someone who is of such earthly-mindedness that he has the potential to be no heavenly use at all.

Why is it that we live with such lack of persecution? Perhaps it is because we are not distinctive. We are, as Tozer said, the best-disguised set of pilgrims the world has ever seen. We have bent over backwards to be so. In the 1950s we'd say, 'We're not like you.' In the 1990s we say, 'We're just like you.' People say, 'Yes, we know we are just like you – so why in the world will we listen to anything you have to say?'

When is the church at its most distinctive? When it is most distinct; when, by its belief and its behaviour, it calls in contrast the world in which it lives.

Verse 13: These 'evil men', he says, these 'impostors' – they will go from bad to worse. It's a very sarcastic statement here. They are actually increasing in their momentum, but they are going in the wrong direction. The only advance that they make is backwards. Their whole operation is set in reverse. They are killed by their own swords, delusion is their weapon, and by delusion they will be slain. And again in verse 14 – 'But as for you ...' – contrasting the wisdom of Timothy with the foolishness of the crowds, and calling out to his young lieutenant, 'Come on now, Timothy!'

'Continue in what you have learned and have become convinced of, because you know those from whom you learned it, and how from infancy you have known the holy Scriptures, which are able to make you wise for salvation through faith in Christ Jesus' (3:14-15). In other words, he reaches into Timothy's background and, as it were, sets it up before him on the screen. 'Now Timothy, think about this. Think about what it is you are convinced of. Think about where you learned that and think about the strength that it gives you to recall your teachers. The people around you are interested in new-fangled notions, they are unprepared for old-fashioned truths, because we bring an unchanging word to bear imaginatively on a very changing world.' The basis of Timothy's continuance is first that he would be strengthened by the reminder of those who taught him, and then that he would be equipped by the very Scripture that they proclaim.

One of the nicest of many nice things that have happened to me this week was to meet a lady who told me that she was my Sunday school teacher in Glasgow. I never knew her name or that of her fellow-teacher until this week. Why did I want to know her name? Because it was after that Sunday school, one Sunday in Glasgow, that I went home on a Sunday afternoon troubled, troubled by what I had heard and whatever they had said. And I asked my Dad, 'How old do you have to be to have Jesus as your Saviour?' My father, in his wisdom, picking up on the work done by these – until this week – unnamed ladies, led me to faith in Jesus Christ. It was a genuine thrill to look her in the eyes. She hadn't a clue that I was anything more than a cantankerous pain in the neck.

We can all do this. We can bring them to our mind's eye: those who have nurtured us in the faith; parents, loved ones, teachers, lecturers, friends. We bring them to our mind's eye, and their continuance is a means of our encouragement.

People ask me how I prepare for preaching. I always say the same thing. 'Well, I come to the Bible, and I think myself empty and I read myself full and I write myself clear and I pray myself hot.'

'Oh,' they say, 'that's good! Did you think that up?'

'No, that was Leith Samuel at a preaching day at London Bible College. I didn't just write it down, I remembered it. I didn't just remember it, I do it. And I bless God for that and the likes of that, and so do you.'

Do this exercise sometime. Rehearse in your mind's eye those from whom you have learned the Scriptures, and bless God for their memory and thank God for their continued influence in your life. And I tell you, it will lift you a wee bit above the clouds and the rain.

God's revelation

As we close, verse 15. It was from infancy that he had known these things about salvation, 'The holy Scriptures, which are able to make you wise for salvation through faith in Christ Jesus.' The Bible is a book about Jesus and the Bible is therefore a book about salvation. The whole Bible is about God's revelation to us and how we who are unworthy might become children of His grace.

In the Old Testament Jesus is predicted, in the gospels Jesus is revealed, in the Acts Jesus is preached, in the epistles Jesus is explained and in the Revelation Jesus is anticipated. ('Oh,' you say, 'you got that from somebody didn't you.' Yes I did! From Alec Motyer, it's very good, write it down.) You know the Bible from infancy and it is brought to you for salvation through faith in Jesus Christ.

We know where it came from: verse 16, its source is God. It is all 'God-breathed'. Not that the Scripture was in existence and God breathed into it, but rather that Scripture was brought into existence by the breath of God. We know where it's from and we know what it's for: verse 17, 'so that the man of god may be thoroughly equipped for every good work.'

And how will that happen? Timothy is a faithful pastor who teaches and rebukes and corrects and trains in righteousness (cf verse 16). What a wonderful reminder to us of the sufficiency of the Bible!

How are men and women then to be nurtured in our day? How are we to ensure that they will be kitted out for the challenges of the next century? By ensuring that the word of God is brought to bear upon their lives. Sadly, some are out to sea, rudderless and ill-equipped for the voyage; it is our responsibility to equip them with a conviction in relationship to Scripture – a life-transforming grasp of the Bible. It is the word of God that makes men and women of God. And despite the fact that there is much that militates against it in our day, it is surely here that we must take our stand.

2 Timothy 4

As we turn together to this final chapter of 2 Timothy, I want to take just a moment to say thank you to each of you for the immense privilege that it's been for me to be here for these five days. I'm very grateful also to the Keswick Council for extending the invitation to me. But I also want to thank my mentors and my colleagues in ministry, the people that I've been spending the week with, and publicly to acknowledge my gratitude to Parkside Church, Ohio, where I serve. They have been praying for us this week, and I don't take that for granted; nor do they. Finally, and not in the least at all, I acknowledge my indebtedness to my wife Susan, without whose partnership in ministry I would never feel free to be away; and who, though separated from us by 3,000 miles, has in a sense been at my right hand through all of this week.

Paul is now about to move out of his office, as it were. That is what his letter has been about. His departure is imminent; he is about to vacate his chair. And there is no doubt in Timothy's mind that it is going to fall to him to take that seat, and to fulfil the responsibility that is now his in the cause of the gospel.

The vacancy is going to be left as a result of Paul's departure. Verse 6 refers to his imminent death. It's not that he sees himself quitting on the job, or failing as a result of exhaustion or indifference. He's going to breast the tape as best he can, but he knows that he needs to go. After three decades of faithful service in the army of the Lord Jesus Christ, in the midst of doctrinal and moral confusion, the apostle is about to entrust the truth of the gospel to a young man who is more prone to lean than he is to lead. We saw in chapter 1 that he has urged Timothy to guard it and keep it, to be prepared to suffer for it, to base his life and his ministry upon it; and now in this final chapter he is urging him to be bold in proclaiming its truth.

The sense of urgency pervading these verses is matched by the intimacy that is also conveyed in them. Here we get an insight that is somewhat unique to the heart of the apostle; his humanity comes out with great clarity. While his concerns are as vast, one can say, as the extension of God's kingdom throughout the world, nevertheless he is not immune to the need for friendship, for the encouragement that warm clothes will bring, and also for the help of good books.

Paul's exhortation to Timothy (4:1-4)

But first of all, we have this stirring charge to 'preach the Word' (verse 2). Its context (verse 1) is graphic, a reminder to Timothy that the call to preach had not come about as a result of human contrivance but as a result of a divine commission. And he underscores the solemnity of the responsibility that falls to Timothy by exhorting him not in his own name, and not even in that of his apostleship; but in the presence of God and of the Lord Jesus Christ.

The exhortation expanded

Having issued the exhortation, Paul explains it. He mentions three incentives to faithfulness. First, Jesus is going to appear. Second, His kingdom is going to be ushered in, in all of its fullness. And third, men and women are going to face the judgement.

This is the theological underpinning of this exhortation to be a preacher of the word of God, to be conveying the truth in his day. They were truths which Timothy's generation needed to hear, as indeed does every generation. Samuel Johnson said of an earlier century, 'The Master has set a day when He will separate the sheep from the goats; and this is a truth which our frivolous age needs to hear.' And despite the fact that as a result of unbelief – or perhaps of ignorance or lack of interest – men and women may devalue and discount the claims of the Lord Jesus Christ, the Lord's servant is charged with fulfilling his calling in the awareness of Christ's right to judge, the certainty of His return and the fact that He will one day reign supreme over all. 'At the name of Jesus every knee should bow, in heaven and on earth and under the earth, and every tongue confess that Jesus Christ is Lord, to the glory of God the Father' (Phil. 2:10-11)

It is within that sort of environment that Paul says to Timothy, 'Now, this is what you need to be doing.' W. E. Sangster, the Methodist preacher who was active in Britain at the turn of the century, said, 'Preaching is in the shadows, the world does not believe in it.' We may feel that our presence in these large gatherings on each day of this week at Keswick suggests that that is not so, but the fact is that we are somewhat atypical. There is a sense, moreover, in which, if we are realistic, we could well say that our modern condition is more grave than that identified by Sangster. It is certainly true that in the United States preaching is, increasingly, in the shadows; the church does not believe in it. There are prominent individuals moving around America at present with influence over young men in ministry, suggesting to them that if they are going to be effective in Bible teaching into the new millennium then they are going to have to discover how to speak in fifteen-minute blocks – no one can or will listen for longer. They should give up on biblical exposition, say these individuals, and learn to deliver entertaining and humorous topical studies. Their message comes like a siren call in the midst of that confusion.

But the fact is that preaching is more than the meanderings of a man's mind from behind a pulpit. That is made clear by the constituent elements in the task, which are unfolded for us.

It hardly needs to be reiterated, but let's not miss the fact that it is the *word* that is preached. In the rest of the chapter he refers to the same when he mentions 'sound doctrine' in verse 3, 'the truth' in verse 4, 'the faith' in verse 7. We must not take that for granted. It's not the preacher's responsibility or privilege simply to dream up his own ideas or convey things that are of concern to him. Rather he is to be under the instruction of the word of God himself, and to be conveying the same to others.

Now again, each of us today may feel ourselves very much in accord with this. But I want to tell you that I don't believe this is largely the case. I'd like to quote to you something Jim Packer said when he was speaking in Scotland to ministers about the responsibility of preaching. 'Christian preaching is the event of God bringing to a congregation a Bible-based, Christ-related, life-impacting message of instruction and direction, from Himself through the words of a spokesman.'

I think every word of that is tremendously helpful. But the fundamental issue is that we believe that when the word of God is truly preached, the voice of God is really heard. For it is God Himself bringing a message through His word, via the lips of a mere mortal. Therefore any preoccupation with the speaker is ultimately unhelpful both to the speaker and to the listeners. Not that we denigrate the existence of human gifts; surely God could have spoken in other ways but has chosen to use human abilities. Nevertheless it is to God alone we look, both to hear from Him and then to give Him glory as a result of what it is He has conveyed.

When you adopt that definition it quickly becomes apparent that by that standard not every performance from behind a pulpit can be called 'preaching'. The kind of cool chatty approach that calls attention to oneself doesn't qualify. The dull and boring approach, that has all the conviction of a man reading from the *Yellow Pages*, doesn't qualify. And when that is what congregations experience, any sense of expectation in them has been eroded. They do not attend the Lord's Day in worship believing that God's voice is about to be heard, because their conviction regarding it has been eroded by a man-centred preoccupation, focused by the preacher on himself – or, having done no preparation at all, he simply drones on for a while and then drifts off into some kind of oblivion, and people are rather glad that he's gone.

Now, says Packer,

> Instead of heading for worship with an expectation of an encounter with God, in both giving Him praise and hearing Him speak, the average congregation in a spirit

of detached passivity come as observers to measure the
performance, rather than as participants waiting on the
word of God. Instead of sitting up expectantly praying,
'Master speak, thy servant heareth, waiting for Thy
gracious word', they sit back, relax, and wait to see if
anything the preacher has to say will catch their interest.
Since many in our churches have been brought up under
knowledgeable fellows speaking with emphasis, they can
hardly be blamed for their attitude. Just as it takes two to
tango, so it takes an expectant praying congregation,
along with a preacher who knows what he's about, to
make an authentic preaching occasion.

And that is why, in that kind of sentiment, Spurgeon told his
congregation that if they would pray for their pastor, their pastor
would be able to preach the exact same sermons to far greater
effect; because we do not pray for the work, prayer is the work and
preaching is merely gathering up the results of the battle that has
been waged before God's throne in prayer. When the people of
God begin to conceive of it in these terms then it will transform
both the listener and the speaker.'

Now this is borne out in the phrases that follow. 'Be prepared'
(verse 2) literally means 'stand by': it's the doctor on call, with
bleary eyes and drinking lots of cups of coffee, dreading the phone
call – yet ready for it, at a moment's notice, to pull him or herself
together and go down onto the ward. It's the Second World War
dispatch rider loitering on his motor bike but ready at a moment
to be dispatched with information of vital importance.

'So,' he says, 'you're going to need to be the kind of individual,
Timothy, who is taking and making opportunities, when it's
convenient and when it's inconvenient. You should never allow
laziness to divert you from the privilege.' We are to 'be prepared in
season and out of season'; and when we get to the task, there are
various elements involved – correction, rebuke and
encouragement. All of these won't necessarily happen all of the
time, but it is dangerous when in the ministry of the word
somebody gets stuck on one track and begins to bury a
congregation under a vast heavy weight of correction and the
people are bowed down under it. And it is dangerous when a

church becomes a dreadfully nice place where the minister bends over backwards to make sure everybody is encouraged. The balance of God's word is the balance of God's word. Correction for those who are thinking wrong, rebuke for those who are living comfortably with sin, encouragement for those who are down in the dumps.

And I always say to young men now in ministry, 'If you would just expound the Scriptures then you will take care of this. You don't have to have it at the forefront of your mind all the time. It's good to remember it, but the balance of Scripture will ensure that there is correction, there is rebuke and there is encouragement.'

The way it is to take place is also clear. What is the spirit of the individual who is engaging in this? Well, he must act with great patience and careful instruction. Jesus had to look at His twelve and say to them, 'Have I been so long with you and still you do not understand?', and I derive great encouragement from that. As time goes by in pastoral ministry, and there are things that you've been longing to convey and see become a central part of your people's life and experience but it just doesn't seem to dawn on them – you find yourself saying, 'Have I been so long with you and still you do not understand?' The temptation then is to try to rattle a few heads, or stir people up by means of forcefulness. The manner is 'great patience'. We always remember good patient instructors, don't we? – the teachers who put their arms round our shoulders, who were wise enough to know whether a question was simply a diversion or whether it was a realistic cry for help.

In 1976 I used to visit a lady in a nursing home who suffered from some kind of motor-neurone disorder. She had been Matron of the Royal Infirmary in Edinburgh, but now was bed-ridden, able to hear but unable to hold her eyes open for more than a brief second. I used to read to her, and we would discuss what I'd read. When the time came for me to tell her I was moving on she said to me, 'I want to let you know that I often needed to rebuke or correct the nurses in my charge. But I want you to know, Alistair, that I made it my commitment never to rebuke a junior nurse without my arm around her shoulder.' I wish that I had remembered that more than I have done.

Great patience – and careful instruction. If we merely rebuke error and do not instruct in righteousness, we might break an individual's spirit without their life ever being changed.

Do you remember at school, when you took your exercise book to your teacher, and he or she wielded a red pen until your book looked like a piece of modern art? You trudged back to your seat, taking scant comfort from the fact that there was a section at the bottom of the page that had no red marks on it. Of course there wouldn't be, you hadn't written anything there. And you dreaded that your class-mates, or worse, your parents, might see the book. Often teachers like that killed one's interest in the subject. Not because it was wrong for them to mark your mistakes in red ink, but because it seemed that the whole reason they had been put in a classroom was to let you know how lousy you were at a particular subject.

Let us then, as pastors, teachers, Bible class leaders and Sunday school teachers, be aware of the effect of a strident tone and of constantly urging our people to a standard up to which we ourselves do not live.

Let me say too that preaching is not less than teaching, it is more than teaching. People ask me, 'Would you say you are a preacher or a teacher?' It's a particularly American question! I reply, 'I am a preaching teacher and a teaching preacher.' What I mean by that is that I believe preaching is teaching plus application, direction and summons. So there is that exhortatory element, founded upon the didactic element of opening up the truth that is before us.

So that is Paul's first exhortation. 'Preach the word.' Why is it so important?

He tells us in 4:3-4. 'For the time will come when men will not put up with sound doctrine.' Interesting! 'They won't put up with it – so do it.' He doesn't say, 'There will come a point where people will not be interested in preaching, so give up preaching and just tell a lot of stories, sing a lot of songs, or do drama – or whatever it may be. No,' he says, 'I want you to preach the word with great diligence, when you feel like it, when you don't feel like it, in season and out of season.'

Careful instruction, great patience, for people don't want it. Interesting!

There's no pragmatic approach to building a ministry here, whereby we give the people what they want. If you as mothers gave your children what they wanted as regards food in their early years, you would be pushing them around in wheelbarrows and their faces would all be covered in ice cream. But you didn't give them what they wanted (well, maybe a little here and there!) You knew you needed to give them a balanced diet, that they needed starches and carbohydrates and fruit and vegetables. 'An apple a day keeps the doctor away.' And now you see them growing in physical maturity, because you were wise enough not to capitulate to their silly ideas.

You may say that's not a very nice way to think about your flock. Well, I don't mean that's the exclusive nature of what they're like. But we all have silly ideas; that's why God has established a structure. That's why He has given a father to be the head of the home and a mother to be with him in partnership. That's why He has given to the eldership the responsibility of leadership in the church.

Nor is preaching simply a man with a product trying to overcome consumer resistance, as is often suggested to us today; you have a salesman, he has a product and you have a potential market. The potential market is not remotely interested in your product; therefore you need to do everything you can possibly do to overcome consumer resistance to buy your product. I don't like that. There are restaurants in America where the waiters come out to you on roller skates. Why? I have a sneaking suspicion the food's no good, it's a diversion (I realise that is unfair to good restaurants that have good waitresses on roller skates, but even so ...)

This is the contrast. Motivated by personal satisfaction – 'to suit their own desires' – people 'will gather around them a great number of teachers'. The preachers will be united by one factor: a willingness 'to say what their itching ears want to hear'. And, Paul says to Timothy, you will find yourself ministering in an environment where people increasingly want teachers who simply tell them what they want to hear. Many will be willing to assign themselves that task – but you, Timothy, you're not to be like that. The number one question in these individuals' choice of church is simply, 'Will I be told what I want to hear?' They do not first listen and then decide whether what they've heard is true. They decide what they want to hear and then select teachers who will oblige by toeing their line. So they bounce from congregation to congregation, from place to place.

It's a sad and sorry thing. And of course, the more restaurants there are in the town the more places there are for you to go. You don't have to stay at Aunt Mabel's Pancake House, there are lots of places you can go to. Sadly, American Christianity is marked by people moving from place to place to place to place. It's what Chuck Colson calls 'The McChurch mentality'; if you don't like the burgers at McDonald's, you can move to Burger King; if you don't like it there, you can go to Kentucky Fried Chicken; then on to Wendy's ... there's always another place you can go and have them serve it up to you just the way you want.

Can I say to some of you who are planning to leave your church for less than biblical reasons: won't you stay, and make a commitment to pray for your teaching minister, for the ongoing work of the gospel? Don't scurry around from place to place looking for somebody who will make you feel comfortable. It may be in God's plan for you to feel distinctly uncomfortable at the moment, in order that you might know the comfort that He can bring.

Paul's concern for Timothy (4:5-8)

Now, because of the crazy environment in which he is ministering, Timothy must continue to preach the word of God, and he must be sure that he doesn't lose his spiritual and theological equilibrium – isn't that what he's saying in the opening phrase of verse 5? This is the second imperative: first preach the word, secondly keep your head.

It would be so easy for the prospect of Paul's departure, coupled with the itching-ear syndrome, to knock Timothy completely off his balance. And so Paul issues this strident call: keep your head; the danger is that you will allow your head to be spun all over the place.

I want to tell you, 2 Timothy 4:5 is my verse. I scribble it down for myself regularly, I remind myself of it frequently. The danger is that when we need to be steady, alert, calm and cool, we begin to flap and go crazy and annoy everyone around us. So this is a wonderful word of encouragement to all, particularly perhaps to some whose heads are being spun. Maybe there's a more successful ministry down the street, at least in terms of numbers attending.

Maybe there are people within our leadership team who are discouraging us dreadfully. We feel that it might be a good idea to throw in the towel, to lie down on the grass, and not to take the baton on for the next four hundred metres. But the word of God comes and says, 'Now listen – just keep your head, and do so in all situations.'

It will mean you will have to 'endure hardship'. If Timothy was going to continue to refuse to compromise on the basis of truth, if he was going to uphold these principles of biblical certainty in an age of confusion, then he was going to suffer hardship. And whenever the biblical principle becomes unpopular the temptation comes, especially for a young man in ministry, to downplay those factors which cause offence. Paul says, make sure you don't do that, keep your head in every situation, in a situation of hardship.

Secondly, you must make sure that you are involved in evangelism, that you 'do the work of an evangelist'. D. E. Hall said, 'I would not appoint a man or a woman to the mission field unless they had first learned to wrestle with the evil one. For if they have not learned to wrestle with the evil one then they will wrestle with their fellow missionaries.' In other words, when a church loses sight of the battle ground, loses sight of the over-arching objective to see unbelieving people become committed followers of Jesus Christ – when that characteristic goes, then there will be all kinds of things come in to take its place. They won't all be bad, but they won't be the best thing.

We reminded ourselves yesterday that the Bible is a book about salvation and that Timothy is to be committed to proclaiming the good news. In doing this, he must 'discharge all the duties of his ministry'. In other words, don't shirk all the bits and pieces. There are all kinds of things involved in pastoral ministry. Not all of them are those for which we are immediately prepared. They don't all attract us in the same ways that others do. That's true of everybody's job. There are few people who like everything that they do every day.

Paul says, 'Don't run away, leave nothing undone that you ought to do. The environment around you may tempt you to silence or to compromise. You may find that it dulls your spirits, that it weakens your resolves. But let me urge you on all the more. The tougher the times and the greater the public lack of interest, the more diligent we need to be in keeping our heads and fulfilling the task.'

The exhortation expanded

And now, again, he explains his exhortation. What is the reason? Because, says Paul, I am on my way out. Verse 6: 'For I am already being poured out like a drink offering, and the time has come for my departure. I have fought the good fight, I have finished the race ... Timothy, you are going to have to take the next lap.'

Do you notice the juxtaposition between the opening two words of verse 5 and the opening two of verse 6? 'But you', 'For I'. Studying the Bible is not difficult. If you're reading in English you just need to understand the English language. Read Numbers 15 for homework. There you will read of the drink offering, the final act in the sacrificial ceremony that brought a closure to all that had gone before. Paul picks up on that when he writes to the Romans and he urges them, 'I want you to present your bodies as a living sacrifice' (cf Rom. 12:1). Now he says, 'That's essentially where I am. I don't think that my second defence is going to go better than my first. I think that I'm probably out of here.' He was talking in realistic terms. 'It's my departure that's coming and my life is just passing away. I'm pouring it out now like a drink offering.'

It's a wonderful illustration of the Christian's view of death. The word here for departure, *analusis*, is a word that meant various things in the Greek of the day. It was used of the farmer unshackling his oxen from their yoke and allowing them to roam in relaxation; it was used for striking a tent and heading for a permanent dwelling; it was used for weighing anchor and heading to that final harbour that is the destination. Paul says, 'That's it for me. I'm going to be relieved of the yoke, I'm going to be weighing anchor and heading for my heavenly harbour, I'm going to be striking tent and heading for my permanent dwelling.' There's no sense of grim desperation here, is there? There's no sense of agonising over it.

He's in a dismal dungeon – and yet, what a wonderful reminder to us that God has made of death for the Christian a narrow sunlit strip between the goodbyes of yesterday and the hellos of tomorrow. For us Christians, what we fear most we never experience. We are going to fall asleep in the arms of Jesus and we are going to wake up and we will be at home. The sun will be shining through the windows, and we will hear our Father's 'Well done'. So that event holds no terror for the Christian. What it will mean for us in the eking out of our lives may be painful. I'm not sure that I like the prospect of the process. But let us learn here from Paul. 'I'm going to be departing,' he says.

In the light of that, he looks back over his shoulder and says, 'I have fought the good fight, I have finished the race, I have kept the faith' (4:7). What a wonderful thing to be able to say! Timothy could underline it. He knew that Paul had struggled on many occasions; the metaphor is a good one. 'The glorious fight that God gave me – I fought that. The course that Christ set me – I ran that.' It underlines for us the steady persistence that is involved in Christian living. For Paul since his coming to Christ it had not been a few forty-yard sprints. It hadn't even been a cross-country run. It had been a marathon that was going on right until he breasted the tape. 'I press on towards the goal to win the prize for which God has called me heavenwards in Christ Jesus' (Phil. 3:14). He had been a guardian and steward of the gospel, he had kept the faith in the way he now urges Timothy to do. He had retained his own personal faith, trust and confidence in the Lord Jesus as he now urges Timothy (and us through this letter) to do.

From there he looks forward, in verse 8. Verse 6 is the present tense – 'Here I am.' Verse 7 is the past tense – 'There I was.' And verse 8 is the future tense – 'This is what I'm looking forward to: a crown.' It's not his exclusive expectation, but rather the expectation of all who have been justified through faith in the Lord Jesus Christ on that day. He longed for the appearing of the One from whom the unbeliever will hide in shame. He is looking forward to a crown.

See his confidence! Nero may be about to declare him guilty, but he looks to the Lord, who is the righteous judge. Nero may send him to his death, but the Lord the righteous Judge will reward him on that day. And his testimony of faith, there in three tenses in 6, 7, and 8, serves as an encouragement to Timothy, to whom he now gives a further and final word of instruction which reveals the sensitivity of his heart and the intimacy of his friendship.

Paul's request to Timothy (4:9-18)

Again, the imperative – 'come to me quickly'. All through this letter we have sensed the ties that Paul feels towards this young man Timothy. 'If I am ever to see you again,' he says, 'you need to come to me soon.' Presumably his concern about the winter is that if he didn't reach him before its onset the difficulties of travel would probably prevent his coming. He mentions three times about him coming; look for them yourselves.

It's not difficult to sense from Paul's words his almost tangible loneliness. He is in a dismal dungeon, separated from the opportunities that were previously his, no longer able to fulfil the things to which he is exhorting his young lieutenant, and aware of the fact that people have been leaving him all over the place.

The exhortation expanded

Some had left for reasons of ministry: Crescens and Titus, verse 10, and certainly Tychicus, verse 12. But the real blow had been struck by Demas who, 'because he loved this world, has deserted me and has gone to Thessalonica.' Read Colossians and Philemon and you will discover that Paul and Demas had been close, they had been related to one another. But now he was gone. Paul doesn't say, 'Well, *che sera, sera*, whatever, it doesn't matter. I've got a few left – so what, if Demas left.' No, there is a deep sadness in his life. And it appears there was a personal element in the defection: 'Demas has deserted me.' In ministry these things are sad, and you sense the sadness.

Why did Demas desert? Was he afraid? Was it a relationship with a woman? Did he fall in love with 'today' and lose the sense of the 'then'? We don't know, but he stands out as an individual who represents discouragement to the servant of God at a time when his greatest need was encouragement. Remember, we are leaving a legacy.

The desertion of Demas is more than matched by the loyalty of Luke. Verse 11: 'Only Luke is with me.' That's the good news and the bad news – where are the rest? 'Our dear friend Luke, the doctor,' as he refers to him in Colossians 4:14; in Philemon 24 he is referred to again as a fellow-worker. There's no indication that Luke was a great evangelist or an effective Bible teacher, but he was loyal to the Lord Jesus, he was loyal to the servants of Jesus, he was loyal to the gospel and in his capacity as a Christian doctor he made a powerful contribution to the kingdom by way of the kindness of his heart. And I say to you again, kindness will live on in the hearts of men and women long after mental cleverness and eloquence has been forgotten.

When my mother died twenty-six years ago, many people wrote us cards with Bible verses, but it was actually the lady round the corner who did all my father's ironing, left with two teenage girls of eleven and fifteen, who comes to my mind most. Not to denigrate the card writers, but I've forgotten the verses, and I've never forgotten her knocking at the door and handing over another load of ironing. Don't let the evil one come to you on a day like this and tell you that you're not going home to anything spectacular – to the laundry, to visit the lady up the street, to call on the elderly neighbour to ask him if he needs any eggs from the shops. Listen, those are the things that are so often making a dramatic impact for the kingdom. 'Live such good lives among the pagans that, though they accuse you of doing wrong, they may see your good deeds and glorify God on the day he visits us' (1 Pet. 2:12). Don't desert like Demas. Be loyal like Luke.

And don't let's forget the ministry of Mark. Don't you love this, 'Get Mark and bring him with you' (4:11). Pardon, Paul – did I hear you correctly? Isn't this the character of whom you once said, 'You can take Mark anywhere you like, but he's not coming with me!' Didn't you say that, Paul?

'Yes I did.'

'Were you right?'

'Well ... let's just say he's helpful to me in my ministry now.'

What a wonderful encouragement is contained here, that God is a God who turns defections into blessings, that He is the God who nerves the feeble arm for the fight, He turns the pain of failure into the privilege of usefulness. All of us have 'done a Mark' at some point on the journey, I'm sure. How wonderful that God does this.

Verse 13 is an interesting verse, as we approach the end of the passage. 'When you come, bring the cloak ... and my scrolls, especially the parchments.' There are a couple of things here. First, here is this spiritual giant and he wants his jacket. He didn't say he had no need of a jacket, he had his own spiritual warmth. He needed his jacket. 'When you come, don't forget it.'

Also, 'bring my scrolls'. What were they? We don't know. People have done PhDs on the strength of these scrolls. Are they the Old Testament Scriptures? The early narratives of Jesus' life? The equivalent of his passport? We can't say with certain. All we can say with certainty is that they were important to Paul, and that's all that matters. 'I'm cold, bring my jacket; I'm bored, bring my books; I'm lonely, come and see me.' Do you see Paul's humanity? That's how we often feel. 'Hey, could you bring me a book?' 'Dear Mum, please send me my anorak, and if you could drop by at the campsite I would love to see you.'

And all the more so, because he records the antagonism of Alexander the metalworker, who was more of a hindrance than a help. He says the Lord will take care of him (verse 14). 'I'm going to commit my cause to Him who judges justly – but I need to mention Alexander because I want you to be on your guard against him.' Not because he was opposed to Paul as a personality, not because he didn't like the way Paul did things, but because he strongly opposed the message of the gospel.

That is the great concern in our day. It's not a personality conflict, it's the issue of the gospel. We need to warn God's people against those who strongly oppose the gospel, whether it's politically correct to do so or not. 'Alexander the metalworker did me a great deal of harm. I'm not going to go further than that,' says Paul. 'I will commit my cause to Him who judges justly. I need to warn you, Timothy, because the character's on the prowl and he opposes the gospel.'

Not only had he been opposed by Alexander, but he had been unsupported by his first defence (verse 16). The preliminary hearing before the trial had been an occasion of desertion. But he wasn't embittered. Look at that lovely sentence, 'May it not be held against them' (4:16). In other words there was no spirit of resentment. It's not, 'I remember what he did to me then.' The only reason he mentions Alexander by name is because Alexander was opposing the gospel.

There are many others who made all kinds of personal attacks upon him, but he doesn't mention their names. In fact, he says, when I think about them, 'may it not be held against them'. Because, after all, 'The Lord stood at my side and gave me strength.' What a lovely word! And the enabling was for a purpose: 'so that through me the message might be fully proclaimed and all the Gentiles might hear it. And I was delivered from the lion's mouth' (4:17). What an encouragement to Timothy as a young man. 'I was like Daniel,' he says, 'in the lion's den. I went in before the largest, the highest tribunal of the day, before the Roman Empire, maybe even before the Roman Emperor himself, with the whole world looking on, and the Lord has kept me safe. And the Lord will rescue me from every evil attack' (verse 17). I was delivered in the past, I am kept in the present, I will be delivered in the future. And He's going to bring me safely to His heavenly kingdom. To him be the glory for ever and ever. Amen!

Final greetings (4:19-22)

Just when you are about to close your Bible, he adds another little section. I love all these names, and I can't wait to meet these people. Remember that old song?

> You've heard of little Moses in the bullrush,
> you have heard of fearless David and his sling,
> You have heard the story told of dreaming Joseph
> and Jonah and the whale, I often sing.

There are many others in the Bible, and I should like to meet them all.

I want to meet Pudens, don't you? and Onesiphorus – I'm going to see the two of them. What you have here are not Smarties or Refreshers, you've got Allsorts! The point is simply this. As wonderful as the presence of the Lord Jesus is to Paul, and as wonderful as the prospect is to him of the return of the Lord Jesus, both His presence with me and the prospect of His coming for me are not intended to be a substitute for the joy of human friendship and human fellowship. We need one another. And if you've no idea what your ministry is to be when you get home from Keswick, go back and do some visiting. Drop in a note, or call by, or whatever it may be. Because this is a little reminder to us of the way fellowship works. Priscilla, Aquila, Onesiphorus, Erastus, Trophimus sick in Miletus – I beg your pardon, you left him sick in Miletus? Doesn't it say in Acts 19 that your hankies had healing powers? Miracles of healing are not at the command of their performers. Human experience in the biblical record make it perfectly clear that there are reasons in the divine council of God for a believer's sickness as well as for a believer's health. And to teach other than that is to teach from an empty head and a closed Bible.

Now let me finish by pointing you to two phrases. Verse 22: 'Grace be with you', and the final phrase of verse 18: 'To him be glory'. Let me summarise it like this: 'From Him grace, and to Him glory'.

'Timothy,' says Paul, 'you need to be useful to the Master. Don't be ashamed, aim for God's approval, continue in the faith, keep your head intact, don't deviate, be kind to everyone, patient, tender-hearted ... just run the race to the finish.'

And that's my word to you. Let us run the race to the finish.

Some have already finished their race. I asked my colleagues and mentors at Keswick to sign my book this morning, so that I would remember having been here when I'm old and cold and settled in my ways. I looked back to the page where I asked people to sign five years ago. And there was the signature of dear John Caiger, whose memory is a fragrance to us all and a challenge to finish the race. We could all supply other names, not just from Keswick but from our own situations.

If we live for seventy years, that will be nice. That would mean that at forty-six I am well into the last two hundred metres of the race. When Eric Liddell was interviewed by the *Edinburgh Evening Post* after winning the 400 metres in the 1924 Paris Olympics, they asked him, 'What was the reason for your success in the 400 metres?' I love what he said to them. 'I ran the first 200 as fast as I possibly could, and then with God's help I ran the second 200 even faster.' To those of you born a little earlier, don't buy this notion that the future of the church is in the children. You are the future of the church! Your theological grasp, your experience of God's faithfulness, your laying hold of God in prayer, is undergirding the very framework into which another generation comes.

So let us press on. From Him the grace, and to Him all the glory.

THE ADDRESSES

The Promise

by Mr Dick Dowsett

Acts 2:1-41

A very old song asks the question, 'Were you there when they crucified my Lord?'

Well – were you?

Many of you would quote what you may perhaps call your 'life verse': 'I have been crucified with Christ and I no longer live, but Christ lives in me' (Gal. 2:20) – 'I was there! It happened decisively once for all, long ago, but now, praise God! It's true for me.'

'Were you there when the Spirit came from heaven?', asks the old song.

It happened long ago at Pentecost, as decisive an event as Calvary; but 'you ought to be there' in your own history, it ought to be true of God's church today. When the church asked Peter what he was doing evangelising Italians, Peter, his knees knocking, reported what had happened to Cornelius's household: 'As I began to speak, the Holy Spirit came on them as he had come on us at the beginning' (Acts 11:15). They were there, when the Spirit came from heaven.

The details were different just as they are different for you and for me, but in essence what happened to the early believers at Pentecost should be ours in the church today.

Let us think first, then, about the significance of their

experience, as Luke, under the inspiration of God's Spirit, writes it up for us.

The significance of their experience (2:1-4)

He describes it first of all as the wind of the Spirit: 'Suddenly a sound like the blowing of a violent wind came from heaven ...' (2:2).

A violent wind

When I was a small boy my mother was addicted to the singer Kathleen Ferrier. I was brought up on:

> Blow the wind southerly, southerly, southerly.
> Blow bonny breeze, bring my lover to me.

But there's nothing of the bonny breeze about Acts 2. It sounded like a violent wind. That's important. It was like the sort of gales we live through regularly in Glasgow (though when it happens in the South, they call it a hurricane!). It was the sort of breeze that uproots my fence and messes up the garden; the sort of breeze that we used to have in the Philippines that once lifted the roof off my Filipino colleague's house and put it on top of the next door neighbour's roof. (He was not pleased to have no roof, and his neighbour was not pleased to have two). This violent wind is not a gentle waving among the fellowship, to ease us in the sweat of life.

Brothers and sisters, our God is not manageable. He cannot be dictated to by committees. As Jesus said to Nicodemus, the wind blows where it wants; and at Pentecost the wind of God – the creative wind of God that was there at Creation, the life-giving wind of God that made Ezekiel's valley of dried bones into a mighty army – the wind of God blew and the church took off.

It was windy in Jersey when I was there a couple of weeks ago. On the beach I saw a wee lad (well, a fairly muscular wee lad), sitting on a sort of go-cart, but he wasn't going anywhere. Then he took a massive kite and threw it into the wind. The wind caught it and I'm glad that I wasn't standing in his path, as he zoomed across that huge beach on the south coast of Jersey.

Are you going anywhere with God? Has the Spirit the wind in your sails – or are you just sitting there?

A fire that did not destroy

Consider the significance of their experience as the fire of the Spirit. I usually have to explain this when I'm talking to children, because in the childrens' books they picture the apostles almost as if they have turned into candles on a birthday cake. It wasn't like that. It was much more what Moses experienced in the wilderness, where he sees a bush on fire that was not burnt up. And it was just like that, that night in that early fellowship. You could see the presence of God upon people and yet they were not consumed.

Does that surprise you? It ought to, if you know anything about the sin in your life and in mine: that the holy awesome God –Holy! Holy! Holy! – should come in upon the fellowship, that the fire of God should be there and that we are not destroyed. This is because it's after Calvary, isn't it.

And yet this fire of God is the fire that John the Baptiser prophesied, when he said that he could get people wet, but that Jesus could change them on the inside and make them really clean. 'I baptise you with water. But one more powerful than I will come, the thongs of whose sandals I am not worthy to untie. He will baptise you with the Holy Spirit and with fire' (Luke 3:16).- And what was the fire to do? 'He will burn up the chaff with unquenchable fire' (verse 17).

And thus, says Luke, he preached the good news to them. Not the good news that God wants to give you a lovely warm glow, but the glorious news that he wants to burn up our awful rubbish. It's amazing! And these people were being dealt with by God. Not that they became a perfect church; anybody who thinks that the New Testament church was 'Wow!' in a way that was radically different from us, has not, it seems to me, ever read the epistles. But they were a church that was beginning to change by the fire of God, and it showed.

The filling of the Spirit

The third thing that we need to consider is in verse 4. 'All of them were filled with the Holy Spirit and began to speak in other tongues as the Spirit enabled them.'

We know, of course, that in Ephesians 5:18 we are commanded, 'Be filled with the Spirit.' It's commanded, so we know that it is possible for every Christian. But the fact that it's a command and not a nice little statement of fact means that, though it is commanded for every Christian, it is not inevitable that every Christian is filled with the Spirit. We may actually just be filled with self.

But they were to be filled with the Spirit. And the interesting thing is that Luke is not writing an abstract theological statement. He didn't say, 'I know they were filled with the Spirit because I read it in Berkhof', or whoever's systematic theology you might like to study. He reported, 'We know they were filled with the Spirit because it showed.' You could see it. What could you see? Well it showed in their behaviour, didn't it.

I have been absolutely gob-smacked at the extraordinary new world religion that has taken the world stage this year, in which people take weeks off work to worship and donate small fortunes to be in on it. This religion creates a tremendous sense of devotion, a proud commitment, a sense of belonging and passion; its followers sometimes yell, sometimes cry, sometimes kiss and hug one another and sometimes fall to the ground. I was told last week in a phone call from Brazil that in one small town 28 people active in this new worship had been admitted to hospital with major cardiac arrest.

I'm referring to the religion of the World Cup.

I remember a young man telling me, 'Even in Glasgow, when I go to the football I can cry when they miss a goal and I can kiss the bloke next to me when they win, and I don't even know his name. But when I go to church, if anybody gets passionate I'm really upset about it.'

Why do so many Christians want their faith to be so cheap and optional, so passionless, so unemotional, so manageable? Pentecost meant observable passion and excitement that led some unbelievers to say, 'Hey what's going on? We want to get in on this,' and made others say, 'Can you believe it? It's a load of drunks.' I think that those observers, visiting some of our churches, might have said that we've had an overdose of a sedative! But when the Spirit came, there was passion, brothers and sisters. It showed in the way they behaved, in that sheer delight in Jesus.

And it showed in what they said. They began to speak in other tongues (2:6, 8, 11). Each one heard them speaking about how wonderful this God of the violent wind, this God of fire who comes into the midst of His people, is. They heard it, they talked about it.

Some of us in the body of Christian belief praise the Lord in tongues, and we say that it is something that we use to praise the Lord; a private matter. 1 Corinthians 14, perhaps, speaks about that. But this is not what is being spoken about here. Here what we see is a group of people filled with the Spirit, who are longing to share. They are a people, as described by Peter in 1 Peter 2:9, who are made 'a chosen people ... that you may declare the praises of him who called you out of darkness into his marvellous light'. This is what Acts 1:8 is all about. The Spirit comes, and they've got to be witnesses. They've got to tell. And they are longing to share.

In 1 Corinthians 14, the tongues spoken of which people don't understand are a sign to unbelievers that they are outsiders. They say, 'What a crazy lot these are.' But here (especially in verse 6), the tongues of Pentecost were understood as a sign to unbelievers that they were included, and that God wanted to get through to them that day.

So Peter explains what is going on in terms of Joel's teaching – not about tongues, but about prophecy. For people were asking, 'How come these people say it in a way that makes sense to me?' He replies that they've experienced an outpouring of God's Spirit; God speaking to them, and them speaking for God. These people at Pentecost were no longer setting the scene, hoping that God would come on stage. God had come on stage. It was obvious. The people were filled; it showed in their behaviour, it showed in their speech.

The impact of their experience (2:5-13)

The first thing to notice is that the impact was:

An international impact

There's an extraordinary list supplied of all the different people groups: as though the Holy Spirit, according to one commentator, is checking who we've reached already. It's wonderful. When I look at some of these people I say, 'Wow, Lord! You really are burdened for them, even though it doesn't look terribly like it at the moment in today's world.' For many of these places are thoroughly resistant to the gospel today.

Yet, do you see? In those days they were all either ethnic Jews or foreign converts, which meant that they almost certainly spoke either Aramaic or Greek. So you could say, the Holy Spirit could actually have economised and just had sort of one translation. Indeed you can see that's the case because there's no mention of Peter having multiple translators. But, you see, people heard them declaring how wonderful God is in their own heart-languages, the languages in which they talked with the kids and with granny, in which lovers talked to one another, in which they chatted over the meal table. And in that language they heard it, and they knew it was for them. It's beautiful, isn't it!

It is the beginning of the outworking of Acts 1:8; first of all in Jerusalem, but the Holy Spirit says, 'I'm on the move. These folk are going home, and look where they are going.'

A prophetic impact

It's also important to notice that they heard God's truth spoken prophetically for them. That's what the prophecy of Joel, quoted in 2:17-21, is really all about. Peter says, 'You've seen the Spirit outpoured, you've heard their prophetic words; now you may call on the name of the Lord and be saved.'

What happened at Pentecost was not that they'd all learned one standard presentation of the gospel and were going to dump it on people, regardless of from wherever in the world they came. What they heard at Pentecost, if Joel's prophecy was fulfilled, was people speaking to them where they were at; so they heard it. Isn't that what we need to pray for, as we witness around the world?

I had a wonderful experience last year during a preaching visit to Japan. One of the pastors said to me, 'It was amazing! I noticed that as you moved from paragraph to paragraph in your talk, you were describing different people in the congregation.' At the end of the next week one of the Japanese brothers said, 'I want to tell you what this person and that person has done in this past week because of what you said last week.' It was absolutely incredible, because I speak about three words of Japanese. I had a translator who jumps like me – which is wonderful – but the thing for which we need to pray is that we won't just say things the way we have always seen them, but that there will be that fusion between the crummy ordinary people that we are, and the Holy Spirit of God.

We need to pray that communication will get through, that people will hear what they need to hear. This is what Luke is talking about. We hear them declaring – in the way we say it, in the way we want to hear it and need to hear it – the wonderful works of God. The Spirit came to glorify God through a prophetic ministry to the world.

A ministry grounded in Scripture

We need to understand that Peter's sermon wasn't a Keswick address. Keswick addresses take a lot of blood, soil, sweat and tears in preparation (you may not think I've got notes, but I have; they're hidden!). What Peter is doing is providing an off-the-cuff, ad hoc explanation because something has happened. He's quoting scriptures from memory. And it's very important to understand what's going on here in relation to the Scripture.

The biblical quality of their experience

Peter's Christian experience was earthed in scripture. Christian experience needs to be biblical experience. You can have plenty of other experiences; if they're not biblical, you'd better watch out. He has an experience of the Holy Spirit that day. He knows he's safe, he knows it's all right because it's just what Joel's written about. Prior to that, and later in his sermon, he talks about the experience that he and some of his mates had, they saw before their very eyes the risen Lord Jesus. Now – did they? It's amazing what people see when they want to. Are you sure they saw? Do you see how Peter knew that it was right? He knew that what he'd seen fitted with the prophecies of David in the Psalms. Did you notice that? It's tremendously important. Jesus was concerned, even when He appeared risen before the disciples, to explain to them, in all the Scriptures, that this had to be. They knew that it wasn't a seance; they weren't simply dependent on, 'Oh, I've had an experience; so it must be true.' Their experience was validated, showed to be spot-on and right, by the Scriptures.

Now that is immensely important. Our experiences are not insignificant, but Scripture is the standard by which all ideas are to be weighed. What you've seen may be true, but how you explain it needs to be biblical, in tune with God's words. So Peter's experience was earthed in Scripture.

A communication grounded in Scripture

But so was Peter's communication to unbelievers. Scan this sermon with me. The first thing Peter says is, 'You've seen Christians who've been extraordinarily changed and it has amazed you; now I'm going to explain to you, from the book of Joel in the Bible, what's actually happened.'

When I was a student at university, the college organist once said to me, 'I've been watching the Christians in college. It's quite extraordinary; they're very loving people, and they have an interesting sort of peace about them. They've got joy, they are very loving, they are very patient, kind and gentle; and they are very disciplined. Do you know why this is?' I said, 'You tell me.' He replied, 'It's because of the very strong organisation of the Christian Union.' I opened my Bible to Galatians 5, saying, 'Well, actually the Bible explains it as what happens when the Holy Spirit starts working in people's lives. It is what's called the fruit of the Holy Spirit.' And he began to wake up.

That's what Peter's doing here. 'You've seen it; now, let me explain it to as the Bible does.' It's very important, he says (cf verse 14), for the Bible's explanation of what's happening concludes with 'Everyone who calls on the name of the Lord will be saved' (verse 21).

So you've got to that bit of the Bible. Now what? Well, you've got a problem. Which lord are you going to call on? Can you call on any lord? People will say to you, 'You believe in God your way and I believe God in my way.' And you wonder: What God do you believe in? 'Oh well, so long as you believe in a god, it's all right, isn't it? As long as you call on a lord, it's OK, as long as you've got faith ...' But Peter's not going to get sold on this one. He begins to talk to them about Jesus, so that they know which Lord they've got to call upon. And when he talks about Jesus, do you notice what he does? He starts by telling them the things about Jesus that they know already. 'You know that Jesus did these absolutely wow! things, because God was with him' (verse 22). 'And you know that He was murdered because you did it.'

Next he says. 'Let me take you further.' Now he brings them to what they don't know. He tells them that God raised Him from the dead, because death couldn't hold on to Jesus. Now that's *really* interesting. He's claiming now that the cross was not an accident, but was God's plan. The resurrection had to happen.

Of course the people might turn to Peter and say, 'But that's just your opinion.' So back he goes to the Bible again. 'Look, it's not just my idea. You can see it in Psalm 16 and you can see it in Psalm 110' (verse 31 ff). He shows them that their own eyes have seen what Scripture promised: verse 33: 'Exalted to the right hand of God, he has received from the Father the promised Holy Spirit and has poured out what you now see and hear.' Now that's important, isn't it? He's talking to unbelievers; 'There's this bit in the Bible, and now you've actually seen it work.' Can you do that with unbelievers in some areas? You can, you know.

He quotes Psalm 110: 'The Lord says to my Lord: "Sit at my right hand until I make your enemies a footstool for your feet"' (verse 34). What's Peter doing here? He is using the Scriptures to make his listeners understand that this discussion about Jesus is not to be filed away in some mental library of interesting thoughts about a Jewish Messiah. This scripture says that if you are an enemy of Jesus, you're in big trouble. And it is part of the strategy to bring them to conviction and to commitment.

Peter's use of the Bible

Let me summarise what I have tried to say about the use of the Bible here. First, in this passage we see that Scripture explains what his listeners have experienced but don't understand.

The Scriptures explain what his listeners saw. They experienced the extraordinary crowd praising the Lord, but they didn't understand. He said, 'Let me explain.'

I think that's tremendously important. Often unbelievers say to you, 'I don't understand this.' A Chinese professor said to me a couple of years ago, 'I've been trying to find out; is it actually possible to know anything for certain about God?' I turned to John 1:18. 'No one has ever seen God.' He said, 'Yes that's right.' We went through other bits of John: 'Yes that's right ... Yes, that's right ...' He was ready. He had experienced all sorts of things, and now I was able to take him to the Bible and explain why he had experienced them. The Bible knew about Professor Wong.

And that's what's happening here. The Scripture explains what the listener saw. Secondly,

The Scriptures confirm what the disciples claimed. They claimed to have seen the risen Christ. And the scriptures from the Psalms showed it had to happen. And thirdly,

The Scriptures convict of the need to get right. Again, very important. The scripture in verse 21, 'And everyone who calls on the name of the Lord ...' invited them to salvation. The scripture in verse 35, '" ... until I make your enemies a footstool for your feet ..."' warned of the consequences of being on the wrong side of Jesus. Under the Spirit's leading Peter knew where people were at, and what scriptures would make sense of it. We need to understand this, brothers and sisters. The Spirit of God is not just given to make you personally wonderful. The Spirit of God is also given so that our bold proclamation of the gospel of Jesus around the world will be properly contextualised and carefully biblical. This book is to make it make sense to people, because it is the Spirit's book.

How the blessing was meant to grow

Thus we end. We need to consider, at the end of Peter's sermon, how the blessing was meant to grow. For in verse 39 Peter did not say, 'Now, if you open your heart to the Lord Jesus, everything will be right for you. You will have forgiveness, and the Holy Spirit will come to you, and that'll be great.'

Even in his evangelistic preaching, Peter was concerned for that Holy Spirit mobilisation to the ends of the earth. So he says, 'I want you to come to the Lord. I want you to repent, to be baptised as somebody belonging to Father Son and Holy Spirit. I want you to submit to learn, I want you to experience the Holy Spirit. But it's not just for you; it's for your kids. It's not just for you, it's for those who are far off.'

Perhaps some of the people would say, 'I'm not interested in the far off, I'm interested in getting blessing for me.' But if you're going to get blessing from God, you're going to get it in line with what God wants. If you're going to become passionate for God, you're going to be passionate for what God is passionate about – and God is passionate that this Holy Spirit experience, that comes as the result of what Jesus did on Calvary, should reach down the generations and far away.

Were you there when the Spirit came?
Were you? Are you filled?

Then, keep singing it; because what has become your story is meant to become the story of many others too.

'A Word Which Divides'

by Mr Tom Bathgate

Acts 4-5

You know, if the book of Acts were a film, I would have called it 'Pentecost Productions'. Doctor Luke is a brilliant director, and it seems to me that he is without doubt filming not dry, dead, boring truth, but truth, or theology, on fire. According to Acts 1:8, he's filming a theology of people on fire. He takes his theme from Jesus' words, 'You will be my witnesses.' Luke picks up his camera and sets about filming God in action through people, because God's plans *are* people.

Acts 1:8 goes further. Jesus adds, 'You will receive power.' And there are things happening in the Acts of the Apostles that defy human minds to understand and human ability to perform. Luke takes his camera and says, 'There's something here about heaven come down to earth. These people are His plans, and they have a power that is beyond themselves. There is wisdom here that is from above, a righteousness that has come from another world. And there's a ministry of compassion, of healing the sick, and of power, in deliverance from demons, that we haven't seen on earth before.' So he's filming a theology of power as well as a theology of people.

But he's also filming a theology of progress. For Jesus is saying that these people, this power and this truth, are going to start in Jerusalem and go on to Judea, to Samaria and eventually to

Edinburgh in Scotland – the uttermost parts of the earth! You can see it, because God is on the march and God is on the move. He's actually making progress. And, ladies and gentlemen, it's the responsibility of every generation among men under heaven to see the kingdom of God constantly advancing.

Faithfulness to Jesus Christ as Lord is not about maintaining where we're at. It's about seeing the kingdom of God advance, through every nation and every ethnic people group, throughout the history of the world. So Luke presents a theology of people, a theology of power, a theology of progress, and – above all – a theology of Pentecost.

Jesus said, 'You will be baptised with the Holy Spirit.' And Luke is watching what's happening. I've a friend who says that the difference between the Acts of the Apostles and the Gospels is that in Acts, Jesus Christ has changed bodies. He's gone from a physical, visible body, back to heaven. He's sent the Holy Spirit, and He's now inhabiting His new body on earth, the church that is ruled by His royal presence and is meant to be proclaiming His royal message: that the kingdom of God has come, is coming and will come.

And Luke begins to film the repercussions.

The relationships that the Holy Spirit creates

'All the believers were one in heart and mind. No-one claimed that any of his possessions was his own, but they shared everything they had' (4:32). What a quality of relationship! It's very important not to minimise or trivialise it. It is more than polite British culture, more than just 'getting on with' people quite different from you in temperament and background. The New Testament word is *koinonia* – 'fellowship'. Someone has pointed out that before *koinonia* became a religious word it had a secular background, and initially meant 'siamese twin'. A union between two little creatures, sharing the same blood stream: fellowship. It was lifted out of that setting, brought into the Christian church and called 'fellowship'. And that's what we're looking at.

Isn't it interesting that, when you are looking at that kind of fellowship, verse 33 then says, 'With great power the apostles continued to testify to the resurrection of the Lord Jesus, and much grace was with them all.' Perhaps it was because they related with such quality that they could serve with such power; perhaps there's something here that's very important; perhaps Luke is trying to show us that those could relate in the love of Jesus, served in the power of God.

Ananias and Sapphira

The camera then moves on to a particular person and a remarkable incident. The trailer for this sobering incident with Ananias and Sapphira is a wonderful person called Barnabas. 'Joseph, a Levite from Cyprus, whom the apostles called Barnabas (which means Son of Encouragement), sold a field he owned and brought the money and put it at the apostles' feet. Now a man named Ananias, together with his wife Sapphira, also sold a piece of property' (4:36-5:1).

A stunning honesty

I think it's remarkably honest that the story about Ananias and Sapphira gets into this history. The camera isn't directed elsewhere. This is an unpleasant, an unattractive story, neither glossed over nor hidden under the carpet. John Stott says that 'Luke did not suppress the sordid episode.' It is remarkable, stunning honesty and a stark reminder of the stubbornness and selfishness that fills our hearts. It's a stubborn reminder that the church of Jesus Christ may be pardoned but it isn't perfect. John Stott says that this story throws light on the interior life of the first Spirit-filled community. It was not all romance and righteousness. I don't think that we are ever to become complacent because we are not perfect, but we shouldn't be overwhelmed when we discover it.

If you had been Ananias or Sapphira, would you have wanted to be mentioned in the Bible like this? No way. If you are introduced to someone, do you want them to be told your bad points, or do you want to be introduced presented with your better side showing? Just as we sometimes prefer to be photogrpahed from our better side: 'Not with my glasses on! No, no, no!', or 'Oh, you might have told me! I'd have got my hair done.' Why are we like that? Because we always want to present the best image. So how would you feel if you were Sapphira or Ananias and someone bumped into you in a coffee shop in heaven: 'Oh, you're the ones that died in Acts 5!' What a thought.

What does that stunning honesty tell you? It tells you something very simple but very powerful that none of us must never forget. You cannot pull the wool over God's eyes. It's the height of ignorance about God and the height of foolishness as a human being, to think that anyone on the face of the earth can hide from God. The Bible teaches that 'all things are naked and opened unto the eyes of him with whom we have to do' (Heb 4:13). A sobering thought. But think about the honesty that's here, and how God is living with His gaze upon our lives.

A Government Health Warning

The story of Ananias and Sapphira, and a cigarette packet, have something in common. Both of them carry a Government Health Warning. The difference is that one is about an earthly government and the other is about a government called the Kingdom of God. There are a number of elements in the warning that Acts 5:1-11 carries.

But before I mention them – what do you do with warnings? In the company where I work a few people smoke. One day I decided to clean the smoking room out and paint it up. The smokers were absolutely stunned. 'But you don't smoke.' I replied, 'I know. I just wanted you to know that as you make yourself more and more unwell you are doing it in comfortable surroundings.' They say that when you go into business, your first hundred days counts. Well, that's how I started; in the smoking room. One day I said to one of the members of staff there, 'Have you read the packet?' She said, 'Which packet?' 'The cigarette packet.' She said, 'Why?' I said, 'Because there's a warning on it.' 'Oh! That. Oh yes, I've read that.' I'm not knocking her or mocking her. I'm using her as an illustration. You can be incredibly casual about warnings. This story, ladies and gentlemen, carries an awesome Government Health Warning; yet we can do with it what a lot of people do about the warning on the cigarette packet. You can say, 'Oh – that! I've read that.'

In this story I believe that there is *a warning about Christian marriage*. There are only two married couples highlighted in this book, and this is one of them, so perhaps there's a warning here about marriages where something is kept back from God; a warning, perhaps, about the quality, depth of devotion and length of devotion in the quality of Christian marriage. Fundamentally what matters about one's faith is not the duration of it but the depth of it, and whether or not I am going on believing now.

Maybe we shouldn't be surprised that this story carries a warning. In the book of Genesis we find that the very first marriage was profoundly and successfully tempted to deceive God and live for self. Perhaps the serpent has learned that if the human race could be derailed by a couple deciding to disobey, then so may the Christian church be derailed by a couple deciding to hold back something from God. It may be that something of the strategy of the Evil One is being thrown up in this story, as a warning to those of us who are married or are contemplating marriage; that it does matter, the depth of our devotion to Jesus: not yesterday, but now.

And presumably Ananias and Sapphira should have been encouraging each other to be following Jesus to full capacity, and not cutting back to cut-price fellowship. Here was a couple who had somehow managed to encourage each other to shallow discipleship.

How about you? How about me? Are we an encourager to our partner or potential partner, to be going on, going on, following Christ? A man in Northern Ireland wrote his own version of 'Amazing Grace'. It didn't take long to write; it was just two words. Sung to the tune of 'Amazing Grace', it was, 'Go on, go on, go on, go on, go on, go on ...' Each partner in Christian marriage should be saying to the other, 'Whatever happens, go on, go on, go on, go on.'

What are we going to do with this warning about Christian marriage?

A warning about the Holy Spirit

You can see another warning in, for example, verse 3: 'Then Peter said, "Ananias, how is it that Satan has so filled your heart that you have lied to the Holy Spirit ...?"'

This story underlines the fact that the Holy Spirit is a person. It took me the first six years of my Christian experience to discover that God did not send Jesus Christ to this world simply to take me off the road to destruction and put me on the road to construction. In fact He sent Jesus to the cross to bring God out of Heaven and inhabit my humanity with His presence. I thought Christianity was all about heading towards heaven, when in actual fact God's purpose was getting Himself out of heaven into my humanity and depositing His life and His presence in me, through the inhabiting gift of the Holy Spirit who comes to live and bring the Jesus-life into our humanity. Thus His character and His conduct are formed in our humanity.

And this story emphasises, the Holy Spirit has been lied to. You can't lie to a thing. The Holy Spirit isn't an 'it', the Holy Spirit is a person – beautiful, winsome, tender, awesome, holy. And this story reminds us that He's a person, that He can be tested. It reminds us that He is God who when He's at work produces a deep consciousness of God's holiness and a deep awareness, as a result, of our own sinfulness. It appears that He wants nothing to do with evil, but only everything to do with producing the moral beauty of Jesus in our character and in our decisions and priorities. And it's easy to forget. It's easy to neglect the fact that the Holy Spirit can be tested and lied to. In fact other New Testament passages show us that the Holy Spirit can be wounded, He can be grieved, He can be received and His activity can be quenched. In Thessalonians we're told, 'Do not put out the Spirit's fire.' (1 Thess. 5:19). It's very easy to pour buckets of water over the Spirit's fire.

A warning about attitudes

When I moved from full-time Christian ministry into the business in 1993, I found the change dramatic – extremely demanding and very stretching, and I felt extremely vulnerable, inadequate and inappropriate. I discovered a huge amount about myself. It was the worst year of our marriage, it was the worst year of my relational style, it was the worst year of attitudes for me in a very long time. I knew something was wrong when one day I went to discipline my little boy and instead of telling him off I pushed him by the scruff of the neck against the wall. You don't feel smart when at night you take a moment to pray and you ask the big question: 'Holy Spirit, how have I wounded You today? How have I grieved You, how have I resisted Your holy presence?'

A warning about saying the wrong word

I have a natural gift for saying the wrong word at the right time. It's a very special gift. Very close behind comes the gift of regret.

1993 was the year when I said and did things that I wish I never ever had. Sometimes they dog my steps. But one day, I realised that I needed to get back into fellowship with the Holy Spirit, and I sat down on my own and I asked the Lord, 'How have I wounded, bruised, damaged the Holy Spirit and His function, His fellowship in me?' I wrote down thirty-five things.

Those thirty-five things don't go away immediately. You can face them immediately and confess them. You can change your mind about them and repent of them. But some of them are done and finished, some of them are done and still affecting you, and some of them go on getting repaired because of the damage you did. But the good thing was the joy that came when I felt, 'I've begun again. I may have a bigger L-plate on my back. I may have had to face up to some home truths. I may have had to sit down with my children and say I'm sorry and ask how I can change and what I should do to be different here. Or sit down with my wife and say, 'What should I do here?'

And it's easy to forget that the Holy Spirit is a person, and He has come to bring into our humanity the gift of the presence of Jesus Christ, a companion God, a God who inhabits our humanity. And it's easy to neglect and easy to forget that we should be cultivating fellowship with the Holy One who inhabits our humanity. Sometimes we need to face up to the reality of who we are and where we are at, and sit down and say in the quietness of a room exclusively with God, and say, 'Holy Spirit, how have I grieved You, resisted You, wounded You? How have I taken buckets of rebellion, self-indulgence, laziness, arrogance, lack of kindness, lack of courtesy, unbelief, wasted time – How have I almost extinguished the Spirit's fire?'

Ananias and Sapphira were involved with the work of the Holy Spirit, but were careless about God's holiness. How do we respond to that warning? Do we say, 'Oh I've read that, heard that, been there, done that, got the tee-shirt, seen the video – I know the Holy Spirit's a person.'

But do we?

A warning about hypocrisy

Both Ananias and Barnabas sold property; both of them brought the proceeds to the apostles. Good. The difference was that

Barnabas brought all of the sale money, while Ananias brought only a proportion of it. There's nothing actually wrong with holding some of the proceeds, because Peter said the property was theirs both before and after the sale. They are under no obligation to sell, they are under no obligation to distribute the proceeds. However, from what Peter says, it appears that both Ananias and Sapphira had agreed to sell the property, pretend that they had given all, and keep back some. So they were guilty of dishonesty and deceit and, in a sense, embezzlement.

It's interesting, however, that it is the hypocrisy that Peter concentrates on. It wasn't their honesty but their integrity that was under scrutiny; they brought only a part but pretended to give the whole. In the Gospels Jesus is very severe on hypocrisy, especially among a believing community – presumably because He Himself was aware of how destructive hypocrisy can be.

Hypocrisy is the desire to appear what you are not. It could mean claiming skills that you don't have; I have interviewed a remarkable number of people for jobs who talk a better game than they play. It could mean implying that your motives are higher than they actually are. It could mean conveying a Godliness that just isn't true. It could mean presenting a sincerity that just isn't real, it's a surface: all that 'Oh praise the Lord, praise the Lord ... How are you today? ... Isn't God good!' could be portraying a knowledge that's far from the truth, a willingness that falls far short of what real commitment is. If it were put to the test it wouldn't stand.

It's interesting, is it not, that this young church will not only undergo persecution from the outside but also hypocrisy from the inside. And both will do severe damage to its cause and its reputation. Something very attractive, I think, has been happening in the life of Barnabas and his service to Christ. It's probably been affecting a number of people in the church. Perhaps Ananias and Sapphira wanted to attract that kind of attention and have that kind of influence, so they pretended that what was true of him was true of them.

Of course, as Peter pointed out, the money wasn't the vital thing. The real point was the mask they were wearing. They were pretending to a commitment, a sacrifice, a discipleship that really wasn't real and about which they probably knew nothing. John

Stott, in his book 'The Message of Acts', says:

> They were not so much misers as thieves and above all
> liars. They wanted the credit and the prestige for
> sacrificial generosity without the inconvenience of it. So
> in order to gain a reputation to which they had no right
> they told a brazen lie. Their motive in giving was not to
> relieve the poor but to fatten their own ego.

What John Stott is describing is a serious sickness. To be more
concerned about the reputation they were going to have, than what
was true and real, is a dangerous condition I would suggest, to be
in. And God the Holy Spirit rooted the presence of hypocrisy out.
Why is that? Because hypocrisy dies in the presence of God.

Many of you will know, I am sure, that the Greek word for
'actor' is the word from which we get 'hypocrite'. Imagine you are
watching a bunch of Greek actors, all wearing masks, on stage. At
the end of the play you all burst into rapturous applause.
'Wonderful hypocrites! Excellent hypocrites! Brilliant, they're the
best hypocrites we've seen in years!' Imagine that. And then they
come off stage and become unmasked and become real people
again, and you expect to meet the real person. You don't expect to
meet the mask and the character behind the mask.

You see there are two things going on here in the early church
that are both remarkable, and from my perspective unnerving. On
the one hand you've got the Almighty pouring out massive and
rich blessings on them all; on the other, you've got the same
Almighty moving in judgement to clean up and purify His church.
As I said when I came to the speakers' prayer and preparation day,
'I've been studying Isaiah 6 on one hand and Acts 5 on the other,
and I've discovered from both that I'm very fortunate to be alive
today.'

I suppose all of us must feel the power of this story. I would
suggest (and please don't think I'm being rude, but I believe it has
to be said) it's probably a miracle that any of us are still alive. And
every person sitting here is a walking, talking miracle when you
read this story. All of us, I would suggest, have to rush with
incredible haste to Psalm 130:1-4. 'Out of the depths I cry to you,
O LORD; O Lord, hear my voice. Let your ears be attentive to my

cry for mercy. If you, O LORD, kept a record of sins, O Lord, who could stand? But with you there is forgiveness; therefore you are feared.'

If there is an area that makes us feel ashamed or concerns us, or that we are so glad that nobody knows about, it's time to bring that to God. It's time to confess, to repent, to determine before Him that with the help, presence and power of the Holy Spirit, we will forsake it, turn from it and walk down the everlasting way.

You see, repentance is the root to freedom. It's not a stick to break your back, it's a springboard into the grace of God. As a little boy I misunderstood what repentance meant, for I thought it was going to lead me into drudgery and misery. So it might, for a little while. But the ultimate end of repentance is that it is the springboard from which you dive into the grace, the mercy, the extravagant, inexhaustible, inextinguishable, unending, never-dying love of God. So repentance is the royal route to freedom.

And the point at which we are prepared to repent, you'll discover, is the last bit of the diving board: 'Boing-g-g-g-g!' – then, into the grace of God.

Word and Spirit

by Rev Hugh Palmer

Acts 8

I've had the privilege of looking at the earliest minutes of the Jerusalem Keswick World View Committee, which I am almost sure are contemporary with the early part of Acts 1. That committee set the agenda for future meetings and produced a mission statement It ran like this: 'You will receive power when the Holy Spirit comes on you; and you will be my witnesses in Jerusalem, and in all Judea and Samaria, and to the ends of the earth.'

The second meeting must have taken place somewhere near the end of Acts 2. Apologies of absence were given; one Jesus of Nazareth was no longer with them. A welcome was extended to the Holy Spirit, and they minuted the founding of the International Friends of Jerusalem Keswick World View. Many family, friends and tourists who had been visiting from abroad had joined the Christian community briefly and then seemed to have returned home. Someone actually even prepared an amendment to the mission statement, and wondered whether they couldn't live with 'You'll receive power when the Holy Spirit comes on you, and others will be My witness to the ends of the earth.' But that was held over for the next meeting.

That meeting probably came at the end of Acts 4. The church

was gathered together for a prayer meeting, and rather than call them out again they had a committee meeting afterwards. The minutes record that the original mission statement was confirmed, and that they gave great thanks for the witness in Jerusalem.

Acts 5 saw one or two disturbances in the church. A couple of members left rather abruptly. Fortunately neither were on this particular committee, but they had another meeting just to check out where they were going. Once again they confirmed the mission statement and gave great thanks for the witness going on in Jerusalem.

The next meeting is somewhere in Acts 6, I think, because the restructured church meets at the beginning of that chapter and re-delegates responsibilities. The minutes of that meeting read very predictably, as minutes do: the mission statement was re-confirmed and they gave great thanks for the witness that was going on in Jerusalem.

The messengers who didn't want the job (8:1-8)

In Acts 8, there was no committee meeting. All the members had left. 'On that day a great persecution broke out against the church at Jerusalem, and all except the apostles were scattered throughout Judea and Samaria' (8:1).

The first people we encounter in Acts 8 are the messengers who didn't want the job. Although they'd been meeting continually there is no evidence that missionary society had been formed. They didn't so much go out as were kicked out.

They discovered early on a principle that recurs in the book of Acts: that we have a God who sometimes closes doors in order to open doors. These are messengers who didn't want the job but found they'd got it. God even uses persecution to further His mission; the martyrdom of Stephen led to great persecution and a great scattering. As Dick Dowsett has told us, the pluses of the martyrdom were that Jesus gained as His name was glorified, Stephen gained, Saul gained, and, he could have added but kindly didn't pinch my talk, Judea and Samaria gained. What was not begun, because of the slowness of the Christians, was achieved at a single stroke by their enemies. There's the power of God for you.

It seems as easy for God to use enemies as friends. Have you ever thought how frustrating it must be for Satan, as time and again so many of his best moves become spectacular own-goals? That's what happened. 'Godly men buried Stephen and mourned deeply for him. But Saul began to destroy the church. Going from house to house he dragged off men and women and put them in prison' (8:2-3). It wasn't a light and easy move. But 'Those who had been scattered preached the word wherever they went. Philip went down to a city in Samaria and proclaimed the Christ there.' God closed a door, in order to open doors.

He has worked like that down the centuries. John Wesley preached in London and was told by the church warden, 'Sir, you may preach here no longer.' It was only because he couldn't preach in the churches that he finally swallowed all his pride and social inhibitions and started preaching in the open air. And when Wesley and Whitefield preached in the open air, thousands and thousands came to hear them.

The story of the missionaries driven out of China by the Communist regime in 1949 is well known. Forty percent of them were redeployed within four years in South East Asia and Japan. The China Inland Mission became the Overseas Missionary Fellowship, and the national church in the last forty years has multiplied by a very large factor.

On a smaller scale, remember the riot in Strangeways Prison. It began in the chapel and seemed to close down a remarkable gospel work. It was devastating – except for the fact that when the prisoners were transferred, they were moved to other prisons, taking the gospel with them.

Individuals, too: a friend of mine, a banker in the City, was made redundant. He began to help others who had been made redundant, to help them how to handle finances and attitudes. I know two or three people who came to Christ because of that initiative. It seemed a devastating blow to him; a door had been closed, but God was actually opening other doors.

It is all very well holding World View meetings, but sometimes we are not very good at actually having a world view. Don't worry; God's got hold of it. 'Those who had been scattered preached the word wherever they went.' Do notice, by the way, that the only group of people who weren't scattered and doing this particular job of preaching the word was the big-wigs, the leaders, the apostles. It was the ordinary Christian men and women who did it; they didn't run off and hide, or keep a prudent silence. They preached the word wherever they went. I don't know whether they got up on soap boxes, or whether they just responded when people asked, 'What are you doing here, why are you so far from home?' But they preached the word.

'Philip went down to ... Samaria and proclaimed the Christ there ...' (cf 8:4-8). The word is going out, but these are the messengers who didn't want the job. 'When the crowds heard Philip and saw the miraculous signs he did, they all paid close attention to what he said. With shrieks, evil spirits came out of many, and many paralytics and cripples were healed. So there was great joy in that city.'

The messenger who didn't have the heart for the job (8:9-25)

When Philip went to Samaria he preached Christ. Samaria had a history of unorthodox worship. The Samaritans had broken from Jerusalem in the civil war of the tenth century BC. They had even built their own temple and had rejected most of the Old Testament scriptures beyond the first five books. As so often happens, when you start turning your back on God it doesn't lead to believe in nothing, it leads to believing in anything.

Simon the Sorcerer practises what seems to be a mixture of magic and spiritism. He gave himself out to be someone great, and people swallowed it. He's a big figure who amazed all the people of Samaria (8:11). He would have been on GMTV if they'd had it. Don't underestimate him, I don't think we should think of Simon as a sort of Paul Daniels or David Copperfield. He wasn't an illusionist. The New Testament is very clear that there are supernatural powers at work in this universe other than God. They are powers of evil – which is why we need to be careful about the pragmatic argument that if it works and it's miraculous it must be from God. We've got to get real about the genuine force of such powers. And even if it were true that they are more obvious where the gospel hasn't taken hold, and for that reason we hear missionaries in foreign countries speak most often about them, I would expect more and more signs in this country to be appearing as the gospel grip recedes.

But the stunning thing is – even Simon believes: 'Simon himself believed and was baptised' (verse 12). I imagine when most us were converted it didn't cause much of a ripple around the community. There may have been one or two eyebrows raised, but I guess none of us were big enough figures to create that kind of a stir. Simon must have been. When the news got out that he had become a Christian, the *Sun* would have headlined it: 'Sorcerer Saved'. The *Mirror* would have labelled it an exclusive:

> Conjurer Converted! Simon, AKA the great power, aged 43 astonished the country yesterday as he got caught up in the revival sweeping through Samaria, confessing that Jesus was even greater than himself. 'I'm hooked,' he declared at his baptism. 'What this Messiah can do is astonishing.'

When Martin Lloyd-Jones was a young preacher in Wales a spiritist who lived near the chapel was intrigued by the crowds going there Sunday after Sunday. She went along herself, and her life was turned round. She later said to the Doctor, 'When I came to your meetings, I realised there was a supernatural power at work in your meetings, just as in mine. The big difference was that the power at work in your meeting was a clean power.'

The sense of excitement and renewal in Samaria must have been remarkable, as Philip preached, people turned to Jesus, and even Simon was converted.

> When the apostles in Jerusalem heard that Samaria had accepted the word of God, they sent Peter and John to them. When they arrived, they prayed for them that they might receive the Holy Spirit, because the Holy Spirit had not yet come upon any of them; they had simply been baptised into the name of the Lord Jesus. Then Peter and John placed their hands on them, and they received the Holy Spirit. (8:14-17)

Listen to where God is leading us tonight.

> When Simon saw that the Spirit was given at the laying on of the apostles' hands' – it's clear that as these apostles

came and laid hands on the new converts, the Spirit was given in some visible, obvious way – 'he offered them money and said, "Give me also this ability so that everyone on whom I lay my hands may receive the Holy Spirit. Peter answered: "May your money perish with you, because you thought you could buy the gift of God with money! You have no part or share in this ministry, because your heart is not right before God. Repent of this wickedness and pray to the Lord. Perhaps he will forgive you for having such a thought in your heart. For I see that you are full of bitterness and captive to sin." Then Simon answered, "Pray to the Lord for me so that nothing you have said may happen to me."' (8:14-24)

I love the integrity of the Bible. Here is their star convert; he's a dud; and they've got the honesty to come clean about it. Here is the messenger who did not have the heart for the job. It's not that he's not keen to do it; he was so keen, he was prepared to pay good money to be able to do it. But he had completely missed the point 'Give me this ability so that everyone on whom I lay my hands on may receive the Holy Spirit.' He wanted power, and for that, his name has gone down in history. The purchase of ecclesiastical office by money is today known as 'simony'. Here's the man who had to be at the centre of everything. It was once said of a German Kaiser that he always had to be the centre of everything. If it was a baptism he wanted to be the baby, if a wedding he wanted to be the bride, if a funeral he wanted to be the corpse. Simon is a bit like that.

Often, when you see a Christian life collapse, you see that the seeds have been there for a long time. Some tragic collapses look very dramatic, but again and again I find that when we know the story, we see that the seeds have been coming. You say, what kind of a man was he? Well look back to verse 9. He was the sort of man who boasted he was someone great. And they called him the Great Power. What a contrast to Philip, because what did he preach? Verse 12 - the good news of the kingdom of God and the name of Jesus Christ. But nothing's changed for Simon. Why does he want the ministry? So that he's the one with the power and he can give it to someone else, so that he stays centre stage. It turns out actually he's not hooked on Jesus, he's just hooked on better magic. Verse 13, 'He followed Philip everywhere, astonished by the great signs and miracles he saw.'

But notice in verse 6, we are told of Philip's preaching in Samaria: 'When the crowds heard Philip and saw the miraculous signs he did, they all paid close attention to what he said.' Simon was only after the power. By verse 19 it's clear that there's no repentance, no turn-around, nothing that's put him out of the centre.

It's a dangerous dream to have, to dream dreams of being on the Keswick platform. Friends, you might be very zealous to follow Christ, but if you want to be the great missionary, evangelist, healer or teacher, listen to Simon, the messenger who did not have the heart for the job.

'To hell with you and your money,' is how J.B. Philips translates verse 20. It is very strong language from Peter. It's much worse than a mere rebuke for a bad error of judgement. 'Repent of your wickedness!' I don't think verse 24 is much of a repentance. It simply says, 'I want to avoid trouble'.

The messenger God used for the job

But the story ends on a different note. The human figure at the heart of Acts 8 is of course Philip; who, like Stephen, was a man full of the Spirit and wisdom, chosen at first to serve at tables. He was just a glorified waiter on a soup run. But God has a way of taking people whose ministry starts humble. The waiter becomes an evangelist. And he is at the centre of this extraordinary revival in Samaria.

Verse 26: 'Now an angel of the Lord said to Philip, "Go south to the road – the desert road – that goes down from Jerusalem to Gaza."' I do wish God would listen to us ... His strategic planning is fairly faulty at times! Does He not realise what a good job Philip is doing in Samaria? The crowds are flocking to the tent night after night, the city's being turned upside-down. And – just when Peter and John the apostles had left, notice – God seems to pull the plug. Philip's whisked out of Samaria on a road in the middle of nowhere.

But Philip is the man God used because he was the man who obeyed God (verse 27). There was a cabinet minister, the Ethiopian

Chancellor of the Exchequer, apparently taking time out announcing his spending revue, to go to Jerusalem to worship. It looks as if he browsed through the airport shop on the way home looking for something on which to spend his last Jewish shekels. He'd got his duty-free, ignored the latest Dick Francis and the steamy pot-boilers, and he was intrigued by a scroll from Isaiah. Fortunately, even going club class by chariot is a bit like going by ox cart so he has plenty of time on the road to settle back and read the scroll.

We Christians with the benefit of hindsight are tempted at this point to think, 'Job done: he's got it, the answer is there in his hands. He's even got Isaiah 53 in his hands – he can't miss!' So it's rather shattering to read on. Philip runs up to the chariot, hears the man reading Isaiah the prophet aloud, does that most un-British of all things: he speaks to someone else when they're travelling. 'Do you understand what you are reading?'

'How can I,' says the other, 'unless someone explains it to me?'

This man has the key scriptures in front of him and he's reading them. But he asked for them to be explained. Friends, let's get clear. The God who's revealed Himself to us and longs for His gospel to be revealed to the whole world hasn't not only given the gift of His Scriptures to reveal Himself, but the gift of teachers to explain it. The Bible on its own can be a closed book. We need to face this – because God has faced it. If He hadn't, He could have left the Jerusalem church in Jerusalem and zapped directly Judea, Samaria and the ends of the earth. Much quicker!

But He hasn't just led the Ethiopian to the Bible, He's led a teacher to the Ethiopian. And what a teacher!

Note that when Philip is driven out of Jerusalem as they preached the word around Judea, Philip is the one who'll go to Samaria, the one who'll where any self-respecting Jew would feel most sensitive – any self-respecting Jew would believe there were good grounds for looking down on that people and avoiding them.

And now we find him with the Ethiopian – the wrong colour (black), the wrong class (a dignitary). You could imagine Philip wanting to avoid him for the opposite reasons he might have avoided the Samaritans. Anyway, there was always the Covenant: by Old Testament law eunuchs were excluded from God's Covenant people. A perfectly good reason for not talking to them!

It's fascinating to speculate just how far that scroll stretched. How many more miles would it have been before the Ethiopian had come to Isaiah 56, and read some very strange and thrilling words:

> Let no foreigner who has joined himself to the LORD say, 'The Lord will surely exclude me from his people.' And let not any eunuch complain, 'I am only a dry tree.' For this is what the LORD says: 'To the eunuchs who keep my Sabbaths, who choose what pleases me and hold fast to my covenant – to them ... I will give them an everlasting name that will not be cut off. And foreigners who bind themselves to the LORD to serve him ... these I will bring to my holy mountain and give them joy in my house of prayer.' (Isa. 56:3-7)

Before he could read it he experienced it. The Messiah had come. That wonderful promise was true, and true for him. He invited Philip to come up and sit with him – Philip, the man with the clues, next to the Ethiopian, the man humble enough to listen to a teacher who could open the book up for him.

There are people searching for God who find the Bible a closed book. If you are one, are you humble enough to let someone open the book up for you and be your teacher? It doesn't have to be a Reverend in a pulpit. Any Christian can be your teacher. When I first came to Christ it was a fellow student who was my teacher. He grounded me in the gospel. I'll be eternally grateful to him. The great majority of you to whom I'm speaking are Christians: are you ready to teach friends to whom God is giving a hunger for Himself? Will we be teachers?

The eunuch was mentioned in Isaiah 53 and couldn't get the hang of it. Philip started with that very passage and told him the good news about Jesus. Do you think you could pull that off? It's a pretty good gift, finding someone wanting to know what it's all about. I know we tremble a little when we discover it's the Old Testament, but there wasn't much choice then. But if it is the Old Testament, do you think you could start from Isaiah 53? If we can't, there aren't many other passages in the Old Testament we've got a lot of chance with? So let's mug up Isaiah 53, that will be a start!

The Old Testament will stay a closed book without a Christian teacher. A rabbi cannot explain it. He can explain all sorts of nuances and allusions, but if one wants the central thrust – 'Who is the one whom God will send as a servant to bear away our sins?' – it stays a closed book. It needs a Christian to explain that it's Jesus. If you have that key, will you be the teacher? Jesus is my missionary motivation. The Christian message is not that we must be good, but that 'while I was still a sinner Christ died for me'. And that's a very different matter.

And he was baptised. The stunning thing is how quickly it happened. Who would let someone be baptised that quickly these days? You'd wonder if Philip hadn't learnt his lesson from Simon! But the answer, and I believe the New Testament pattern, seems to be – if they are a Christian, dunk them. Philip went straight ahead and baptised them. He had taught and explained; the Ethiopian had responded, he was baptised.

Notice that it's the Ethiopian who demands the baptism, not the evangelist. Of course, in the culture of the day baptism was much more obviously significant than it is for so many of us today. Where has the Ethiopian just come from? Jerusalem. What's been going on in Jerusalem? They had been persecuting Christians. Whoever wants to be baptised and then have the mark of a Christian on them – unless they truly believe? They don't need six months of preparation classes if that's their background.

It's hard to get baptism onto a meaningful level in our Anglo-Saxon culture at the moment. But I still vividly remember a Hindu girl who was to be baptised in a little mission church in the East End of London. The service started and there was no sign of her. She appeared, almost at the point in the service where the baptism was to happen. She looked a little flustered but she was there, and they went into the pool. Suddenly there was a disturbance. One of her brothers came to the front and said something like this: 'I know my sister wants to get baptised. I just want her, and you, to know that if she goes ahead with this baptism she is not welcome in the family home. She's of age, she must make her own mind up, but we want you all to know she's not welcome in the family home if she's baptised.' And he left.

Imagine: a stunned and shell-shocked congregation, the

minister standing with the girl in the pool. He turns to her and says the words of the baptism service: 'Do you turn to Christ?'

'I turn to Christ.'

You don't need a three-hour interrogation to determine that she is really a Christian.

The story in Acts peters out here. They botched it again, really. Because the follow-up isn't any better than the preparation! If Philip had got his wits about him, he'd have scribbled a letter of recommendation to the pastor in Addis Ababa and given the Ethiopian a copy of John's gospel so he could learn to read the Bible and get going and grounded. There's an even bigger problem about follow-up. Philip may well now have dreamed about going with the Ethiopian as the great missionary who brought the gospel to Africa.

But God had other ideas. 'When they came up out of the water, the Spirit of the Lord suddenly took Philip away, and the eunuch did not see him again, but went on his way rejoicing. Philip, however, appeared at Azotus [wherever that may be] and travelled about, preaching the gospel in all the towns until he reached Caesarea' (8:39-40).

The big evangelist who brought revival to Samaria? Yes, he was. But he was quite willing to go to the back of nowhere to talk to one person. And even though that one person is very important, Philip is then to be whisked away to preach who knows where.

Before we go on with our service I would ask you not to close your Bibles. I'm going to suggest that we be quiet with Acts 8 in front of us, and let God bring whatever challenge he has to bring to me or to you tonight. It may be that you are one of those who are very nicely settled with home and career – but Lord deliver us from that sort of career mentality, that sees the next twenty years are out because our career says so. Who's running our lives? Whose world view is actually operating?

I'll tell you what I find very striking, and very difficult, in Acts 8. I can have a ministry that is large and important, whether it's in Jerusalem or Samaria, and still I can find that God has other plans for me. That is very unsettling if like me your claim to an international ministry is that you once preached in Tenerife when

I was on holiday. Can I hide behind the fact that I've got a ministry in England? Can I even hide behind the claim that 'I've done my bit?' We have heard from High Time at this Convention. I've been rejected by that mission agency – I'm too young! But you can be over fifty, it can be high time for you; there may well be opportunities still for you.

You may stay firmly rooted to your seats tonight [*when the traditional Keswick World View invitation is issued, to stand as in indication of willingness to serve God wherever He may lead* – Ed.]. But God may have other plans anyway. You may discover that the doors that you felt were your reason for staying so firmly rooted to your seat may close in due course. When they do, remember: when God is closing doors, perhaps even shutting them in our faces, it may be because He's opening others. Home, career, an important ministry, being fifty – none of it means He hasn't got other doors to open.

Those who are actually eager to serve God, who have responded already in their hearts, probably actually worry me the most. Stop and check your motives. You'd never be a Simon, of course. But if we don't think our motives are mixed we don't know ourselves too well. A longing to be at the centre, to be the great this, that and the other, on whatever scale we want to operate, is very near the surface for most if not all of us.

If you want to be the messenger whom God uses, don't think too much in terms of having a great ministry. Will you be the teacher of one person? And even if that person turns out to be important, will you mind if then you get whisked off who knows where and become nothing more than a footnote at the end of the book – someone who put up a few more missionaries, and had four remarkable daughters who prophesied, and that's your lot?

For that's the kind of person whom God uses.

A Matter of Life and Death

by Rev. Philip Hacking

Acts 12

The celebrated football manager Bill Shankley was once asked whether he thought that football was a matter of life or death. He said, 'Not At all! It's much more important than that!' And that is what this remarkable chapter of Acts is all about. It's not the easiest chapter to preach on – as you'll realise over the next forty minutes! But it's a great chapter. Why? Because of verse 24: 'But the word of God continued to increase and spread.' That's our theme; truth on fire. What does the 'but' refer back to? To the death of Herod, that terrible, remarkable event: Herod with all his pomp died suddenly – but – the word of God continued to increase and spread.

This chapter is full of tremendous contrasts. Have you noticed the contrast between the sudden death of Herod and the spreading of God's word? Herod Agrippa I was a man of pomp and power, but he had no control over his destiny and he died a tragic figure. But the word of God kept going. Those awkward Christians he was trying to get rid of just kept on proclaiming, and the word kept on growing: the word being personified.

And have you noticed the contrast between two deaths? Between, at the beginning of the chapter, the death of James the martyr, the first of the twelve disciples to be martyred for the faith; a death of greatness and glory – and the death of Herod.

And another contrast that we'll come to later on – the contrast between the death of James and the deliverance of Peter. Why God, did you allow James to get killed, and brought Peter out? Why one and not the other? Well, I hope we shall see some reasons as we go through the passage.

One of the great things about this chapter is that it reminds us vividly that we are indeed dealing with something more than a matter of life or death. It is more important than that because it's got eternity within it; not just life or death here and now on this planet, but an eternity. And I simply want to ask you whether you believe all that? I think if we did believe it, there would be a new, deep desire to fulfil that great commission.

I can never sing Graham Kendrick's hymn, 'Great is the darkness' without being deeply moved. It's not just about the great celebrations on the final day. 'Watching while sanity dies' is to me very much a description of where we are. And if we believe it's a matter of life or death, then we should be doing something about it.

Some of you, I think, have been coming to Keswick for a long time, and you know there's a sequence of teaching through the week. Maybe you're getting a bit worried; it's not quite working out this year; you can't go through Acts fitting the bits in the right places. For those of you who know the background, Monday has always been the night at Keswick when we preach on sin in the life of a believer. But in a very real sense, I don't think we have got too far away from sin in the life of a believer. In the days when I used to say the old General Confession from the Church of England Prayer Book, I was always more sincere when I talked about the 'things left undone that ought to have been done' than the other kind. Oh yes, certainly I did things I shouldn't have done; but I was more conscious of those sins of omission. And that's one of them; If I really did believe the gospel was a matter of life or death, then I certainly would never rest content till I was out there with all my might and main and love, doing something about it.

I believe there's one more sin of omission. This chapter is about the sovereignty of God. I believe in that with all my heart, and Alistair has reminded us very vividly in his Bible Readings what it means. But the sovereignty of God very often works through the activity of men and women.

There's that remarkable story of prayer (12:12-14). Didn't it occur to you when you read that story. 'My – if God answers prayer as faithless as that, there's hope for all of us.'? After all they, didn't believe very much. An extraordinary moment; I think it's one of the most humorous stories in the Bible, and if you think humour shouldn't be in the Bible then you're wrong. It's there right through the Bible. The poor maid goes to the door and Peter's there. She doesn't even let him in, even though the troops are chasing him around. She leaves him standing at the door, she goes back to the praying group who are praying like mad, 'Lord, deliver Peter out of prison,' and she says, 'He's at the door'.

'Don't be ridiculous, girl! Lord, deliver Peter out of prison.'

That's what they call believing prayer. And yet – and yet – God answered it.

I remember George Duncan of great memory, preaching on this Monday night at Keswick when we think about sin in the life of the believer. He was preaching, in his lovely Scottish accent, on 1 Samuel 12:23, 'God forbid that I should sin against the LORD in ceasing to pray for you.' It made a great impression on me – the sin of prayerlessness.

It has been said by more than one person at Word Alive and elsewhere, though I find it difficult to believe, that a recent statistic said that the average time spent by the average minister in this country in prayer is four minutes a day. I don't know where they get their figures from, but I think it's saying a great deal. As one who has always found prayer difficult and can't cope with these long, long sessions of prayer easily, even I am shattered by that statement. And we meet the sin of prayerlessness vividly in Acts 12.

It's a very vivid narrative, but there are some important verses in it too. I want to talk about this matter of life or death, and I hope you'll keep your Bible in front of you. How does that word of God continue to increase and spread? In two ways.

The sovereignty of God

Many moons ago I read history at Oxford, starting at 55 BC and finishing in 1914. In those days they called it 'modern history' ... But I've always had a fascination with history. I like to think of it not as 'history' but as 'his-story'. History, the Bible believes, is the story of God sovereignly working; the history of the people of God, of God even using a Syrian, a 'rod of my anger', using a Babylonian king, using the most unlikely people; using Caesar Augustus to make sure that Jesus was born in Bethlehem. It's His story.

God's sovereignty in church history

In Acts 12 we see God's sovereignty in two ways: in church history and in world history. This is King Herod Agrippa I. Please don't ask me how he was related to all the other Herods – they were a strange and motley crew and not a very pleasant crew. But Herod Agrippa 1st wanted desperately to propitiate the Jews. He was a Roman stooge, but he wanted people who mattered to be on his side. Things don't change very much when it comes to political correctness!

He wanted to be sure that he had the right people on his side. If that meant the death of James and Peter, so be it. Notice that by now the church of Jesus in Jerusalem was so much 'truth on fire' that it was becoming unpopular. Don't for a moment believe that if a great reviving movement of God broke out among us, the world out there would think how wonderful we are! The more true we are to the word of God, the more we should expect to be persecuted. Whoever will live their lives in Christ Jesus will be persecuted. That's the world in which we are living.

The Roman stooge is determined to get rid of the church. Why? Because the church was being radical. Stephen saw the vision and because Stephen saw the vision and dared to die for the vision, the church was persecuted and scattered. The stories of Antioch, Samaria and the rest are stories of costly sacrifice. They didn't sit down as some great committee and plan – 'How do we follow through the great commission of Acts 1:8?' It was because they, or some of them, got the vision of the truth that the church began to be persecuted and things happened through the suffering church.

I believe there's a message there. I find it hard to preach it, because I know what it can cost. Maybe God is going to teach us some very serious lessons in days to come. But here it was. Herod decided to get rid of James the brother of John and put him to death with the sword (12:2). Do you remember Mark 10:38-39? James and John were something of an elite among the disciples;

their parents had hired servants so they must have been really rather upper-class. And James and John thought they ought to be special. 'Can we have places at Your right and Your left when we come into Your kingdom?' And Jesus said, 'You don't know what you are asking. Can you drink the cup I'm going to drink? Could you be baptised with the baptism with which I'm going to be baptised? Oh yes, they said, not knowing what they said.

Do you think James and John stood by the cross and saw the people on His right and left, when He went into His kingdom, and they wished they hadn't said what they said? But Jesus said, 'Yes, you will drink My cup. You will be baptised with My baptism. You will suffer with Me.'

So James was martyred. What about John? As far as we know, John lived to be a ripe old age. Tradition says that eventually they had to wheel him in his wheelchair to preach. He went on and on and on. Was that fair? James martyred, John living to a good old age? But they both knew what it was to pay a price. A different price.

There's an old Roman coin that bears on one side the Roman emperor's head and on the other side a picture of an ox. That side is in two halves: one is an altar, the other half is a plough. The Latin inscription beneath means 'Ready for either'. The ox may be destined for the altar and sudden sacrifice, or it may be destined for ploughing and hard, hard work until the end. 'Ready for either' – for James the altar, for John the plough. So they both did drink the cup, and it was all part of the sovereignty of God.

There are those who are the martyrs, whose blood is the seed of the church. More than once on this platform I have mentioned my first ever visit to Africa. I stood by a little church and a little graveyard up in the north of Nigeria reading the tombstones. I had been preaching to hundreds of young eager Nigerians where the church was, and still is, growing. And whose were the gravestones? The early missionaries who had one-way tickets to Nigeria. The 'White Man's Grave', they called it. And because they went, this church grew.

But for most of us it's hard work, the plough, the dedication.

Then comes the deliverance of Peter. It's a remarkable story, isn't it? It's possible that it was an inside job, the work of somebody in the prison. The 'angel of the Lord' wasn't necessarily an angelic being from heaven, though he may have been. But it was a divine act, it was supernatural. Eventually, when the door opened of its own accord, that was God at work sovereignly; and when it all happened, Peter knew why. 'When this had dawned on him' (verse 12) – it was all too good to be true! – he worked out three things. 'This is God; somebody is praying; I know where they are praying.' Off he went to the home of Mary, the mother of John Mark.

Let me ask you: have you reflected upon this strange sovereignty of God, that He does sometimes bring dramatic deliverances? We love the stories. One of the new things we now do at Keswick is that the evening speaker gives the Children's Team, who are busy doing other things in the evenings, a version the sermon he's going to give that night. It concentrates the mind, reducing a forty-minute talk down to ten – you may have preferred me to bring that version with me tonight ... I told them a story that really needed the whole ten minutes. In my Edinburgh days, we had a thanksgiving service for a couple in Edinburgh who had been delivered out of the Congo, now Zaire. There had been a terrible outburst of violence there and many people had been killed. This couple had been prayed for and had escaped. We were there to give thanks to God with them and for them, and it was a wonderful thanksgiving occasion, a marvellous testimony, and we were thrilled.

Out from the body of the kirk came an elderly lady, I can see her now. 'Could I please say something?'

I'm always suspicious of people who want to come to the front and say something. I tend to want to approve it in advance. But she seemed innocent enough. and I said she could. She came to the platform and what followed was one of the most moving, electrifying moments of my ministry.

'That was a marvellous story,' she said. 'But I want to tell you mine.' She told us about her son (I think it was her son, I can't now remember; it may have been her daughter). 'He was out in the Congo too and we prayed for him too. He was martyred. But I want you to know that we believe our prayers were answered, because already we've heard of people whose lives have been changed by his faithfulness even to death.'

Do you see? You must not say, 'If only they had prayed for James like they'd prayed for Peter, he'd have got out of prison?' How do you know? How do you know they weren't praying for James? No. Remember, God is sovereign, and He works out, in His story, His good and sovereign will. In His sovereignty in that particular instance, two were delivered and one wasn't; yet both were in the purpose and the plan of God.

And it's part of God's story, it's part of His story. Read Hebrews 11, where the writer accumulates that long list of great people of faith. At the end he finds he hasn't got time to read them all and he starts shortening it. He talks about those 'who shut the mouths of lions' – remember Daniel? – and 'quenched the fury of the flames' – Shadrach, Meshach and Abednego; and 'escaped the edge of the sword' ... 'women received back their dead, raised to life again' – remember Elijah and Elisha – 'others were tortured and refused to be released, so that they might gain a better resurrection. Some faced jeers and flogging, while still others were chained and put in prison. They were stoned; they were sawn in two; they were put to death by the sword' (Hebrews 11:32-37).

But they were all people of faith. They were all doing God's will.

And the challenge I bring to my own heart tonight, which I think becomes more concentrated as we get older, is that we only have one life to live; and in the sovereignty of God, for some of us it will be long and for some it will be short. I find the story of Robert Murray McCheyne very moving. He died in his twenties. yet by God's grace moved that nation of Scotland.

So I bring it to you tonight: 'His-story' – the sovereignty of God in church history. I want to play my little part in it. I want to be in the centre of God's will, I want to do His will, I want to be there, I want to renew my dedication. How about you?

God's sovereignty in world history

The story of Herod's death is very dramatic indeed. He accepted the title of God, he accepted the praise of people. He let them put him on a pedestal. He committed a great sin of pride.

God is not mocked.

Herod died a rather gruesome death; Josephus, the Jewish historian, writes about it too. Of course he doesn't talk about the angel of the Lord. He talks about Herod seeing an owl that was an ill-omen; and he talks about his death. I read a commentary that assured me that medically what really happened was a hydatid cyst[1]. (I'm always intrigued by these titles. In my congregation in Sheffield we had so many doctors I didn't dare do more than read what the commentators said. There were so many doctors in our church, it was the healthiest place in the world.) But do you see what Luke says? There's no doubt at all. Verse 23: 'Immediately, because Herod did not give praise to God, an angel of the Lord struck him down, and he was eaten by worms and died.' That's the Bible version.

Let me say just say one thing about that. Who struck him down? An angel of the Lord. It's the same phrase that's used earlier about the one who delivered Peter out of prison. I am so glad that last night Steve Brady gave us that 'inside view' of what was happening in the early story of the Acts of the Apostles. We can never go back, but it's good to read of those events. People sometimes say to me, 'How I wish I were living in those great days of the Acts of the Apostles, when wonderful things happened. Wouldn't it have been marvellous?' I reply, 'Do you really mean that? You want the deliverance from prison – and you want to see the angel of the Lord smiting people down? You want the story of a lame man being healed – and of Ananias and Sapphira dropping dead?' We tend to choose the bits we like. But they are all part of Acts.

And the solemn thing about the story of Herod is that God is working sovereignly in history, in world history. So I can pray about things that are happening in the Middle East, in Northern Ireland, in the Sudan; the sovereignty of God is there, just as much as He is at work within the church. The two intermingle. But I want to, I must, believe in that sovereignty of God; and sometimes it includes the bits we don't like.

Now that I'm retired I wander around preaching here, there and everywhere, an itinerant preacher in various denominations. The other Sunday I was preaching in the Methodist church. As an Anglican minister I never took the slightest notice of the Anglican lectionary, which prescribes set readings for various times. We just did our own series of sermons. But the Methodist Church is very keen on the Anglican lectionary, so in that Methodist church I

---

1. It is a particularly nasty fluid-filled sac caused by the larva of a tape-worm—Ed.

decided to follow the lectionary. The reading was the story of Esther – a great story. As all good Christians know, it's the only book in the Bible where God's name is not mentioned. Yet – it's a most extraordinary thing – there's no book where God is more sovereignly seen than the book of Esther. When things come to a climax, when there seems no hope, there remains the belief that God is sovereignly at work, even placing that Jewess where she should never have been, in the harem of King Xerxes (Ahasuerus); the belief that she was there for a purpose in the sovereignty of God.

So first of all then, that's to all to do, that the word of God is increasing and spreading through the sovereignty of God.

Human activity

But secondly (and briefly), it happens through the activity of men and women. We have a part to play, and that part is prayer.

God doesn't have to use our prayers, but He chooses so to do. The theologians have a nice phrase for it: 'the dignity of causality'. We actually have the dignity of being used within the sovereignty of God. So you can never say, 'Well, God is working out His purpose, there's not much point in praying, He'll do it in any case.' Oh no He won't! Your prayers are part and parcel of what God wants to do.

In Revelation 8:4-5, prayers go up like incense and come down like fire and earthquake. That is when prayer really gets going – it's all part and parcel of God's sovereignty. In James 5:16 we're told that that 'the prayer of a righteous man is powerful and effective', and he uses Elijah as an illustration. If you were asked what Elijah's greatest quality was you would probably say what a powerful preacher he was and what a courageous man of God. But James says, what a mighty man of prayer he was. As I look back on my ministry, I realise that if I had prayed with as much fervour as I have put into my preaching, I would have been a far better man and a far better minister.

I think this story is in Acts at least partly to show us the importance of prayer. It's vivid, it's humorous in a very real sense, and it's a story of things happening. Out there the angel is bringing Peter out of prison; up there are a group of people praying.

Look again at verse 12. There is a rather lovely aspect to this story of prayer. John Mark was brought up in a home where not only his mother prayed but everybody else did as well. It was a home where people naturally gathered to pray. I agreed with what Alistair Begg said this morning – there is no plus and minus about being brought up in a godly home. It's all plus. And what we need is more and more godly homes, not more religious ones. John had that privilege; and eventually he came good.

I'm fascinated by this home. I can't prove it but I'm sure it's the same home where they prayed in Acts 1 and 2. When Peter is out of prison, where do they pray? And is it not probable that it was the home where they met in Acts 1, that it is the same home where they met with Jesus when He instituted the Lord's Supper? I can't prove it, and I've no doubt that there's some who'd tell me I'm all wrong. But I think it probably was.

And if it was, then two verse in Mark 14 become really precious to me. They are not powerful, just interesting; it's nice to be interesting sometimes. In Mark 14:51-2, Mark has told the story of the Last Supper. Now everybody had gone out into the garden, the troops had come and everybody ran away and left Jesus. And 'A young man, wearing nothing but a linen garment, was following Jesus. When they seized him, he fled naked, leaving his garment behind.' Why on earth put that in? Well, because it's Mark himself isn't it? Surely it's Mark's little personal signature: 'I was there'. Can't you imagine a teenager, hearing the noise of this remarkable event outside and wanting to know what was going on? And he got a bit panicky, and he ran away, and he remembers that he fled naked; when kids flee naked, they remember. He remembered all that. Now I can't prove all that, but come back to Acts chapter 12 and what I can prove is that Mark's home was a home where many people gathered to pray, and that's the secret of Peter's deliverance.

I ask you: do you pray much in your home? I'm all against Christians being artificial in the way they pray. As an itinerant preacher I've sometimes been present at family prayers where I've sensed the rebellion of the kids and have understood why they sometimes rebelled. Let's not be artificial, please! But homes ought to be places where it's natural to pray. I hope that one little result of this Convention might be that we will do something about what might happen if they are.

As we've seen in that vivid narrative, they didn't pray with a tremendous amount of conviction and assurance. But they prayed nonetheless, and I'm sure that, remembering that story, they would pray later with greater conviction.

I was asked a few months ago by a church that wasn't an evangelical church to talk to them on the subject of how we should pray at the end of this millenium. Being a simple soul I thought that we ought to pray at the end of this millenium the same as we prayed at the beginning of it, but clearly they didn't think so.

So, I decided to go back to the prayer of Abraham in Genesis 18, which I reckon was as far before Christ as we are after Christ; I went back to 2,000 years before Christ and saw how Abraham prayed. And after his prayer, in Genesis 19:29, it says that God remembered Abraham and delivered Lot. There weren't ten righteous men in Sodom, but God was better than His word because Abraham prayed, Lot was delivered. And when you think of people who never pray for themselves, when you think of a nation whose leaders very rarely pray for themselves, our task is to be their intercessors. God remembered Abraham and delivered Lot.

So you see, don't you, that in the sovereignty of God He uses this great activity of men and women in prayer. He is sovereign, I don't dictate to Him, prayer is not like the slot machine where you put your money in and you pull the goods. Oh no! God is your master, my master. But He uses my prayer and yours in His purposes.

Do you remember how the story of Esther goes? Mordecai says to Esther, 'Look, only you can help to save our nation from this awful ethnic cleansing' – which we still see in our world. 'Only you can do it.' And he says this to her: 'For if you remain silent at this time, relief and deliverance for the Jews will arise from another place, but you and your father's family will perish. And who knows but that you have come to royal position for such a time as this?' (Esth. 6:14).

He's saying, 'Esther, God is sovereign, and He'll have to work out His purposes, but if you don't play your part you and your family will suffer.'

I believe the church of Jesus Christ will conquer. I have no doubt about the final victory, the gates of Hell will not prevail, but I do know that we may miss out on much of that blessing unless we recognise that we have been called to the kingdom for such as this. And if it is a matter of life or death, we have a great responsibility to make sure that we do something about the lost.

May I make it very simple? I come across some in Scripture who continue to avoid that responsibility, of whom it is said that they will not enter the kingdom of heaven. I think we sometimes let these things happen because we don't really believe that they are going to a lost eternity because of the way they live.

But that's what the Bible says. So if I really cared deeply, I could never compromise my position. I could never stand before my Maker on the Day of Judgement and say, 'Well, you see, in my day, people didn't bother about these things.' It's a matter of life or death, and I'm called to the kingdom for such a time as this.

There is the sin of carelessness and there is the sin of prayerlessness. And we are called for such a time as this. God has His men and women for the hour. You may have wished to live in another hour, but this is the hour in which you live.

One more illustration before I close. I remember as a young man of fifteen listening to the radio when England was batting in a Test Match against South Africa. A famous Derbyshire batsman, Cliff Gladwin – a large, rough-hewn man – went in to bat with two runs needed for victory and three balls left to play. And as Cliff passed the umpire he said in his good Derbyshire accent, 'Come the hour, cometh the man,' which, being translated is, 'I'm the man for the hour.' And did Cliff Gladwin smite the bowler for a six? – No, they got four leg-byes off his very ample backside and the hour had come. Come the hour, cometh the man.

The hour in which we live desperately needs the kind of witness that can change things, in a matter of life or death. You and I, whether we like it or not, are God's men and women for this hour. We're going to sing in a moment a hymn that contains the line, 'We go in faith, our own great weakness feeling.' And I would like to think that this evening some in a quiet moment of commitment to the Lord will make a new dedication in this matter of life or death, whatever it may cost, to go out and serve. I stood down there as a young man and made that commitment: 'Whenever and wherever'. I'm not making that kind of appeal today. But I hope we are challenged to be prepared to dedicate whatever life we have in front of us, whether it be long or short, to reach people for that which is even more important than life or death. Or the challenge may simply be that, challenged by our praylessness, we will dedicate our lives to go on praying, to be renewed in prayer.

When Esther got the message, she said with great courage, 'I am going. If I perish I perish.' It doesn't sound terribly optimistic, but it's utterly realistic. May God give us that quality!

Growing Pains

by Mr Jonathan Lamb

Acts 13-15

Not long ago I spoke with a friend of mine who had just taken her driving test – always a pretty demanding experience, but for her particularly traumatic. She told me about the hill start test. She'd struggled for what seemed ten minutes trying to select second gear. Fortunately she had a very patient examiner. He peered over his glasses as she tied to get into gear, his pen hovering over his clipboard. And as he saw her stress levels rising, he said to her these encouraging words : 'Don't worry, love, they're all in the same box. All you've got to do is to sort them out.'

The story seemed to have a Pauline ring, because Paul often stressed that combination in his epistles. He would say, 'We are all members of the same family, we all belong to the one Father, we are all indwelt by the one Holy Spirit, we have all been redeemed by the one Lord Jesus Christ, we are all in the same box.' But many if not all of his letters spend a great deal of time talking about how those cogs should mesh together – how to sort them out. And I think that is one of the issues we face in a text like Acts 15. It was a fundamental issue in the first century, and it's certainly a fundamental issue for our church as we approach the twenty-first century. Whenever Christians are in fellowship there are sure to be differences of all kinds; cultural, temperamental, social, doctrinal.

225

And in these situations, if a church is to survive at all (let alone make progress), it must learn to come to terms with those differences.

Sometimes differences very quickly move towards divisions, and I'm sure you identify with this. You've probably heard the story of the minister who was asked if he had an active congregation. He replied, 'Oh yes, yes they're very active! Half of them are working with me and half of them are working against me.' So often it does seem a particularly insidious, Satanic strategy, that when growth in the church, opportunities for mission and new challenges in evangelism are present, Satan himself will do all he can to create divisions amongst God's people. He will exploit every opportunity to create lines of fracture between fellow Christians. And it seems to be the case in Christian mission around the world, in my understanding, that as we see that kind of expansion there will be a special temptation to Christians to engage in internal disagreements. I'm told that many of those who return from the mission fields, who leave the missionary enterprise – it's called missionary attrition – do so not because of the difficulties of encountering a new culture, or problems with the food, or the challenges of confronting other religious groups. Many return simply because they cannot get on with their fellow Christians.

We have arrived at such a moment in Acts 15, Luke's story of the spreading flame. It describes an event that had a potential for creating a deep division within the Christian community. In fact it was to become a critical turning point in the growth of the church, and if handled unwisely would have the potential to blow apart the entire expansion of the church and the missionary movement. It focused around a theological issue and a practical issue. Theological: How are we saved and how are we incorporated into the Christian family? And practical: How do Christians from different backgrounds learn to live together?

I hope that we will find, addressing those issues, as well as the way in which those early believers tackled that, will be real help to all of our churches, where we have to learn how to cope with growing pains, particularly the pains which come from the differences and disagreements.

The challenge of growth (15:1-5)

One of the great blessings of the gospel that Peter proclaimed in his sermon in Acts 2, as we saw earlier this week, was this: 'The promise is for you and your children and for all who are far off' (2:39). In Acts 15 we are twenty years on since Peter proclaimed that message, and already what Peter implied was beginning to be realised. Gentiles had been brought to faith and those who were far off were now becoming members of the Christian community in city after city. It was ones and twos at first but eventually it became huge numbers.

Look back at Acts 14:17. Paul and Barnabas, sent out by the church in Antioch on their missionary journey, came back with extraordinary news of how God was at work and all that He had done, and how He had 'opened the door of faith to the Gentiles.'

As Steve Brady told us, the Antioch Christian community was a very colourful mix of Jews and Gentiles. The Jewish Christians in the mother church up in Jerusalem were beginning to adjust to the fact that Gentiles too were coming to faith. Ten years after the conversion of Cornelius that trickle of Gentiles coming to faith was becoming quite a flood. And in that context, a number of the Jewish Christians up in Jerusalem were beginning to ask some serious questions.

There was probably a small pressure amongst those Jewish Christians, made up of people who were particularly concerned that though more and more Gentiles were coming to faith, they were becoming Christians but they were not submitting to the law of Moses. The Jewish Christians were happy about Gentiles hearing the good news, but as far as they were concerned Israel was the appointed agent. Surely all nations would come – and it would be through Israel; it would mean also submitting to the institutions of Israel.

So in verse 1 this influential pressure group decided they must come down from Jerusalem and visit Antioch to address what for them was becoming a very serious issue. 'Some men came down from Judea to Antioch and were teaching the brothers: "Unless you are circumcised, according to the custom taught by Moses, you cannot be saved."'

It's very important to understand what a critical moment this was, what a turning-point in Luke's description of the growth of the church. A flood of Gentiles was coming to faith, and this group of believers from Jerusalem were saying in effect, 'No circumcision, no salvation: faith in Jesus is not enough.' As Stott puts it in his commentary, they must let Moses complete what Jesus began. This wasn't just a slightly different cultural emphasis between these Christians. It struck right at the heart of the apostolic mission. It was a potential division, that would affect the entire forward movement of the gospel there in the first century and indeed onwards.

You'll see therefore why there was such a sharp response in verse 2: 'This brought Paul and Barnabas into sharp dispute and debate with them.' In a moment we'll see that there are some differences with which Christians must learn to live. But this was a challenge right at the heart of the gospel, the one thing over which Paul and Barnabas knew they could never compromise. It was going to be a very uncomfortable confrontation, but Paul could see that anything that implied that faith in Christ's work upon the cross was not enough had to be strenuously resisted.

The Jewish delegation was effectively rebuilding the wall between Jews and Gentiles which Jesus on the cross had demolished. They were trying to lay on the shoulders of those Gentiles the heavy Jewish yolk of the law. No wonder that hearing such teaching put those gentile Antioch Christians into a spin (verse 24). When they received that message, that faith in Jesus is not enough, they realised that they were being subverted by it. And no wonder: whenever anyone preaches a Christian message that advocates 'Faith in Jesus – plus something else,' it is sure to disturb Christians. You will find Christians always lack assurance when there is some hint of a 'performance addition'. Even if that extra – that faith in Jesus plus some other activity, if it's ninety nine percent of Jesus' work, but just one percent of my own, there will always be that sense of uncertainty, that lack of assurance amongst Christians.

So it unsettled the Antioch believers when they were told that their faith in Jesus and His work on the cross was not quite enough. And it was clear that the only thing that would settle them was a full and open debate. 'So Paul and Barnabas were appointed, along with some other believers, to go up to Jerusalem to see the apostles and elders about this question' (15:2).

Now we shouldn't imagine that this is just some first-century technical issue remote from the way in which we live today. In every age there are such pressure groups. In Britain's churches today, I'm afraid to say, there are those who would want to lead us astray, who obscure the truth of the gospel. And it has been wonderful working through 2 Timothy with Alistair and seeing with what clarity Paul held on to this truth: faith in Jesus Christ and His completed work on the cross.

Before we move on, it's very important to notice in verse 4 how the group was received in Jerusalem. Here in the heart of conservative Jerusalem, Paul and Barnabas and their companions – a group of liberal Christians in the mind of this Jewish mother church – how were they received, in the light of this major confrontation? They weren't received with cynical suspicion. 'They were welcomed by the church.' If only disagreements in church life could be held in that kind of atmosphere. How are disagreements held in your church? I've been to one or two church meetings in my time and it's often a rather difficult issue. Sometimes it's just a little disagreement about what hymn book you should use, or what colour the walls should be, or – as I heard proposed not long ago – whether you should use the baptistry for a sand-pit for the mothers and toddlers. But sometimes there is a fairly serious issue at stake, and you go into the meeting and see some people sitting with their arms folded; and written across their foreheads is 'This is war.'

The spirit of the disagreement in Acts 15 was one of sharp disagreement and confrontation. Yet in that context you notice that at every stage there is a willingness to debate those issues face to face, to confront those disagreements, to welcome those Christians who may look at the matter differently. They were open together to examine the evidence. I was involved in one church where for a time there were very distasteful anonymous letters being sent between Christians; I received one myself as a leader of the church. That is never the way to handle disagreements or to make your views known. Here in Acts 15, despite the disagreement, there was always face-to-face examination of the problem. Christian relationships, brothers and sisters, are often poisoned by a failure to confront issues openly and in a godly way.

Those early Christians were determined to try to work through this major disagreement. Michael Griffiths once wrote: 'There is little evidence in the New Testament that it ever seems to have occurred to the apostles that problems could be resolved by the simple expedient of hiving off to form a new congregation.' It's what the Moslems call a mosque of one-and-a-half bricks – me and the other person who half agrees with me. But the believers from Antioch were welcomed to Jerusalem, and they began then to consider this critical question openly.

The priority of the gospel (15: 6-19)

They called an official gathering of the church leaders, and there was considerable debate. A series of speakers presented very powerful evidence in facing up to the disagreements. Peter spoke, he was supported by the testimony of Barnabas and Paul, and finally James, acting a kind of chairman, drew the discussion to a close. I want us to notice three issues that surfaced.

God's initiative

Peter begins in verse 7 by stressing that the Gentile mission was something that God Himself had inaugurated. Ten years earlier, as Philip reminded us, Peter came face to face with the challenge of being God's spokesperson to the Gentiles, particularly in that dramatic encounter with Cornelius. 'That was God's clear purpose,' Peter said. 'God called me to that.' Notice how he emphasises that all of this is God's initiative. Verse 7, God made a choice; verse 8, God accepted these Gentiles; verse 9, God made no distinction between Jew and Gentile; verse 9 again, God purified their hearts. It's all to do with God's initiative that the gospel is speeding on in triumph and is going on into nation after nation.

On the back of what Peter said, you will see that Barnabas and Paul reinforced that apostolic witness to God's initiative. 'The whole assembly became silent as they listened to Barnabas and Paul telling about the miraculous signs and wonders God had done among the Gentiles through them' (verse 12). Here was further confirmation to these Jewish believers of God's approval of this mission to the Gentiles. It is God's initiative, and the apostles witnessed to that. Always, missionary advance – indeed, your conversion and mine – is down to God's initiative.

God's acceptance

There is also, in this Gentile mission, witness to God's acceptance; the witness of the Spirit. In verse 8 Peter argues that the Gentile believers have received the same Holy Spirit and have been accepted by God on the same condition as Jewish believers: faith in Jesus. That's the sole condition of salvation and entry into God's people. There are no racial, social or religious requirements. Peter says, just for the Jews, so for the Gentiles, faith in Jesus Christ through whom God's grace is brought to sinners.

It's not going to be the law, Peter says. In fact it hasn't even worked for us, it's not a means of salvation for anyone, Jews included: it is 'a yoke that neither we nor our fathers have been able to bear' (verse 10). Salvation comes through God's grace to Jew and Gentile alike, it's received by faith to Jew and Gentile alike, hearts are cleansed by the same Holy Spirit for Jew and Gentile alike.

Peter's speech ends in verse 11 with a little intriguing twist. He doesn't say, 'So the Gentiles are saved like us.' He reverses it. 'We believe it is through the grace of our Lord Jesus that we are saved, just as they are.' Just as the Gentiles. No discrimination, no distinction – whoever you are, by grace you are saved through faith, Peter says, sounding very much like Paul.

Peter saw very clearly that if that were not accepted as the foundation of the gospel, then the forward march of the church that Luke is recounting would be completely paralysed. Of course, it was a quite revolutionary sentiment for those Jewish believers in Jerusalem; it's just as radical today. God is at work by His Spirit amongst all kinds of people, without discrimination; in nation after nation, in all kinds of ethnic groups and social classes. By His grace He's calling into His family the most surprising and unexpected of people.

Is God's acceptance reflected in the way in which we receive one another within the Christian community? The most unexpected people come to faith through the same Lord Jesus, by the same Spirit, and yet sometimes feeling excluded in the Christian family. I was talking not long ago to a Christian in Siberia in the Russian Federation who was a fine art student from a very pagan background. He had a remarkable conversion. He'd heard the good news of the gospel, and from a very pagan (actually, occult) background, he'd come to faith in Christ, it was a wonderful miracle. But he was poor, as most students are in that part of the world. He couldn't afford to change his clothes, which was very typical of a fine art student. He was a smoker, which is also very typical. He went to church – there weren't many evangelical churches to choose from in his city. He was a young believer, wonderfully saved by the same grace of the Lord Jesus Christ. And after a couple of Sundays he was almost excluded, in fact he was effectively asked to leave, because of his appearance and his failure to stop smoking. So he went to another church; and exactly the same thing happened.

Do not condemn our Siberian brothers and sisters. Our own churches can sometimes be very similar, erecting all kinds of barriers and failing to see that God is at work – sometimes in surprising ways, producing miracles by His Spirit and By His grace – in bringing people to faith. Of course those people have to mature and change. There may be lifestyle issues that have to be addressed. But somehow we have to capture what the early Christians saw: that the Christian family is one created by God's grace, by the same Holy Spirit, and should reflect the kind of acceptance which God Himself demonstrates.

We have a celebration this week at Keswick for those with learning difficulties, and we're delighted that that track is going so well. During the open time of sharing one of those present described how hurt he had been when he had been asked to leave the church because he was making too much noise.

All such attitudes sometimes create a sense in fellow believers that they must stand outside, that they are not truly welcomed in. They sense that there is some kind of discrimination going on and some kind of distinction being made. But what Peter is saying in this wonderful statement in verse 11 is that it is not just for one ethnic group or social class. God's family is multi-ethnic, multi-cultural, multi-coloured. It's a new society that God is creating.

God's purpose

When, in verse 13, James got up, the church in Jerusalem would have pricked up its ears a little more intently. James was a very prominent leader; probably something of a champion of the more conservative believers, so they would have been ready to listen. How was James going to sum up this very difficult disagreement?

His choice of words in verse 14 is fascinating. He begins with a very nice little touch of local colour, calling Peter by his Jewish name Simeon. 'Simon [NIV] has described to us how God at first showed his concern by taking from the Gentiles a people for himself.' His Jewish listeners could not have missed the point. A people for Himself, a people for His name – those were buzz words for those Jewish Christians in Jerusalem. It was a phrase used frequently in the Old Testament to describe the privileged status of Israel, the covenant community. And now James was applying it in such a way as to include other nations: Gentiles are also a people on whom God has placed His name, they belong to Him. And God was not asking them to surrender their national or ethnic identity, He wasn't asking them to conform to any institutional regulations. Their primary identity was in Christ.

I think that's a particularly important point today. I work a lot in countries where there's a great deal of discussion about ethnicity. In our continent and indeed in our nation there is much talk of nationalism, of national identity and ethnic identity. The Christian gospel does not ask us to surrender that kind of identity, but what it does say is that our primary identity is in Christ. And that's what James is saying. These Gentiles now belong to that name, they are part of that family.

So going on with his presentation in verse 15 he says, 'The words of the prophets are in agreement with this.' And he cites Amos (verses 16-18), who prophesied that the blessings which the Messiah would bring would be shared not only by restored Jews (which I take him to mean in verse 16), but also (verse 17) for 'all the Gentiles who bear my name.'

So there is the force of the presentation by Peter, Paul and Barnabas and James, all affirming, in this sharp disagreement about how one becomes a Christian and is incorporated into the family of God, the priority of the gospel: God's initiative, God's acceptance, God's purpose. All believing Gentiles belong to God's people. There is no discrimination and therefore no barriers to fellowship. In verse 19 James sums up, 'It is my judgement, therefore, that we should not make it difficult for the Gentiles who are turning to God.' God accepts them. How could we possibly do otherwise?

In today's fractured world it's not just Europe, it's not just

Britain – these lines of fracture run right through our society; the divisions created between us by our generations, our social status or our race. And the reconciling power of the gospel of grace is a very moving witness in our world.

I was involved with a group of Serb and Croat believers during the Balkan war. Their primary identity was in Jesus Christ. As a powerful expression of fellowship, that group of believers from those two warring nations linked arms and sang in Serbo-Croatian the chorus,

> There is only one God, there is only one King,
> there is only one body, that is why we sing,
> 'Bind us together, Lord.'

Colleagues of mine in IFES in Rwanda and Burundi in IFES have categorically refused to take sides in the Hutu-Tutsi conflict. Believers from both camps refused to take sides in the middle of that ethnic strife. Because they belonged to that one name – that name of Jesus – and to that one family, they refused to divide on other issues. That's a powerful witness in those nations. It cost them their lives but they were determined to stand for their identity in Jesus. There's solidarity in that family.

Now in the light of those examples, I wonder sometimes: when we see the kinds of divisions that sometimes inflict themselves upon our churches, when Christians divide over personality clashes or the type of music in worship, or when congregations segregate by age or by temperament, when they discriminate in their fellowships by race or sometimes even by class, we should ask one another a question, and that is, what kind of gospel do we believe in? If that is what Peter is proclaiming here, God's initiative in bringing all men and women irrespective of class, irrespective of race, irrespective of ethnic identity, all men and women to faith by that same gospel, the same grace, the same Holy Spirit, we have to ask ourselves, do we believe in that gospel and express it in our believing communities.

There is neither Jew nor Greek, slave nor free, male nor female, but you are all in one through Christ Jesus.

Foundations of Fellowship (15:19-20)

After his summary James then proposes the very wise decision, which obviously meets with the approval of everyone: 'We should write a letter to the Gentile believers, we should deliver it to them, we should encourage them.' It's a two-fold decision: verse 19, 'We should not make it difficult for the Gentiles who are turning to God,' and verse 20, 'Instead we should write to them, telling them to abstain from food polluted by idols, from sexual immorality, from the meat of strangled animals and from blood.'

Those two ideas were the basis or foundation of fellowship.

No unnecessary barriers

James is saying, and wants written in the letter, that he wants no unnecessary barriers to fellowship. There are to be no entrance conditions imposed upon these Gentile believers. Nothing further should be required of them than faith in Jesus Christ. That is the sufficient foundation for fellowship and for being part of the family of God.

I hope you noticed, that was the decision of the leaders of the church and of the whole church. Verse 22: 'Then the apostles and elders, with the whole church, decided to choose some of their own men and send them to Antioch with Paul and Barnabas', to carry this letter. It's very impressive to see how they handle this conflict. They decided in a number of ways to express their solidarity with these gentile believers in Antioch to demonstrate their brotherly acceptance of them. They wrote the letter (verse 23), and its opening statement is designed to build bridges: 'The apostles and elders, your brothers...'. Then after writing the letter they not only sent it but they also sent believers from Jerusalem to reinforce it: verse 27, 'We are sending Judas and Silas to confirm by word of mouth what we are writing.' Then they ministered in Antioch: verse 32, 'Judas and Silas ... said much to encourage and strengthen the brothers.'

Do you see how everything about this decision to work together, to ensure the harmony of God's people, was building bridges? They wrote the letter, sending it personally to meet face to face. It is a ministry of encouragement. That's how they handled disagreement. They'd made the decision which seems to have had the approval of the whole church. So it seems that even the pressure group that provoked this story in verse 1 had graciously accepted this decision (that's an argument from silence, but Luke says nothing about further factions and difficulties over this issue). God's people were together in that decision. They had understood the priority of the gospel and therefore the foundation of fellowship.

I want to ask you very simply this evening: is that true in your congregation and mine? Or are there unnecessary barriers to fellowship in your church? Are there people who feel excluded – by comments, perhaps, by jokes, even physically excluded – who really belong by virtue of their faith in Jesus, God's grace, and the same Holy Spirit at work in their lives? Do we practice some kind of ecclesiastical exclusiveness in our churches? Do we erect barriers to fellowship? Because if we do, we have to come back to texts like this; to look at the gospel and say, 'Which of these barriers really do need to be dismantled, so that we become a true gospel fellowship – one which exemplifies this new society and new community?'

I sometimes wonder too about fellowship between fellow evangelical believers in the same town: what kind of partnerships can we express between groups of believers who sometimes hold each other at a distance for denominational reasons? You may have heard of the story of the Pure and Simple Faith Baptist Movement, and the mutual hostility that flourished between it and the rival sect in the same town, the Only True Original Baptist Church of the New Testament. The elders of the two chapels never spoke to each other. On one occasion an elder who had dangerously moderate leanings encountered an elder from the other church in the street. He decided to try to start a conversation. He nodded at the other and remarked, 'I passed your chapel the other day.'

'Thanks,' came the reply, 'I appreciate it!'

Our witness to the gospel of reconciliation will only be credible when we demonstrate that the true foundations for fellowship are the gospel; and when we refuse to re-erect barriers, whether racial, social, economic or ecclesiastical which Christ, through His cross, has torn down. Our Christian witness in our towns and in this country and certainly in Europe, is marred by such inappropriate divisions and barriers. I remember preaching some years ago in Bulgaria where they've reversed the normal cultural signals for yes and no (it is changing a little as they become increasingly Westernised). I didn't know that, and I was very disturbed as I preached to see a number of people beginning to shake their heads. So I decided I needed to preach a bit more passionately – and unfortunately their heads began to nod a bit more passionately.

If we did that in our culture we would be giving two contradictory signals. Sometimes we Christians are very much in danger of doing that in our mission, in our evangelism, in our Christian witness. We say something like 'All one in Christ Jesus', but fractures in our churches and divisions between Christians say something quite different. Let me read you something that is very up-to-date. 'The public takes notice of all this division, and not only derides us but becomes hardened against all religion. When we try to persuade them, they see so many factions they do not know which to join, and they think it's better not to join any of them. Thus thousands grow in contempt of all religion by our divisions.' It was actually written 350 years ago by Richard Baxter.

No unnecessary barriers – that's what the letter said. We are not going to make it tough for these fellow believers from other nations, other backgrounds, to be members of our family.

No unnecessary offence

James's second point was not a theological but a practical issue. It represented a recommendation that would enable Christians from different backgrounds, Jew and Gentile, to live together in harmony.

Verse 20 doesn't make immediate sense to us living at the end of the twentieth century: repeated in the letter, it said they were 'to abstain from food sacrificed to idols, from blood, from the meat of strangled animals and from sexual immorality' (verse 29). But they were very practical recommendations for the gentile believers in many of the churches; certainly down there in South Galatia, for Paul was probably talking the same issues in Galatians 2. There were many believers from gentile background in those churches with whom these Jewish believers were now having to rub shoulders. They'd been taught for centuries to observe certain food laws and to be very careful about making contact with Gentiles – and now all of a sudden they were being thrown together from their different backgrounds actually eating meals together and breaking bread together.

Not all of those Jewish believers were quite as emancipated as Peter and Paul; some still had scruples about what they should eat. So James very wisely proposes in this letter that gentile believers should be sensitive to other believers' scruples. 'Don't create unnecessary offence in your Christian fellowship,' he says.

I believe this is a vital lesson for us too; a very important thing in our churches. There is a doctrine in the New Testament which I think is much neglected. It is the doctrine of difference, the ability to live together with these kinds of secondary differences and still enjoy fellowship. If you don't believe me, it's worth studying Romans 14 and 15 which is all about that theme; how Christians with their differences, whether temperamental, cultural, social, or even doctrinal even within our churches, are to handle disagreements and live together with those differences. That's another subject but, it seems to me, one that's critical. And again, you see, it says something about our belief in the gospel. It says something about our ability to live together as one family.

Do you remember how Jesus prayed about that, in terms of our witness - that people would know we were His followers, that we were believers in this gospel of reconciliation, by the way we behaved together? (e.g. John 17:20-23). Well, this council decision, then, stressed that Christian fellowship meant firstly no unnecessary barriers – no discrimination – and secondly, no unnecessary offence. Rather, it was a fellowship that expressed both truth, the priority of the gospel, and love. I would call it loving compromise that James appeals for in that fellowship.

And that is the real benefit of these growing pains. If your church is going through difficulties or differences, if you are a growing church; if you are working for the Lord, then you'll face them right now. Some will question whether you're right. There will be a few differences and disagreements. All of our churches go through that. We should be thankful to God for the opportunities that those difficulties, differences and disagreements represent.

Conclusion

I summarise with three words.

Priorities

These differences, these growing pains which those first churches experienced and which we do, enable us to assess priorities as they did in Jerusalem. We need to be absolutely clear about gospel priorities. 'By grace you are saved, through faith.' That's what they saw in this discussion. We can never compromise over those priorities. It's that shared commitment to priorities that will then allow us to be sure that there is no discrimination, and which also means that we will be very careful to avoid the distractions and the diversions which Satan is sure to bring to our churches and to us, to make sure that we don't grow. If our priority is clearly the priority of the gospel, we can cope with all kinds of other differences within the Christian family.

Harmony

In the light of those priorities we will be enabled to live together in loving compromise. We will have not constant conflict between different generations in our church, not one faction being offended by the cultural sensitivities of another, but the ability to live together in our rich diversity with this harmonious fellowship.

Growth

The growing pains themselves, properly handled, will result in further growth and the advance of the gospel. Acts 15 is a missionary text; the result will be more nations hearing the word. But I think it's specially true of our churches too. If we handle these differences correctly, there will be growth at two levels. Look at 16:4-5 which picks up on the decisions that were made in Jerusalem: 'As they travelled from town to town, they delivered the decisions reached by the apostles and elders in Jerusalem for the people to obey. So the churches were strengthened in the faith and grew daily in numbers.'

That was the result of these growing pains: a qualitative growth as they were strengthened in the faith and a quantitative growth as they grew daily in numbers. When we Christians live like this, there will be that kind of growth. This kind of church, this kind of gospel fellowship, is deeply attractive to people who are living in a fractured world, in a world of divisions. Seeing a new community like this growing is deeply attractive. That's why the church grew, and that's why the church can grow. By grace you are saved through faith.

Let me read you some words as I finish, which were I believe penned by John White. I think they are very expressive of this theme.

> Christ died that humans of every type be reconciled to God and to one another. The genius of Christianity is that it makes possible on-going fellowship between people who could not otherwise tolerate, let alone enjoy, one another. Christ gets refined socialites hobnobbing with migrant farm workers, middle-aged squares weeping with rebels and swingers, Blacks, Indians, Jews and Whites, praying earnestly together, and management and labourer sharing each other's problems. In a world divided by class, commerce, race, education, politics, the generation gap, and a million clashing interests, Christ alone can make incompatibles mesh.'

We are all in the same box. All we've got to do is work it out!

'Come Over and Help Us'

by Dr Steve Brady

Acts 16

Some years ago Sir David McNee, ex-president of the Christian Police Association and one-time Commissioner of Police, was addressing a group of evangelists at Swanwick in Derbyshire. He described the police examinations that are designed to keep officers skills in shape and to develop them. A question for constables hoping to be promoted to sergeant went something like this.

> You are proceeding along the High Street on your normal course of duties, when in your peripheral vision you notice that a car swerves across the road and into an oncoming van. As you rush across to the scene of the accident you notice a number of things immediately. First, the dazed van driver is a well-known rascal who has skipped bail. Second, the driver of the said car is the wife of your station inspector and she smells very strongly of alcohol. You also notice that the tax disc is out of date. While you are deciding what to do, to your horror a tanker, to avoid the said accident, veers into a bank of shops. Before you know it the tanker driver has emerged saying he thinks there's one or two people injured, but even more worrying, his load is a highly flammable

which he thinks is about to explode. Will you please call for help? As you are deciding on your priorities, from a side road a woman comes out screaming that her little boy has just fallen into the canal and is drowning and she can't swim – will somebody please help!

And then the question was: 'Enumerate, in order, your priorities.'

The chap who came top simply wrote, 'Remove uniform and mingle with the crowd.'

We live in a world of need. And how do you, faced with so many screaming, competing demands, prioritise your life and work out what it is that God wants you to do? Well, let Acts 16 come to our rescue this evening. And my outline is a very simple one: Seek the Lord; Spread the word; Stand the bill.

Seek the Lord (16:6-10)

There are a number of intriguing questions here. Is this Holy Spirit the same as the Spirit of Jesus? And how were they 'kept' – or, not allowed – 'by the Holy Spirit' (verse 6), and not allowed by 'the Spirit of Jesus' (verse 7) from taking various routes? We don't know.

Have you ever found guidance difficult? I find it almost logarithmically more difficult the longer I've gone on as a Christian. Is it a sign of my spirituality decreasing? It used to be so clear when I was a young believer. Well, let this passage encourage you. Here is an apostolic band finding it difficult to discover the precise will of God at this particular juncture. Don't you love the great honesty of the word of God? They decide at one level, they say, 'How are we going to cope? Where are we going to go?' And God wonderfully intervenes.

There are three sub-sections I want to very quickly deal with on the matter of seeking the Lord in guidance.

Get going.

Have you ever tried to move a car that's stationary, with the engine turned off? Have you tried turning the wheels and then beginning to push it – especially when it's wet and muddy? Fun, isn't it? It's so hard pushing something that is stationary and trying to steer it. And it's very hard to push stationary Christians into God's will.

These Christians were already on the move for God, doing what He had clearly already called them to do. Some of us have a romanticised view of guidance. We don't do anything. We never read the Bible, we hardly ever pray, we swan in and out of church, we're never quite sure why nobody's ever asked us to do anything significant. We believe that one day the phone's going to ring and somebody's going to say, 'Hello this is the Billy Graham organisation; your name came up this morning. Would you like to be Dr Graham's successor?'

Do you really think it works like that? Here were folk who were already moving for God. All they needed now was direction. You are looking for direction for life? Well, get involved with where you are already. 'What's that in your hand?' says God to Moses. 'Well it's a staff.' And God uses that staff in a remarkable way in the coming years. He takes what he's already got, he's already moving for God.

Stay sensible

Isn't it odd how we so often lose our common sense when we come to guidance? Some people get very mystical. They have a prayer meeting about what tie they are going to wear and they come down and say, 'Do you like the tie, do you think it goes with this outfit?'

Paul is working to a plan here. He decides to go to Asia. This is his missiological plan: to target areas of vast population. So he thinks, 'I'll go to Asia, there are a number of big cities over there: there's Ephesus, with 300,000 people and a cult to Diana the goddess. That'll be a great city to target!'

God says, 'No, no, no, I don't want you to turn to the left.'

So Paul says, 'Well, then, let me turn to the right. Let me go east. I'll go to Bithynia where later there'll be famous councils. Let me head for Bithynia.'

And the Lord says, 'No, I don't want you to go that way either.' Why? God, don't you care about these places? Yes, He does. Paul eventually makes it to Ephesus and Peter, perhaps, ultimately evangelised around Bithynia according to 1 Peter 1, though we don't know for sure. But just this particular time in Paul's life, God says to him, 'No I don't want you to do that.' But he's thinking Christianly already. That's why we need to read the word of God, why we need to develop a Christian mind.

Romans 12:1-2 talks about not conforming to this world, but being transformed by the renewing of our minds. That's why we get into the word of God. People say that's brain-washing – well it's heart-washing, thank God; and it's mind-washing, unlike the filth around us. But having done that, having stayed sensible, and saying 'Lord do I turn left or right?' that old verse from Isaiah comes to mind, 'Whether you turn to the right or to the left, your ears will hear a voice behind you, saying, "This is the way; walk in it."' (Isa. 30:21). And as he tried to go left and tried to go to the right, God said, 'I don't want you to go that way, Paul.'

Get going, stay sensible – but make sure that you also,

Be receptive

I think it was Roy Clements who first described Christian guidance as being like a London taxi driver. Before you become a black cab taxi driver, for months you have to study for 'The Knowledge'. A friend of mine did this, spending months on a motor scooter going round all London's nooks and crannies with a clipboard, building up a vast knowledge of Greater London. When he became a taxi driver he spent a lot of his day cruising around or standing in a taxi rank. But now and then the radio would kick in and he would be told, 'Go and pick somebody up in Bayswater ... There's a lady outside Harrods with a whole pile of shopping ...'

As we develop a Christian mind, for most of the time we are spiritually cruising round, seeking to keep in touch with God. And every so often at critical times – such as happened here in Acts – God breaks in. The radio, as it were, crackles into life. We say, 'Lord, what is it You want us to do? You said don't go this way, don't go that way – so which way?'

During the night the apostle Paul had a dream. Some of us get very excited about that, but it will put matters in perspective to remember that Pharaoh in Genesis 41 and Nebuchadnezzar in Daniel 2, both Godless men, had significant dreams as well. Having dreams is not necessarily God's only way, but it is one of the ways God uses here, in the book of Acts, to direct His people.

The dream comes. How are we supposed to know what to do? In the dream he sees a man from Macedonia saying, 'Come over and help us.' You've no idea how much ink has been spilled by commentators trying to work out who this man is. Some say it was

Luke himself (probably Philippi was his home city). William Barclay makes the interesting suggestion that it may have been a vision of Alexander the Great, who wanted to marry East and West. Paul has in his heart the marrying of East and West, into one world for Jesus Christ. It's an intriguing thought, even though I don't think there's any evidence whatsoever about it.

How did Paul know the man was from Macedonia? When I was a young pastor in the East End of London, a man and his wife came to me after I'd been preaching my heart out. He said, in a very broad Scouse accent, 'It was great to hear a proper sermon this morning. We've been down the road getting five-minute sermons, we've been starving, like.' I said, 'Are you from Liverpool?' He said, 'How do know that, then, like?' I said, 'It's just a gift; just a gift.' And I imagine the Macedonian had a distinct accent too.

When Paul had his vision he didn't then say, 'Hey! Thus saith the Lord – we've got to go to Macedonia.' He was working in a team, so he shared it with others. Notice that very important plural, 'After Paul had received the vision we got ready.' That's the intimation that Luke by this time had joined them. 'We got ready at once to leave for Macedonia, including' – it's a plural verb; Paul shared it with them, and they said, 'Well, we can see that this is God's will.' There is safety in finding guidance, in getting others involved with you. Remember Alistair Begg's story of the young person who felt called to be a missionary, had no idea where to, and eventually saw an advert for Brazil nuts ... and how fortunate it was that she hadn't seen a Mars bar first ...

But what is going on here? What's the underlying theological basis of what's happening? It's this. We all know Ephesians 2:8-9, 'For it is by grace you have been saved, through faith - and this not from yourselves, it is the gift of God - not by works, so that no-one can boast.' But why do we stop there? Verse 10 is so encouraging: 'For we are God's workmanship.' In the Greek it says we are his *poiema* – His poem, His work of art. 'We are God's workmanship, created in Christ Jesus to do good works, which God prepared in advance for us to do.' Isn't that fantastic?

Sometimes people say of Christian work, 'It must be very hard, doing what you are doing.' I want to tell you that in the right place, it's the simplest thing in the world, to be doing what you were made for. And if you are in the place God wants you to be, if you are prepared for that good work, then there is a certain sense of ease about it. At one level you are just doing what you are made for. And some of us tonight are going to discover that God has made us for Africa, for India, for South America, or maybe Steeple Bumpstead in the middle of nowhere in Essex. But God has made us for there. It's no accident, it's no fluke, when it comes to guidance. It's not a matter of landing on your feet. It's a matter of finding out what God has on His heart for you.

Spread the word (16:11-40)

Luke is being selective here. At the end of the chapter he talks about the brothers, and eventually Paul will write to the church at Philippi; there's every indication of a large growing and vibrant church there. But Luke is selecting these stories of conversion.

Any one of us with any sense would do that, wouldn't we? Some churches do literature blitzes and distribute some startling testimonies out of the stories of their two or three hundred members. They select. Now if you're blitzing Highgate you don't as a rule send round stories of converted house-breakers and car thieves, or announce that Damien and Floyd, the converted cons, will be coming round any day soon. And if you come from where I do in Everton in Liverpool, you don't send round a testimony from a local fellowship by Lady Leandra Farquahar-Jackson, testifying to the wondrous delivery of her yacht from a tornado just off the Florida Keys. That just doesn't immediately strike a chord in the average Scouser.

So Luke selects three cameos of what conversion's about. They are interesting because they al;most incidentally give us three forms of evangelism as well. We could call them the conversational, the confrontational, and the consequential.

Conversational evangelism (11-15)

For instance, we bump into this well-to-do lady, Lydia. That may be her name, or it may mean she was a Lydian woman. She's a business woman, she's into fine purple, she's got a big house and servants; in our parlance she is well heeled. And she's a worshipper of God. She's not a Jewess but she's interested. Paul and his associates were looking for somewhere to pray because there weren't the requisite ten Jewish males that you had to have to have a synagogue. So Paul, unable to find where he usually began – a synagogue – went down to the River Gangetes. And there they found a place of prayer.

Paul has had a Macedonian call from a man; he sits down and starts speaking to a woman. The original word simply means that they are having a conversation; they are talking. And as they talk, they get round to the Lord Jesus. And Paul shares the gospel with her, and as she listens God does the work and opens her heart.

'Faith comes from hearing the message, and the message is heard through the word of Christ' (Rom. 10:17). We must keep the Bible in our evangelism, and yet be sensitive and flexible as we do so. Paul is sharing the gospel – that's the human element; preaching, sharing, casual conversation and 'gossiping the gospel'. As Paul does so, God is at work and He opens her heart. And the light dawns.

We've all got Lydias in our churches and on the edges of our churches. They want to worship God, they are genuine seekers. The penny hasn't yet dropped. And rather than battering them over the head, telling them what Godless sinners they are all the time and that's why they are seeking, they need to be told about the Lord Jesus, and to pray that the Spirit would open their hearts to receive Him. What a privilege to tell them that!

There is a human element here and a divine element. Some Christians are always tugging on divine sovereignty. Like rowing a boat with just one oar, they go round in circles. They become hyper-Calvinists. And some Christians are always tugging on human responsibility; they row the boat in different circles. They think it's all down to us, as if God can't do anything.

Charles Spurgeon was once asked how he reconciled divine sovereignty and human responsibility. He replied, 'I never try to reconcile friends, they belong together.' Paul spoke, God worked. Paul spoke, Lydia listened, the Spirit opened her heart. It's the anatomy of conversion. 'Take my lips and let them be/Filled with messages from Thee,' prayed Frances Ridley Havergal. You and I have those opportunities too; at the school gate, at the job club, in the workplace over coffee or over lunch, at the sports club.

Confrontational evangelism (16-19)

And now we bump into a poor soul who's possessed with what is called a 'spirit of python'; it was believed of the Delphic Oracle that Apollo the god incarnated himself in a snake. His devotees, who were affected by this snake's spirit, became his mouthpiece.

Of course in the area of the occult there is often sleight of hand and similar trickery. I split my sides when I see Mystic Meg on the TV lottery programme – if she's so clever, why doesn't she just pick the numbers herself and collect £20 million? But having said that, we are fools if we do not recognise that there are very real occult, psychic realms. The Bible clearly tells us so.

This girl wasn't just psychologically unhinged. She was demonically oppressed and possessed. What is interesting is how Paul deals with it. This passage gives problems both to those who deny the demonic and say it doesn't happen today, but also to those who see demons everywhere, so that before they do anything they have to name and claim the spirits and bind them so they can get on with the gospel. It's interesting that Paul didn't do the latter. He got on with preaching the gospel and for many days he didn't take the demon on. That's an important point, both for charismatics and for non-charismatics; he took his time. And this woman kept making a row. She was telling the truth, but, as a wise old Puritan said, 'Don't even believe the devil when he tells you the truth.' Why didn't Paul say, 'Well, this is good! She's doing P.R. for us'? I imagine because of that kind of frenetic note in her voice when she was beside herself. God doesn't need the devil to publicise His mighty works.

So this is what some would call, in theological terms, a power encounter. And Paul, not so much fed up with her as grieved in his spirit for this poor kid being used and abused by folk making a fortune out of her, commands in the name of Jesus Christ this thing to leave her. Immediately it does so.

> Jesus! The name high over all,
> In hell, or earth, or sky;
> Angels and men before it fall,
> And devils fear and fly. *(Charles Wesley)*

This is confrontational evangelism. Listen, folks: we can't always have friendship evangelism. We can't always be nice about things. We are in a battle and there are no demilitarised zones. And there are people who are fast bound in sin and nature's night. Increasingly, with New Age and everything else around us, and the rise of the occult and pagan religion and all sorts of other stuff, we are going to encounter this kind of thing in England's green and pleasant land. And some of us as pastors know about that first hand.

Consequential evangelism (20-40)

We'll return to the circumstances of Paul in prison as we close. But here is someone who, in the middle of the night, is led to Christ. And it's the consequence of a remarkable incident. Paul and Silas, in this Roman colony, are put in the charge of a jailer – almost certainly an ex-veteran. If Lydia is from the higher echelons of society, and the slave girl is from the very lowest, then this man is from the middle classes. That's what Luke wants us to see.

So here are Paul and Silas at midnight. They are in the darkest part of the prison. It's black, it's dingy, their feet are in the stocks, they're still lacerated from their beating. And they are singing and praising God, and the other prisoners were listening. I wonder what some of them were saying? 'Shut those guys up!' ... 'No, *you* shut up, these guys have got something to say that's worth hearing.'

And as they carry on singing suddenly an earthquake takes place.

You might say, 'Oh isn't that fantastic and dramatic! Paul must have been saying, "Hey, here come the cavalry!"' You're in a dark dungeon, it's black, you've been beaten up pretty badly, your feet are in the stocks, and then comes the earthquake – and you're thinking to yourself, 'Oh, isn't God good!' You and I know the end of the story. We read it that way. I don't suppose Paul and Silas felt like that for a moment – but there was a tremendous tremor, and they are all released.

The jailer knew that if he had lost any condemned prisoners his life was forfeit. He was certain they must have escaped so he decided to fall on his sword. 'Do yourself no harm, we're all here,' said Paul. And there was a dramatic conversion: 'Sirs, what must I do to be saved?'

'Believe on the Lord Jesus Christ and you will be saved – you and your household' ... And 'at that hour of the night, the jailer took them and washed their wounds', and they spoke the word of

God to all in his household (cf verses 30-33). Oh, he comes to Christ.

Why have the Alpha Course and such things been so successful? Because, in some measure, it's locked into something we've lost in the West. We believe in individual salvation, of course we do. But we've forgotten that God works through family and social networks as well. The churches that are successful with the Alpha Course are successful because their members have networks of folk they can bring along. The tragedy with some of us who've been on the Christian road for quite a while, is that we've got no non-Christian friends any more. And that's why we're sometimes against evangelism – we've got nobody to bring. We need to get out of our ghettos.

So here in Acts the networking goes on. It's like the old saying – forgive the politically incorrect language – 'Man's extremity is God's opportunity'. All around us are people who've hit a skid patch in life. Disaster strikes, they lose a life's partner, a loved one; they face a life-threatening disease, they lose their job, they're told some bad news; of for whatever reasons they have a mid-life crisis or whatever. And in one way or another they are saying, 'What must I do to be saved?' For them, they may simply be asking, 'How can I get my life together again?' But whatever the question, the gospel of Jesus Christ is always the answer.

Let's distil a number of principles from these three conversions.

The gospel is for all sorts of people. The early Jew prayed and thanked God every day that he wasn't born a Gentile, a woman or a slave. But here in Acts 16, Gentiles, women and slaves, are converted.

The gospel is the same, but the circumstances in which people are converted differ, sometimes dramatically. A great preacher from a previous generation, a Scot named John T. MacNeil, was recounting an imaginary conversation between the man born blind in John 9 (where Jesus spat on the ground, put the mud on his eyes and said, 'Go and wash in the Pool of Siloam') and Bartimeus, to whom Jesus just restored sight. They are comparing notes. And the man in John 9 says,

'So how did you feel when He spat on the ground?'

'I don't know, he didn't spit on the ground.'

'Well, you know when he made the mud pack and He stuck it on your eyes, what did that feel like?'

'Well He didn't put any mud on my eyes.'

'Well, you know – when you went to the Pool of Siloam and you washed and you saw your face for the first time, how did you feel then?'

'Oh, I was in Jericho, nowhere near the Pool of Siloam.'

The man in John 9 looks at Bartimeus and says, 'I don't believe for one moment you've been genuinely healed.' And, says John T. MacNeil, at that moment two denominations were born: the mudites and the anti-mudites.

You may have come with a whimper and they may have come with a bang. What matters is that you have come to Christ.

In every account, prayer is closely associated with what's going on.

Come, my soul, thy suit prepare,
Jesus loves to answer prayer;
He Himself has bid thee pray,
Therefore will not say thee nay.

Thou art coming to a King,
Large petitions with thee bring.
For His grace and power are such,
None can never ask too much. (John Newton)

Christianity makes people different and generous. Lydia and the converted jailer, instead of being takers and getters, become hospitable givers. If our conversion in the heart doesn't lead to a change in our lives, there's been no conversion in the heart.

And fifthly – in case you've missed it – *the hero of these narratives is not Paul, Silas, or Luke but God Himself in His mercy, grace and sovereignty.* Imagine if Paul had gone as he wanted east to Thyatira. He'd never have met Lydia because she wasn't there; God had already taken her to Philippi. Have you ever noticed that? Lydia was no longer where she had been born. But God knew where she was.

And God knew what He was doing when He allowed Paul to be in prison and under the circumstance and everything else, because He knew there was a jailer there who needed converting too.

God moves in a mysterious way
His wonders to perform;
He plants His footsteps in the sea,
He rides upon the storm.
Deep in unfathomable mines
Of never-failing skill
He treasures up His bright designs,
And works His sovereign will. *(William Cowper)*

And finally,

Stand the bill

Remember what this is about. It's about a man who's beaten up and thrown into prison. It's the New Testament principle of suffering now, glory later.

The vice-principal at London Bible College in my day was known as 'Derry Mac'. He once said memorably, 'God only had one son without sin. He has no sons or daughters without suffering.' For others to hear the gospel, it's going to be costly. To take the gospel into Britain's villages, inner cities and new housing estates means somebody has got to pay the bill.

When I was a kid I went to Bible College to train to be a cross-cultural missionary in Brazil. The last place I wanted to be was in England. As a teenager, I would sometimes weep as I sang a great old missionary hymn by James McGranahan,

Far, far away in heathen darkness dwelling,
Millions of souls for ever may be lost.
Who, who will go – Salvation's story telling –
Looking to Jesus, counting not the cost? …

See, o'er the world, wide open doors inviting;
Soldiers of Christ, arise and enter in!
Christians, awake! your forces all uniting,
Send forth the Gospel, break the chains of sin!

If we're not interested in evangelism and mission, we've missed the heartbeat of God. Alistair Begg and I were privileged to be at college with a young, beautiful Welsh girl from Caerphilly who had the face of an angel and a voice to match. She went out at the call of God to the mountains of what was then Rhodesia, where she worked with the Elim Missionary Organisation. And in June 1978, the so-called Freedom Fighters came and butchered those missionaries to death. She paid the ultimate price, she stood the bill, she gave her life proclaiming that Jesus died and rose, so that eventually some of those Freedom Fighters found freedom indeed in Jesus Christ.

It costs to follow the crucified. It's the principle of following the gospel. Who, who will go? Tonight is our World View Evening. I imagine that if we could ask the apostle Paul, 'Was that beating in Philippi worth it?', he'd say, 'What, worth it? To have all these folk in heaven with me? You'd better believe it!'

Ann Ross Cousin, in a great hymn, 'The sands of time are sinking', wrote some additional verses imagining the saintly Samuel Rutherford in Aberdeen jail in the days of the Scottish Covenanters. Far away from his flock at Anworth on the Solway, he's missing them and thinking about them.

> Fair Anworth on the Solway, to me thou still art dear;
>   E'en from the verge of heaven I drop for thee a tear.
> Oh if one soul from Anworth shall meet me at God's right hand,
>   My heaven will be two heavens, in Emmanuel's land.

Is it worth it, the value of a soul? Yes. Because whatever the cost we'll have all eternity to get over the pains and setbacks of this earthly life and pilgrimage.

God needs Christians who, with all the painful priorities surrounding them, screaming at them, will not take off their uniforms and mingle with the crowd. He wants men and women of faith and courage and tenacity and vision who will get into uniform and serve the King of kings. 'Come over and help us' is the cry of a needy, broken, fractured world. Who, who, who will go?

Keswick 1998

Tapes, Videos and Books

Catalogues and price lists of audio tapes of the Keswick Convention platform ministry, including much not included in the present book, can be obtained from:

ICC (International Christian Communications)
Regency Mews
Silverdale Road
Eastbourne
East Sussex BN20 7AB.

Details of videos of selected sessions can be obtained from:

Mr Dave Armstrong
STV Videos
Box 299
Bromley, Kent BR2 9XB.

Some previous annual Keswick volumes (all published by STL/OM) are still in print, and can be ordered from,:

The Keswick Convention Centre, Skiddaw Street,
Keswick, Cumbria CA12 4BY;
from your local Christian bookseller;
or direct from the publishers, OM Publishing, STL Ltd,
PO Box 300, Carlisle, Cumbria CA3 0QS, England

Keswick 1999

The annual Keswick Convention takes place each July at the heart of England's beautiful Lake District. The two separate weeks of the Convention offer an unparalleled opportunity for listening to gifted Bible exposition, experiencing Christian fellowship with believers from all over the world, and enjoying something of the unspoilt grandeur of God's creation.

Each of the two weeks has a series of five morning Bible Readings, followed by other addresses throughout the rest of the day. There are also regular meetings throughout the fortnight for young people, and a Children's Holiday Club.

The dates for the 1999 Keswick Convention are 17-24 July and 24-31 July. The Bible Reading speakers are Don Carson and Nigel Lee respectively. Other speakers during the fortnight include Derek Bingham, Ian Coffey, Ronald Dunn, Ajith Fernando, Liam Goligher and others. For further information, write to:

The Administrator
Keswick Convention Centre
Skiddaw Street, Keswick
Cumbria CA12 4BY
Telephone 017687 72589